Foreign Policy Implementation

Foreign Policy Implementation

Edited by

STEVE SMITH
MICHAEL CLARKE

London
GEORGE ALLEN & UNWIN
Boston   Sydney

George Allen & Unwin (Publishers) Ltd,
40 Museum Street, London WC1A 1LU, UK

George Allen & Unwin (Publishers) Ltd,
Park Lane, Hemel Hempstead, Herts HP2 4TE, UK

Allen & Unwin, Inc.,
Fifty Cross Street, Winchester, Mass. 01890, USA

George Allen & Unwin Australia Pty Ltd,
8 Napier Street, North Sydney, NSW 2060, Australia

First published in 1985.

British Library Cataloguing in Publication Data

   Foreign policy implementation.
1. International relations.
I. Smith, Steve, 19-- - II. Clarke, Michael 19-- -
327 JX1395
ISBN 0-04-351066-3
       0-04-351067-1 (p/b)

Library of Congress Cataloging in Publication Data

Main entry under title:
   Foreign policy implementation.
Bibliography: p.
Includes index.
1. International relations. 2. United States—Foreign relations
administration. 3. Great Britain—Foreign relations administration.
4. France—Foreign relations administration. I. Smith, Steve,
1952 - II. Clarke, Michael, 1950 .
JX1391.F64 1984   351.89   84-14604
ISBN 0-04-351066-3 (alk. paper)
       0-04-351067-1 (p/b)

Set in 10 on 11 point Goudy by V & M Graphics Ltd, Aylesbury, Bucks
and printed in Great Britain by Thetford Press, Thetford, Norfolk

Contents

Contributors

David Allen is senior lecturer in politics at the University of Loughborough.

Paul Byrne is lecturer in politics at the University of Loughborough.

Michael Clarke is lecturer in politics at the University of Newcastle.

Christopher Farrands is senior lecturer in international relations at Trent Polytechnic.

Walter Goldstein is Professor of International Politics at the State University of New York (Albany).

Steve Smith is lecturer in politics at the University of East Anglia.

Roger Tooze is senior lecturer in international relations at North Staffordshire Polytechnic.

Brian White is senior lecturer in international relations at North Staffordshire Polytechnic.

Acknowledgements

We would like to thank Annemarie Rule (Newcastle) and Christine Jope (UEA) for their help in preparing the manuscript. Our main debt, however, is to Anne Martin at UEA who did so much in the way of typing the final manuscript and mastering the eccentricities of a new word processor. Without her cheerful help there would have been very serious problems in the implementation stage of this project.

STEVE SMITH and MICHAEL CLARKE
25 January 1984

1

Foreign Policy Implementation and Foreign Policy Behaviour

Steve Smith and *Michael Clarke*

The shooting down of the Korean Airlines Boeing 747 on 1 September 1983 by Soviet air defence provides a dramatic example of the problem with which this volume is concerned. Immediately the US government reacted by claiming that the shooting down was a deliberate act, which reflected not only Soviet attitudes towards the lives of innocent people, but also the clinical efficiency of their air defence. However, as the story unravelled, the picture changed dramatically; within a few weeks of the incident it was explained more in terms of failures of the air defence system than successes, and more in terms of standard operating procedures than deliberate and considered policies emanating from the highest levels of the Soviet government. Indeed, as more evidence became available, more and more questions were raised as to what the USA's role had been in the incident, and why the Korean plane was there in the first place.

This is not the occasion to debate the whys and wherefores of this incident, interesting as they are. What this issue raises, however, is precisely the concern of this volume, namely, the ways in which decisions are implemented. For when US leaders were explaining, and denouncing, Soviet behaviour in shooting down the plane, they were engaged in the exercise of imputing intentions to that behaviour. Given that decision-makers are faced with a set of actions by other states in the international system, their task is to judge the motives underlying that behaviour from what they know about the state concerned. This is essentially an exercise in rational policy analysis: we see what behaviour state X has undertaken and, on the basis of our knowledge concerning its ideology, history, culture, interests, and so on, we judge what goal that behaviour is directed towards. Our analysis proceeds in this way, balancing the arguments for and against certain intentions, much as we might do when attempting to explain the behaviour of an individual. Now, of course, such an explanatory process rests on an assumption that behaviour is goal-directed and purposeful. This assumption has received considerable treatment in the literature of the social sciences, and many problems have been noted. For the purposes of this volume, the key problem is that the assumption is undermined to the extent that it is the case that foreign policy behaviour is caused by something other than goal-directed and purposeful decisions. The literature of foreign policy analysis has led to a number of alternative causes of foreign policy behaviour (bureaucratic politics, groupthink, misperception, belief systems), all of which reduce the explanatory power of the assumption. What this volume focuses on is the question of how far the implementation process determines foreign policy. To return to the Korean airliner incident, clearly our assumptions as to Soviet intentions would be affected by whether the shooting down of the plane was a desision taken at the highest levels of Soviet government or was the result of over-rigid enforcement of standard operating procedures. Either way, the result of the incident was to cause US–Soviet relations to deteriorate further, so that subsequent events such as those in Grenada and the Lebanon in October–November 1983 were interpreted from a more mutually suspicious and pessimistic basis. In such a situation whatever the cause of the foreign policy behaviour of each of the superpowers, the tendency is to assess it as purposeful, as emanating from the top of the political structure and as essentially expansionist. In this light it is essential to be able to ascertain to what extent factors apart from decision-making have resulted in the state's foreign policy behaviour. As such a factor, implementation matters.

This collection of essays focuses on the implementation of foreign policy decisions. It not only argues that the implementation process may cause foreign policy to turn out in a way unintended by decision-makers (an empirical perspective), but also assumes that thinking about foreign policy behaviour from an implementation perspective encourages us to ask slightly different types of question about how foreign policy emerges (a theoretical perspective). In the existing literature the implementation of decisions is assumed rather than examined. The fundamental assumption of the theoretical literature in foreign policy analysis is that the central problem to be explained is the decision. This volume is concerned with the analysis of foreign policy behaviour from a different perspective – one which, we believe, throws light on that behaviour and on our ways of explaining it.

The foreign policy analysis literature focuses almost exclusively on the decision as that which has to be explained: explain foreign policy decisions and you have explained foreign policy behaviour. This literature has a number of distinct theories and myriad methodologies, but the dominant feature of it is a concern with explaining decisions. On this basis the focal points of theories may be very different (domestic inputs, images, bureaucratic politics, groupthink, national interest, and so on), but each is concerned with explaining why decision-makers took certain decisions rather than others. Indeed, it can be claimed that to the extent rival theories of foreign policy behaviour can be distinguished, they are concerned with competing explanations of decision-making, with their utility assessed by their success in this explanation.

Now, in this view of foreign policy, precisely because it is a causal one, that which precedes the decision becomes the locus of our explanations. Methodologically, then, our focal point determines our causal purview. This does not mean that implementation is ignored, but it does mean that it is treated in a certain way. For one thing, it is often assumed to take place without major 'slippage'. In many respects it is treated as a natural follow-on to the decision. However, it can be argued – and certainly is in the case of Allison's (1971) work on the Cuban missile crisis – that implementation is not automatic, and that it may be subject to considerable slippage, although such slippage is seen as clearly observable. The point here, though, is that this is a very restricted notion of implementation in that it is still seen in terms of the focus of explanation, namely, the decision. Even cases of slippage are explicable as being exceptions, normally for bureaucratic reasons, and as additions to, rather than part of, the policy-making process.

Given the widespread nature of this assumption concerning implementation, it is not surprising that implementation has not been seen as a major area of importance in the explanation of foreign policy behaviour. As such, even empirical studies of foreign policy behaviour usually concentrate on the inputs to, and the process of, decision-making, with any consideration of the post-decisional process relegated to footnotes or, at best, a brief epilogue.

However, the most important issue that implementation raises for the study of foreign policy behaviour is that it shifts the focus from the *decision* to *behaviour itself*. This is of critical importance since it is the behaviour, and not the decision, to which other states' decision-makers have to respond. To be sure, the decision is clearly an important determinant of behaviour but it is *a* determinant. The literature of foreign policy analysis, however, has tended to see the decision not as a determinant, but as that which is determined. To this extent the focus of foreign policy analysis has made it difficult to explain the dynamics of international relations; it is not simply an interaction between two sets of decision-making processes. The implementation perspective forces us to consider the extent to which behaviour was the intended consequence of decisions, or was the unintended consequence of the implementation process. As such it offers a potentially very powerful perspective for the examination of explanations of foreign policy behaviour.

The starting-point for this volume is, therefore, that there is a vast gap in the literature; but, to repeat, it is not simply that this gap has an empirical dimension, it also has a theoretical one. With regard to the former it means that by concentrating on decisions, the extent to which actual behaviour is determined by slippage, or even by accident, is ignored. With reference to the latter it makes the task of explaining the dynamics of international relations much more difficult. To the extent that behaviour undertaken is affected by the process of implementation, then implementation may significantly affect the responses of other states' decision-making processes. As a further example of this phenomenon, one can cite the case of the sinking of the *General Belgrano* during the Falklands/Malvinas conflict. Much of the discussion in the press both at the time of the incident and afterwards concentrated on whether or not the British government had explicitly ordered the sinking. While this is an interesting empirical question (in that it is important to know who ordered the sinking of the ship), its theoretical importance is much greater. This is for the simple reason that the sinking came at a critical time in the negotiations for a peaceful settlement undertaken by the Peruvian government. Now, for the Peruvians and for the Argentinians, the question of whether or not the sinking was ordered was central to their explanations of British attitudes towards the peace settlement. Clearly, if the sinking was directly ordered by the Prime Minister, this indicated a rather different attitude towards the negotiations than if the sinking was the result of delegated authority to a local commander who, by necessity, would not be aware of the behind-the-scenes discussions. Equally clearly, this example indicates the centrality of focusing on behaviour; had the British government been totally committed to a peaceful settlement, then the actual behaviour would have been very much at odds with the decisions made by the government. As it was, the other states had to react to the behaviour and impute intentions to that. For these reasons the issue of implementation represents an important linkage in explaining the dynamics of international relations.

However, in addition to these reasons for studying implementation, the perspective also involves a major shift of emphasis in the study of foreign policy behaviour in that it encourages us to ask more implementation-minded questions than are conventionally covered. In this sense we can speak of the implementation perspective as offering a new way of examining foreign policy behaviour. For example, we all understand that foreign policies have *outcomes* in the uncertain environment of the international system, but that this is not the same as considering the specific *outputs* of a decision-making system: that is, the particular tasks that it must perform in order to give effect to whatever it is that is called a policy. In a sense it is the gap between foreign policy-making and foreign policy effects. Certainly, foreign policy analysis is aware of the gap, but the literature that deals with foreign policy outputs is not properly a body of literature on implementation. Familiar descriptions of the 'instruments of implementation', or the spectrum of pressures from 'pure coercion' to 'pure persuasion' are valuable in themselves, but they do not describe the *techniques* of implementation as such; they are concerned with the behavioural or institutional *content* of policy rather than how it is applied. In effect, there has been a continuing inconsistency in foreign policy analysis in that the techniques of taking decisions are much considered, whereas the implementation or performance of them has tended to be ignored, taken for granted, or described in different terms.

This is curious for two reasons. First, a number of studies of specific issues have shown a clear awareness of the importance of the implementation stages of policy. For example, Allison (1971) focused directly on the problem in his influential book, *Essence of Decision*. The puzzle is that so little of this has found its way into the general and theoretical literature on foreign policy-making. The way in which Allison has been invoked has not led to a noticeably greater concern with implementation. Where it is considered, it is normally regarded as the administrative and managerial part of foreign policy. Secondly, the explicit recognition that foreign policy should be characterized as a 'process' means that it is a nonsense without an explicitly political study of implementation. For however this process is characterized – as a 'dynamic system', as 'adaptive', as involving 'feedback' – it is imperative, if consistency is required, that the analysis be capable of describing implementation as well as, and as part of, decision-taking. These inconsistencies are not peculiar to foreign policy analysis, however, and the purpose here is to outline a perspective on implementation on the basis of existing literature. There is a great deal of foreign policy material that is potentially relevant; the problem has been that implementation has remained an implicit notion.

It is not hard to understand how this comes about, for the study of policy-*making* is concerned with the activities and attitudes of formal political leaders, institutions and definable groups, whereas the study of policy *outputs* is more concerned with the working of informal groupings, lower-level officials and half-understood procedures. This is not to say simply that the examination of decision-making is deficient, but to argue for a shift in emphasis from the intellectual content of policy to its functional outputs. Foreign policy studies have always acknowledged, of course, that it is important to do this. But beyond the realizations that everyone in a foreign policy machine is a potential decision-maker, and that the process of implementation is as political an act as anything else that passes for decision-making, it has proved hard to say anything more specific about this aspect of the subject. There is, however, a growing literature on policy studies that lays much more emphasis on the politics of implementation. The mystery is why such literature has not had a harder look at foreign policy, since the very nature of foreign policy – its distinctiveness from domestic policy-making – makes it an excellent candidate for the study of implementation.

If we consider the more particular questions that an emphasis on implementation raise, it is clear that foreign policy issues illustrate many of them in their most stark form. First, it is important to consider the general nature of whatever we characterize as a decision. Decisions are characteristically ambiguous, both intentionally and unintentionally. To use ambiguous terms may be the only way to make a decision acceptable to those responsible for making it, or it may be a strategic decision that by nature involves extensive refinement, or it may simply be conceptually or linguistically unclear to those to whom it is communicated. All these generalizations are implicit in Frankel's (1963, p. 202) distinction between 'initial' and 'sequential' decisions. As regards intentional ambiguity, Puchala's (1975) study of the failures of EEC members to implement legalistic and explicit EEC regulations is a good example of the ability of political actors to introduce ambiguity into any directive if they wish, or again, different orders may simply conflict, or may conflict because they arise from different sources. The famous case of the failure of the US Defense Department to withdraw the Jupiter missiles from Turkey and Italy in 1962 was hardly an act of bureaucratic disobedience, but more a conflict between immediate orders to withdraw the missiles and standing orders not to upset NATO allies gratuitously, since Dean Rusk, George Ball and Paul Nitze were all involved in sounding out the Turkish and Italian governments on the issue throughout 1962.

What must be stressed is that decisions make different patterns of demands for implementation. We must be clear initially what form and degree of implementation is required by a particular decision. Some may not require implementing, or may require it only in the indefinite future; some may be declaratory, merely to posture, or procedural, for their own sake; some may conflict with established patterns; some may be incapable of being carried out; and some may be programmatic decisions, as in some cases in the field of foreign aid, where a structure and plan of action is prerequisite to a decision being taken.

Even beginning from the highly simplified assumption that something can be called a recognizable decision, it is clear that our first shift of emphasis is to consider the implications for implementing agencies of whatever is arrived at. There is a particular relevance for foreign policy here in that so many decisions in foreign policy are incapable of being implemented, so many are merely postures, and the business of foreign policy is not commonly concerned with the relatively simple production of goods and services. There is surely an interest, and a need, to try to identify patterns of the implementative requirements of foreign policy decisions. The very difficulty of getting to grips with a decision 'to do something' in foreign policy makes it an intriguing area for research.

A second shift of emphasis is to see the international arena as an arena of policy implementation and to ask what special characteristics of the nature of international politics make a difference to how decisions are carried out. We must recognize, for instance, that in any policy process the metaphor of 'chain of command' is less accurate than the metaphor of 'coalition'. That is, that leaders are concerned to establish a coalition of implementing agencies to perform aggregate parts of the overall function that is required, and they must *maintain that coalition over time*. Giving orders is clearly not enough. Furthermore, implementing agencies are all players in the implementing arena and are subject to any number of other pressures. So coalitions may have to be established in very unfavourable conditions. These are general problems of implementation, but they are all much more stark in the context of foreign policy. The problem of building implementing coalitions among agencies of different states, the problems of holding coalitions together over time in an environment where giving orders is not only insufficient, but often downright impossible, and the contrast, on the other hand, with the fact that many foreign policy-making structures are relatively centralized, all pose very clear-cut examples of the problems of implementation. The attempt, therefore, is to look at the context of foreign policy as a distinctive environment of decision-making processes.

A third shift of emphasis is in the question of control and monitoring of decision procedures. Clearly, much that emerges from the policy machine as 'output' is not the response to an act of choice by a formal decision-maker at all. More likely it will be the result of standard operating procedures, or a misapplication over time of standard operating procedures. This, therefore, raises another important series of questions concerning the difference between conscious policy-making and the policy output that a decision system might produce. This is not to say that we are concerned only to apply insights from management science to foreign policy. Rather we are interested in the distinctiveness of foreign policy, which makes certain *techniques* of control and monitoring either more or less relevant to our cases.

There are two main ways in which controls might be viewed. First, they may be seen as the degree of involvement of initial decision-makers in the resulting sequential decisions. What is interesting in this context is the degree to which the framers of a policy can actually contribute to its impact. Halperin's (1974) analysis of control is illustrative: the more a President can involve himself in the subsequent decisions by influencing, testing, or even sidestepping the bureaucracy, the more likely it is that the initial decisions will bear a closer relation to actual impact. A neat example is offered by President Nixon's personal decision to visit China in 1971, where the arrangements, while elaborate, were continually under review by Nixon himself and his personal assistant, Henry Kissinger. A more conventional form of this type of control entails the use of horizontally structured intermediate organizations, to refine initial decisions, and co-ordinating agencies, thus enhancing the capacity for top-level involvement in the impact of policies.

This, then, is a fairly institutional way of thinking about problems of control. While valuable at that level, it concentrates primarily upon the agents of government and not upon the whole political arena that our examination of implementation suggests is necessary. If we think in terms of governmental attempts to control the whole environment in which sequential decisions are taken, then explanations of mere 'involvement' which are common to this first aspect of control will only be part of an explanation. A second, and more coherent, approach to this issue would be to consider also the types or varieties of control available to all the various agencies in the implementation process, since it is reasonable to assume that different agents will be better placed to use different procedures to influence their environment, and that control procedures will vary up and down the hierarchy. Many examples of different types of control could be mentioned, from pure monitoring procedures, or appeals to reason, to the use of intermediaries, involving blackmail or patronage, to deception or, most simply, to brute force in the sense of physical restraint as a control on behaviour.

Both Hood (1976) and Anderson (1979) offer typologies of control procedures. What emerges from both is that controls can be classified in terms of sanctions (physical or otherwise, but not highly communicative), exchange systems (involving the manipulation of different groups as intermediaries), or what Anderson stresses are appeals to values. Under this category would be the intriguing range of what might be described as self-policing controls and enforcements. As before, examples of all such controls are not hard to find in existing writings but are never applied to thinking about implementation. If we accept that control in implementation terms involves more than just keeping ahead of the bureaucracy, we might then usefully think of the *types* of control available and of the types *used* at various levels by different governmental actors within their political environments, and hence in their relations with each other.

Thus it can be seen that an implementation perspective offers far more than simply filling in empirical and theoretical gaps: it forces us to look at foreign policy in a different way, seeing different issues as relevant, and asking different questions. In this way it is complementary to, rather than a substitute for, existing theories. This volume does not seek to argue that the implementation perspective should be adopted as the only way to understand foreign policy; what it does argue is that it is of considerable use in the very complex task of explaining the welter of phenomena covered by the term foreign policy.

With this aim in mind, we have chosen a set of case studies that we believe will show the gap in existing portrayals of foreign policy behaviour. These case studies have been chosen to provide examples of implementation from four perspectives. First, we have selected case studies from more than one country precisely because we believe it is necessary to indicate that the issue of implementation is not the product of a set of institutional and procedural arrangements specific to one state.

Secondly, we have focused on a range of settings for studying the implementation of foreign policy, namely, national, bilateral, multilateral and international. Thirdly, we have chosen case studies of implementation in different types of issue-areas, so as to include examples of the implementation of economic, political and military policies. Finally, we have picked out examples of different types of decision, notably crisis and routine decisions, so as to cover the possibility of restricting our analysis to one type of decision.

In each case we hope to explain how the process of implementation affected the relationship between decision-making and behaviour; that is, we hope to give a series of detailed examples of the relationship between foreign policy behaviour and actual decisions. In many cases that behaviour was significantly different from that planned by decision-makers as a result of difficulties emerging when implementation was undertaken. This, of course, could be due to a series of factors; for example, changing values, standard operating procedures, bureaucratic stalling, unpredicted outcomes of discussions, breakdown of communications, the failure of negotiations and even the unsuccessful outcome of military action. Any of these factors could result in there being a vast difference between the intended and the actual foreign policy behaviour. As such, this perspective offers potentially vast payoffs in contrast to the static analysis of decision-making, since it offers a link between decision and reaction that is unavailable to decision-making theorists for whom implementation is a black box, and is assumed rather than assessed.

Given that the case studies focus on such different types of state, issues, settings and decisions, it was decided that it would be unrealistic to set out a rigid framework of implementation within which each of the case studies could be examined; the variety was simply too great. Nevertheless, it was decided to present a set of questions as to the nature of implementation, which could serve as a guideline for the research and analysis of the case studies. In this way they represented the kinds of question that arose from our initial thinking about implementation *per se*, before the results of the case studies were known:

(1) What *issue* was involved? This requires a historical outline of the issue to be examined in the case study.
(2) What *decisions* were involved? Having outlined the general issue to be examined, it is necessary to specify the decisions involved in terms of three criteria:

    (*a*) *type* – were the decisions secret/crisis/routine, etc.?
    (*b*) *Actors involved* – who took the decisions, one government, one bureaucracy, or an international organization?
    (*c*) *area of foreign policy concerned* – were the decisions concerned with military, political, prestige/status, or economic issues?

(3)   What were the *actual decisions?* Having classified the decisions according to theoretical criteria, the actual empirical evidence about the decisions will be discussed. In this way the case study will look at what decisions were taken, when and by whom. This is of central importance if we are to establish the existence of a gap between decision and behaviour.

(4)   How was the *implementation of the decision* attempted? Given that decisions were made, what were the processes by which implementation was undertaken?

(5)   What were the *results of the attempt at implementation?* This requires an examination of the actual behaviour undertaken by the state(s) concerned in order to ascertain the outcome of the whole decision/ implementation process. Specifically, though, this question forces us to focus on the further question of whether the implementation process led to very different outcomes from those intended by the decision-makers.

In the concluding chapter (Chapter 9) we look at the implications of the case studies in terms of what they tell us about the relationship between decision and behaviour, often a strange relationship brought to our attention by the use of the implementation perspective. It also investigates the extent to which our case studies indicate patterns in the role of implementation in determining foreign policy behaviour. Above all, our hope is that the findings of this volume indicate that implementation cannot be taken for granted as something that follows on automatically from a decision; in this way we hope to contribute incrementally to the task of explaining foreign policy behaviour.

2

The Hostage Rescue Mission

Steve Smith

At 4.57 p.m., Washington time, on Thursday 24 April 1980 President
Carter aborted the attempt to rescue the fifty-three American hostages
held in Tehran. This rescue mission was finally given the go-ahead on 15
April following an initial decision on 11 April. In this sense, this case study
has all the hallmarks of classical crisis decision-making; yet a much more
powerful explanation of the outcome of the event can only be developed
by examining the process by which the decisions were implemented. In
fact, this case study is an excellent example of the proposition outlined in
the introduction to this volume (Chapter 1) that the implementation
perspective not only sheds a different light on, but also offers a more
powerful explanation of, foreign policy behaviour than does the
traditional focus on decision-making. Here we have a paradigmatic
example of the way in which the behaviour of a state took on a very
different form from that intended in the decision-making process; this
resulted from problems in the implementation of that decision.

The issue involved in the decisions pertinent to this crisis was a very
simple one: what to do to rescue the fifty-three American hostages who
had been held in Iran since 4 November 1979.[1] On that day a group of
400–500 Iranian students stormed the Embassy in Tehran during an anti-
American rally. They seized sixty-three employees as hostages, demanding
that the Shah of Iran, who had been admitted to the USA for medical
treatment on 22 October, be returned to Iran for trial. The hostages would
not be released until this happened. Three other US diplomats, including
the Chargé d'Affaires (Bruce Laingen), had been at the Iranian Foreign
Ministry at the time of seizure and were granted asylum there. The next day
Ayatollah Khomeini condoned the taking of the hostages and his son paid
a visit to the Embassy. From that day onwards the US government was
involved in an extremely intricate and complex set of negotiations to
ensure the release of the hostages (Salinger, 1981; McManus, 1981;
McFadden *et al.*, 1981). During these negotiations a variety of mediators
were involved from a range of international, governmental and non-
governmental organizations. Of these, one of the most successful was
Yasser Arafat, whose close contact with the Iranian revolutionaries was

instrumental in arranging for the release of thirteen female and black hostages on 18–19 November (McFadden *et al.*, 1981, pp. 192–3). These negotiations went on at a number of levels, often involving secret contacts between US and Iranian officials (Salinger, 1981), for 444 days until finally the hostages were released a half-hour after Ronald Reagan became President of the United States, on 20 January 1981.

The negotiations that led to the release of the hostages were the result of four months' work by the Algerian government, serving as intermediaries since the Iranians refused direct contact. The final agreement involved three governments, four central banks and twelve US commercial banks, and the transfer of some $8 billion via escrow accounts (Salinger, 1981, pp. 330–6).

The immediate US reaction to the seizure of the hostages took place on two levels: the first involved economic sanctions against Iran; the second, an attempt to utilize international law and international public opinion to force the Iranian government to release the hostages. As the crisis progressed the USA became involved in attempts to persuade its allies to join in economic sanctions, a move that succeeded just two days before the rescue mission took place. On the legal front the United Nations unanimously passed a resolution demanding the release of the hostages on 4 December 1979, which was followed by an unsuccessful visit to Iran by UN Secretary-General Kurt Waldheim on 1–4 January 1980. A similar call by the International Court of Justice on 24 May 1980 went unheeded.

President Carter's initial public reaction was to stress the importance of putting the lives of the hostages first. On 10 November he asked American citizens to be calm and refrain from any words or deeds that might endanger the lives of the hostages; on 7 December he stated that, as long as the hostages were not harmed: 'I am not going to take any military action that would cause bloodshed or arouse the unstable captors of our hostages to attack or punish them' (McFadden *et al.*, 1981, p. 197). This action was strongly criticized by some for undercutting America's negotiating position (Heritage Foundation, 1980, pp. 12–13). However, whatever this public position meant, it was at best ambiguous. Reports leaked from the White House from day one of the crisis onwards indicated that military action was an option; indeed, this was made plain in a White House statement issued on 20 November 1979, which explicitly spoke about solutions other than negotiation, ones recognized in the Charter of the United Nations. In fact, military options were prepared as early as 6 November 1979. As will be discussed below, these went through a number of plans and stages, although it was not until the end of March 1980 that President Carter felt there was a feasible military plan.

By early April 1980 President Carter and his advisers felt that it was clear that the hostages were not going to be released as a result of negotiation. Informal contacts with members of the Iranian government revealed that they did not expect the hostages to be released for 'months and months' (Jordan, 1982, pp. 266-7). When this news reached the President he called Harold Brown, the Defense Secretary, and said: 'Harold, my last remaining doubt about the mission has been removed. Tell Colonel Beckwith to proceed' (Jordan, 1982, p. 267).

It is now necessary to examine the decisions involved. Given the wealth of information that has subsequently become available, it is clear that there were three overriding features of these decisions. First, they were made by a very small group of people. At most of the relevant meetings there were only seven or eight participants. Secondly, they were made in the utmost secrecy; President Carter did not even write anything about them directly in his personal diary. Thirdly, they were crisis decisions, concerned with a very ambiguous and novel issue as well as one which had a massive impact on the political future of the administration. They were concerned overwhelmingly with military issues, despite the attempts of Secretary of State Cyrus Vance to bring in the wider issue of the political ramifications.

The actual decisions to undertake the rescue mission were made on 11 April and 15 April 1980, although as is often the case, these were the formal ratifications of developments that had long been in progress. As soon as the hostages were seized Carter's National Security Adviser, Zbigniew Brzezinski, telephoned Secretary of Defense Harold Brown and instructed him to prepare a plan for a rescue mission (Brzezinski, 1983, p. 487). This led to a plan being discussed by Brown, Brzezinski and General David Jones, Chairman of the Joint Chiefs of Staff, on 8 November 1979. This plan called for an airborne assault on the Embassy by a specially trained team, who would then take the hostages to a nearby airfield to be transported out of Iran. The problems with this plan were related to the logistics of the operation–working at a great distance from the USA, with helicopters not usually utilized for such missions and with little time to train the force. More saliently, however, was the problem that there was a lack of intelligence as to the precise whereabouts of the hostages in the Embassy. In fact, the USA did have a special unit specifically designated for such operations: it was, indeed, this unit that undertook the eventual rescue mission. This force, codenamed Delta, and under the command of Colonel 'Chargin' Charlie' Beckwith, was formed in 1977 to provide the USA with an anti-terrorist unit.

Late in October 1979 Delta carried out its first validation exercise in Georgia, and it was on the night that this ended that the US Embassy was seized in Tehran. As Beckwith recollects: 'The minute I got that call, several of us rented cars and drove back to [Fort] Bragg, 'cause I knew this could mean we'd be called in' (Jordan, 1982, p. 258). Beckwith was called to Washington and was asked to prepare a plan to release the hostages. He felt that: 'it was obvious to me that they were just trying to answer the mail. Word was out that Brzezinski had already been there asking questions' (ibid., p. 258). Beckwith's hurriedly prepared plan offered, he told

General Jones, zero-probability of success. He would not be able to undertake a mission with any real probability of success until he knew much more about the exact layout of the Embassy. Beckwith told Jones that unless he knew this, his team (of forty) would take three or four hours searching the fourteen buildings of the Embassy. On this basis General Jones informed President Carter that a mission was impossible in the present circumstances. However, Carter gave permission for the Joint Chiefs of Staff (JCS) to prepare a rescue mission in case it might be needed. In this sense the momentum for the rescue mission goes back right to the first few days of the crisis.

From then onwards the planning for a rescue mission led to two main sets of activity. First, there was a critical need for more information on the location of the hostages. In many ways this has remained one of the greatest areas of secrecy concerning the entire rescue mission. The seizure of the Embassy had left the USA without a single CIA agent in Iran (*Newsweek*, 12 July 1982, p. 17). The only officers were held hostage, and there was no alternative means of contacting their local agents. Therefore, a very secret process of placing CIA operatives in Iran was essential if the rescue mission was to be undertaken with any probability of success. The first CIA agent arrived in December, and commuted in and out of Tehran for debriefing in Athens or Rome. He was soon followed by an Iranian exile, who carried out the preparations for the rescue mission, purchasing seven vans to transport the rescue team to the Embassy. This left the major problem of a lack of precise knowledge of the location of the hostages and their guards. This led to the installation of Richard Meadows, a retired Green Beret, to gather the necessary military information. He was followed by four other military men, and eight Iranian exiles. It is quite staggering that this group was able to plan every detail of the mission undetected,[2] as this involved quite open observation of the Embassy and, in the case of Meadows, 'chatting with reporters and waving to the guards' (*Newsweek*, 12 July 1982, pp. 18–19). Despite several very close calls, and Meadows's own very poor cover (as an Irishman, as they were unable to teach him another language), this team was able to check out all aspects of the mission. On 21 April Meadows signalled to Washington that everything was ready for the mission to proceed.

During this period extensive training of Colonel Beckwith's Delta force was progressing under extreme secrecy. On 20 November 1979 President Carter ordered a task force led by the aircraft-carrier *Kitty Hawk* to join the aircraft-carrier *Midway*, which had been on manoeuvres in the area at the time the Embassy was seized. Around the same time a number of helicopters were moved to a western US desert training site, where the training of Delta for the mission was to be undertaken. By 30 November the mission unit was in place and detailed training began.[3] The initial training was not very successful and in the first integrated exercise, held on 18–19 December, the results were such that it was decided to replace the pilots with more experienced ones (Special Operations Review Group of the Joint Chiefs of Staff, 1980, p. 5; hereafter SORG). By 27 December it was decided to plan to use C-130 aircraft to refuel the helicopters at their desert rendezvous (Desert One). However, it was clear that two major problems existed: the first concerned the weather, since the helicopters would have to undertake a very lengthy flight from their carrier to Desert One, and this would be severely jeopardized if there were bad weather *en route*. The second, and related, problem concerned the reliability of the helicopters. Initially the plan was for four helicopters to be used on the mission. This was subsequently altered to eight, giving seven for launch, six to arrive at the refuelling site and five at the hideout (Desert Two). By mid-February the remaining concern still centred on the difficulties posed by bad weather, the reliability of the helicopters and the need for a site for refuelling.

At this point, and for purely military reasons, a deadline emerged. By 1 May the number of hours of darkness would be down to nine hours and sixteen minutes. The helicopter mission to Desert One would take eight hours, and one hour was needed for contingencies. In addition, by 10 May, the temperature would reach 30°C, which would degrade helicopter performance, and thus require a larger task force. At this juncture it was decided to increase to six the number of helicopters to reach the hideout. By the end of March the task force was on a seven-day response status. It is interesting to note that it was at this time that President Carter began to turn to the military option. On 28 February he had refused permission for a reconnaissance flight into Iran to find a site for refuelling, arguing that this might fail and thereby jeopardize the negotiations. However, he finally agreed that such a mission should be undertaken at a lengthy meeting at Camp David on 22 March. This flight (on 2 April) confirmed the suitability of Desert One as the refuelling site. On 7 April the National Security Council decided that, as negotiations had failed, more decisive action was required. The meeting that approved the rescue mission was held on 11 April; this meeting was most remarkable because of its membership. As well as President Carter, there were Vice-President Mondale, National Security Adviser Brzezinski, Secretary of Defense Brown, CIA Director Turner, JCS Chairman Jones, Deputy Secretary of State Christopher, Press Secretary Powell and Adviser Jordan; this is remarkable because it excluded the one top official who had consistently argued against any military action, Secretary of State Cyrus Vance. As Carter records in his memoirs, 'Secretary Vance was on a brief and much needed vacation' (Carter, 1982, p. 506). The effect of Vance's absence was compounded by the fact that his deputy, Warren Christopher, assumed that Vance had gone along with the plan since he had not briefed Christopher to speak against it in his absence. As Jordan recalls, Christopher turned to him during the meeting and asked, 'Does Cy [Vance] know about this?' Jordan replied, 'The contingency rescue plan?

Of course'. 'No, no', Christopher said, 'does he realize how far along the President is in his thinking about this?' (Jordan, 1982, p. 251). Nevertheless, Christopher outlined a number of alternative options to the use of force: going back to the UN, blacklisting Iranian ships, and so on, all of which would have given the European governments more time to decide on measures to support the USA.

This is one of the more puzzling aspects of the decision to rescue the hostages, and well illustrates the argument that government is not a monolith but a set of bureaucratic organizations, with policy emerging as the result of, at best, compromise and, at worst, simply the combination of their separate policies. For at exactly the same time as these discussions over mounting a rescue mission were reaching a decision to go ahead, the State Department was furiously working to get the agreement of the European nations to a programme of sanctions against Iran. The European allies were far more dependent on Iran for oil and trade than was the USA, and so were loath to jeopardize this economic link. Nevertheless, they were also concerned at the effect of a military response by the USA and, in an attempt to postpone this, agreed to economic sanctions on 22 April. This, of course, explains much of the Europeans' reactions after the rescue mission was undertaken: there was a widespread feeling that not only had they been deceived into thinking that if they agreed to a broad policy of sanctions then the military option would be forestalled, but also that they had been used to create the impression in Tehran that the USA was overwhelmingly concerned with following a diplomatic route to the release of the hostages. This belief was strengthened by the fact that the Carter administration decided, for reasons of secrecy, to tell no European government of the mission in advance (although, contrary to press reports at the time, it is now established that British Prime Minister, Margaret Thatcher, was told) British intelligence had spotted US planes in Oman and had suggested that they were to be used to supply Afghan rebels. This was mentioned to US officials and President Carter felt it necessary to send Warren Christopher to London to brief the British Prime Minister and Foreign Minister about the real purpose of the planes (Carter, 1982, p. 512).

This policy of creating the impression that the USA was placing its hopes in sanctions was even more clearly implied by President Carter's statement on 17 April that: 'some sort of military action against Iran would seem to be the only alternative if economic and political sanctions failed'. He added that he had not decided on any specific military action and was hoping that economic and political sanctions, supported by Western allies, would lead to the release of the hostages, and preclude the need for new steps. Indeed, were military force necessary, it would be aimed at interrupting Iranian trade, as distinct from invasion or other combat operations (*New York Times*, 18 April 1980, p. A1). When the European governments agreed to a policy of sanctions (explicitly stating their fear of hasty US military action), the USA welcomed it and 'indicated that this might defer into the summer any *consideration* of military measures to free the hostages' (*New York Times*, 24 April 1980, p. A1; emphasis added). This statement came just one day before the rescue mission was undertaken; in this sense the fears of many West European leaders that things were 'out of control' and that Carter was ready to try a rescue mission if a European response was not forthcoming was partly accurate. What they did not know was that this European response was seen in the White House as the perfect smokescreen for the rescue mission.

In this light the decision to exclude Vance from the crucial meeting on 11 April seems a major issue in the analysis of this decision. Precisely because Vance was in the forefront of attempts to obtain European participation in sanctions, he would have argued strongly against using these as a cover. As it was, Christopher was deeply concerned that the military option would create serious diplomatic problems for the USA, and voiced this opinion at the meeting. His position was strongly attacked by Harold Brown and Walter Mondale, who argued that the rescue mission was the best way out of the situation. Critically President Carter informed the meeting that Vance had, prior to going on vacation, accepted that if military action was necessary, then he preferred the rescue mission option. At 12.48 the President decided: 'We ought to go ahead without delay' (Brzezinski, 1983, p. 493). Yet as Brzezinski points out:

> In a way, the decision had been foreshadowed by the discussion initiated at the March 22 briefing at Camp David. From that date on, the rescue mission became the obvious option if negotiations failed – and on that point there was almost unanimous consensus within the top echelons of the Administration. (Brzezinski, 1983, p. 493)

When Vance returned from his vacation, Christopher informed him of the plan, and 'he was dismayed and mortified by it' (Brzezinski, 1983, pp. 493-4). Warren Christopher had decided not to disturb Vance on vacation with the news, as he was 'under the impression that Vance, who was taking his first time off in months, had given his tacit, if reluctant, approval to the plan' (McFadden *et al.*, 1981, p. 220). After all, had Vance objected to it, Christopher reasoned, he would surely have stayed for the meeting or left instructions for his deputy (Salinger, 1981, p. 235). Vance met with the President on 15 April and outlined his objections to the plan. First, it was very unlikely to be successful. Secondly, even if successful, a number of hostages would be lost in the process. Thirdly, if the mission succeeded, there was nothing to prevent the seizure of further hostages from the US community (and, more worrying, from a diplomatic perspective, other Western communities) in Iran. Finally, there would be serious political and diplomatic repercussions – Vance asked how the allies would react when they learned that they had been deceived (Salinger,

1981, pp. 235–6). President Carter gave Vance a chance to present these reservations to the national Security Council later that day. At this meeting no one supported Vance, the common response to his position being that it offered no guarantee of releasing the hostages. Added to this was Brzezinski's point that the mission had to be attempted by 1 May or not at all, because of the lack of night-time thereafter. At this juncture Carter said he would go ahead as planned. The remainder of the meeting was spent discussing the possibility of taking prisoners for leverage, and the desirability of combining the rescue mission with a wider retaliatory response. On 16 April the mission was examined in great detail at a secret briefing with the mission's commanders: as a result of these discussions it was decided to raise the number of helicopters from seven to eight (Brzezinski, 1983, p. 495). Despite this, the overall mission commander, Major-General James Vaught, pointed out that the helicopters were still one of the most critical problems. When Carter received Jordan's message that the hostages would not, according to secret Iranian government sources, be released for 'months and months', he gave the go-ahead (Carter, 1982, pp. 511–12). On 21 April Vance, knowing that the mission was to go ahead, offered his resignation, but agreed to delay it until after the rescue mission.

Having traced the development of the process that led to the decision to undertake the rescue mission, it is now necessary to turn to consider the post-decisional period. By 21 April the decision was made; it then had to be implemented. In line with the framework outlined in the introductory chapter to this volume it is important to state, first, what the planned implementation was, and then to see what actually happened. This will allow the examination of how and why the process of implementation altered the desired outcome. At the request of the task force the date of the rescue mission was set for 24 April, primarily because of the degree of moon illumination expected that night. On that evening, at dusk local time (10.30 a.m. EST), eight RH-53 (Sea stallion) helicopters took off from the aircraft-carrier *Nimitz* and flew nearly 600 miles at a very low altitude (to avoid Iranian radar, and with radio blackout (to avoid the mission being detected), from the Arabian Sea to a location (Desert One) about 320 miles south-east of Tehran. Earlier four C-130 transport aircraft had taken off from Egypt with the Delta team of ninety-seven men and their equipment. After refuelling in Oman, they landed at Desert One at 10.30 p.m. local time. The location of Desert One was chosen because it was a secret airstrip (allegedly laid out years before by the CIA) in a very remote part of Iran, west of the town Tabas in the empty great salt desert, Dasht-e-Kavir. The plan called for the eight helicopters to arrive at around midnight local time. They would be refuelled by the C-130s and the Delta team would transfer to them.

Three hours before dawn on the morning of 25 April, the eight helicopters would take off and fly north-west to a second location, Desert

Two, some fifty miles south-east of Tehran. CIA agents in Iran (led by Richard Meadows) would meet them there and hide the helicopters in a 'mountain hideout'. Delta would remain there during the next day, being picked up the following night by Meadows and his team in a fleet of trucks and then taken to a location called the 'warehouse' just inside the city. Following a reconnaissance by Beckwith and Meadows, Delta would drive to the Embassy in a fleet of vehicles driven by exiled Iranians who had arrived on the C-130s. The plan then was for Delta to attack the Embassy (while a smaller team went to the Foreign Ministry to release the three hostages there) and rescue the hostages. In case resistance was heavy, C-130 gunships would be able to provide cover (although it is still not clear whether these would have been in the area anyway). Contrary to many reports at the time, it has since emerged that the plan was for one helicopter from Desert Two to land inside the Embassy compound to pick up the hostages, while others went to a nearby soccer stadium to pick up the rest of the Delta force (*Newsweek*, 12 July 1982, pp. 20–2). From these locations the entire force would travel to an airstrip known as Manzariyeh, about fifty miles south of Tehran. At this airstrip, already secured by another commando team, C-130s would transport the party out of Iran en route to Egypt. There the hostages would be switched to a hospital jet and taken to the US military hospital in Wiesbaden, West Germany, arriving on the afternoon of 26 April. That was the plan.

What happened is, of course, both well known and rather different from what was intended; the rescue forces never got beyond Desert One. About one-third of the way into the mission (two hours after take-off) one of the helicopters received cockpit indications that there was about to be a rotor-blade failure. This indicator warns of a 'potential abort situation' and, accordingly, the crew landed immediately. Another helicopter followed them down, as operations security (OPSEC) required radio silence. The crew found that one of the rotor blades had lost pressure (they are pressurized by nitrogen), but they were unable to ascertain whether this was due to a cracked spar or merely a leaky valve (in which case the mission could have been continued as the integrity of the rotor blade was not threatened; indeed, there has not been a single case of rotor-blade failure in the RH-53 helicopters (SORG, 1980, p. 44). The commander of the helicopter followed procedure and abandoned the helicopter; he and his crew were transferred, along with all classified documentation, to the accompanying helicopter.

However, the other helicopters were by this time encountering a very dense dust cloud, which prevented the maintenance of visual contact. Without breaking radio silence, the crews proceeded, except for the first two helicopters in the formation, which turned back out of the cloud and landed, expecting the others to follow. When this did not occur, they continued the path on instrument navigation. Shortly afterwards, another helicopter suffered a mechanical failure. A motor, which powered a blower providing cool air to a power supply, failed; consequently the power supply overheated and rendered inoperative parts of the navigational equipment. The crew did not have visual contact with the other helicopters, and could not see the ground even from a height of seventy-five feet. Thus they concluded that they could not continue, as they were under half an hour away from reaching a mountainous area. They reversed course and returned to the *Nimitz*, arriving with only minutes of fuel remaining. This decision proved critical since had the helicopter arrived at Desert One, the mission would have continued.

As it was, the six remaining helicopters arrived at Desert One, between fifty and eighty-five minutes later than planned. However, on landing, another helicopter was found to be mechanically unsound. About two hours after take-off, the crew had received cockpit indication of the failure of a second-stage hydraulic system. In fact, a nut had cracked in the system thereby not only releasing all the hydraulic fluid, but also causing the pump to burn out (as it is cooled by its own hydraulic fluid). Although this still left the first stage operational, the risk was that if this failed, the flight controls would lock and a crash would be very likely. The crew had hoped to be able to repair the fault at Desert One. This, however, proved impossible. The other helicopters arrived, but out of order, so that the flight commander arrived next to last and did not know that one helicopter had turned back. The crew of the unsound helicopter decided that they could not repair it and, therefore, said they could not proceed. At this point the various commanders of the separate elements of the rescue force consulted and agreed that since they only had five helicopters, as opposed to the six required for the mission, they would have to abort it. They communicated this to the Joint Task Force commander in Egypt, who relayed it to Washington. The President had already been kept fully informed of events and, therefore, knew about the two failures in the helicopter fleet (and also about the unexpected arrival of some forty Iranians on board a bus and two other vehicles at Desert One – they were detained!). At 4.45 Washington time Secretary of Defense Brown called the President: 'I think we have an abort situation One helicopter at Desert One has a hydraulic problem. We thus have less than the minimum six to go' (Brzezinski, 1983, p. 497). After checking the recommendation of the ground commander (Beckwith), President Carter aborted the mission at 4.57. At this point, as the rescue force began their escape from Desert One, disaster occurred. At 5.58 the President was informed that one helicopter had run into a C-130 and had burst into flames; within a few hours he learnt that there had been eight deaths. The White House delayed any press release until 1 a.m. on 25 April. What had happened was that the C-130s were refuelling the helicopters with their engines running to guard against the possibility of suffering from engine-stall. The one helicopter that had not yet been refuelled could not be supplied by the designated C-130 as it was already very low. So the helicopter crew was asked to move the helicopter to another C-130 (which had extra fuel, since not all of its assigned helicopters had arrived). During this manoeuvre the helicopter hit the C-130. The commander ordered the helicopter crews to evacuate aboard the C-130s rather than try to return to the *Nimitz*. In the rush to do this classified documents were left on the helicopters; these contained information as to the location of the other staging-posts and could easily have jeopardized the extrication of the CIA agents in Tehran who had undertaken the preparatory work.

It is very clear that there is a massive gap between what the decision-makers expected to happen and what actually occurred. President Carter has an equally clear notion of what went wrong, one which does not hint at there being any structural problems in the implementation process:

> The cancellation of our mission was caused by a strange series of mishaps – almost completely unpredictable. The operation itself was well planned. The men were well trained. We had every possibility of success, because no Iranian alarm was raised until two or three hours after our people had all left Iran. (Carter, 1982, p. 518)

Such a reaction, although common among the senior decision-makers (Brzezinski, 1983, pp. 498–500; Jordan, 1982, pp. 270–5), was certainly not universal:

> The accidental crash in the desert and the general failure of the mission have detracted from a discussion of the basic flaws in the operational concept itself. The tendency has been to attribute the failure to simple bad luck when in point of fact the mission had very little chance of success to begin with if one assesses what appear to be basic systemic shortcomings in its planning and execution. Indeed, as regrettable as the accident at Desert One was, it may well have served to prevent an even more serious and costly failure later on in the mission. (Gabriel, 1980–1, p. 8)

This was evidently the concern of the Joint Chiefs of Staff, who set up a Special Operations Review Group (SORG) to examine any possible planning failures. Their report (SORG, 1980) highlighted twenty-three areas of concern in the planning and execution of the raid, although in many of these cases they found nothing to criticize. Naturally the mission has generated a large literature examining why it failed. From these sources, it is possible to isolate fourteen issues where the implementation process seems to have led to a marginally different outcome from that intended by those who took the political decisions in Washington; together these add up to a most explicit illustration of the main theme of this volume, that implementation, rather than decision, may cause foreign policy behaviour. These issues may be analysed conveniently by dividing them into three groups: planning issues, operational issues and contingency issues.

Planning Issues

ISSUE ONE
The first issue that the implementation perspective sheds light on is that of the nature of the plan for the rescue mission. Gabriel has argued that the plan was not only too complicated, but also relied too much on 'gimmickry, exotic skills and non-military elements to compensate for a realistic assessment of battle conditions' (Gabriel, 1980–1, p. 9). Specifically he argues that the assault force was too small for the operation, · the rationale for the size of the force being determined above all by the desire for secrecy. In this light the chances of success would have been very slim (see issue two, below). Further, SORG found that because of the desire for secrecy, the planning was never reviewed independently. They reported: 'the hostage rescue mission plan was never subjected to rigorous testing and evaluation by qualified, independent observers and monitors short of the Joint Chiefs of Staff themselves' (SORG, 1980, pp. 35–6). One result of this was that no final plan was ever written up. This made the task of examining it for any weaknesses very difficult: 'A written plan to supplement oral briefings to the Joint Chiefs of Staff would have provided them a document to study and review in the privacy of their own offices, which might have sharpened their understanding of details and led to more incisive questions' (SORG, 1980, p. 36). For reasons of operations security (OPSEC), then, planned implementation of the decision was never critically assessed outside the immediate commanders of the operation, and even then was never available in one document.

ISSUE TWO
Although OPSEC required a minimum of participation in the planning process, there was one independent analysis of the plan. This was prepared for CIA Director Stansfield Turner on 16 March 1980. There is no mention of this being sent to the President, nor of its being discussed at any of the meetings held by the President to decide whether to proceed or not, although Turner was present at them! What his reasons were for not mentioning the findings of his own agency on the probability of success of the mission, or, if mentioned, why they were ignored, are not known, but the findings were very clearly at odds with the views of the planners. According to the report, the plan would have probably resulted in the 'loss' of 60 per cent of the hostages during the rescue mission: 'The estimate of a loss rate of 60 per cent for the Embassy hostages represents the best estimates (Salinger, 1981, p. 238). Further, the report suggested that no analogous large-scale rescue missions had been undertaken in

urban areas during the previous fifteen years, and concluded that it was equally likely to prove a complete failure as a complete success. Salinger comments: 'The American Government, in sum, had undertaken a rescue mission that its own intelligence service had predicted would result in the deaths of 60 per cent of the people it was trying to liberate' (ibid., p. 238). Whether this estimate was accurate or not is immaterial; what is crucial is that there is no evidence of this being discussed by those who took the key political decisions. After all, the mission had been initially estimated as having a zero-probability of success in November 1979 (Jordan, 1982, p. 258). But at exactly the time when the CIA report was presented to Turner, Brzezinski notes,

> a very comprehensive review of the rescue plan undertaken by Brown, Jones, and me in mid-March led me to the conclusion that the rescue mission had a reasonably good chance of success though there probably would be some casualties. There was no certain way of estimating how large they might be. (Brzezinski, 1983, pp. 489–90)

ISSUE THREE

Despite the complex planning that was undertaken to take care of every contingency, one major criticism of it was that there was not sufficient in the way of rehearsal. Gabriel comments that:

> In one sense it was over-rehearsed while in another it was not rehearsed enough. No less than twenty-four rehearsals were carried out prior to execution. However, only four of these involved most elements of the force. (Gabriel, 1980–1, pp. 8–9).

Rehearsals were, therefore, fragmented. Each section rehearsed over and over again, but not in conjunction with other units. This had two results: first, it reduced the capacity of the rescue force for innovation and flexibility, so that when things went wrong there was no tendency to improvise, only to go back to the pre-planned contingencies. The second was that few members of the team knew anything other than their own tasks; very few indeed had any conception of the overall plan. Thus, as Gabriel concluded: 'In the end, the way in which the mission plan was rehearsed, piecemeal and far too often, produced a force that was so rigid and so committed to an anticipated scenario that its ability to improvise in the face of changing circumstances was lost' (Gabriel, 1980–1, p. 9).

Even then, various key aspects of the plan were not rehearsed. The plan called for two helicopters to land simultaneously in the soccer stadium near the Embassy, but although Beckwith recommended such a rehearsal at a stadium near Fort Carson in Colorado, it was vetoed on grounds of security (*Newsweek*, 12 July 1982, p. 22). Instead a marked-out grid was used but the pilots *never* got the landing right. Furthermore, the final dress rehearsal was described by one participant as: 'the sorriest display of professionalism I've ever seen' (*Newsweek*, 12 July 1982, p. 22); the Desert Two night-time landing rehearsals resulted in the helicopters setting down as far as a mile apart! This difficulty led to very strained relations between the commander of the rescue force and the Marine helicopter pilots. Beckwith has since commented: 'If you're going to do these kinds of things, you better have the right cuts of cloth in pilots.' He has also admitted that he nearly drew his pistol on the pilots at Desert One, calling them 'cowards' (*Newsweek*, 12 July 1982, p. 22).

ISSUE FOUR
In each of the issues examined above OPSEC was the primary determinant of decisions. SORG felt that this problem was the most difficult one to assess: the balance between the needs for OPSEC and its costs in effective planning is a fine one. Yet SORG concluded that OPSEC was too rigidly enforced – thus preventing effective planning, command and training. As will be seen later, it also caused serious problems in the implementation of the raid. They argued that a number of the problems that occurred during the mission either could have been predicted or could have been overcome had OPSEC been relaxed a little; this would not, they felt, have jeopardized the mission (SORG, 1980, pp. 13–14).

However, it is also clear that OPSEC was not applied to anything like the degree ordered by the planners of the mission. To cite the most obvious example, the helicopter pilots 'had no appreciation for secrecy, they called their wives over open phone lines and left codes lying around' (*Newsweek*, 12 July 1982, p. 22). Despite the attempts to hide the intentions of the rescue force from other US service personnel, the very clear priority given to the force and its needs must have aroused suspicion.

ISSUE FIVE
The final planning issue concerns the size of the force. There are two aspects to this: the first concerns the actual rescue unit. The initial plan called for a force of eighty, but this gradually was increased, requiring changes in the number of helicopters from six to eight. This, in turn, led to problems of getting the equipment in the right place and in the right condition in time. As the SORG concluded:

> the failure to fix the size and composition of the assault force at an early point, or at a minimum establish a troop lift ceiling, led to late juggling in the number of helicopters. This appeared to have exacerbated a problem that, even in the early planning stages, was considered the most critical link in the entire operation. (SORG, 1980, p. 27)

Even so, there is considerable evidence that the original planning called for a much larger assault force of 600 men and thirty helicopters. This was cut back, to preserve surprise and ensure OPSEC, but, argue some, to a point where there was little margin for error (Heritage Foundation, 1980, p. 27).

The second aspect of the force size issue concerns the number of helicopters assigned to the mission. When he heard of the failure of the rescue mission, Yitzhak Rabin, Israel's former Prime Minister and Army chief of Staff, asked, 'America doesn't have enough helicopters?' (McFadden *et al.*, 1981, p. 224). The rationale for the size of the helicopter force was that a larger force would have jeopardized OPSEC and would have increased the possibility of discovery by radar. Although *Nimitz* could have carried additional helicopters, it did not, since this would have reduced the number of combat aircraft, which it 'needed' for protection in what was classified as a hostile area. Fuel was not a problem, as the C-130s carried enough to refuel at least ten helicopters. The original estimate was for four helicopters, although this was subsequently increased to six, and then eight. The SORG report concluded that eight helicopters would have given an adequate safety margin for the mission had not the force size been increased as the planning developed.

The problem of the size of the helicopter force relates to two main weaknesses, although only the first of these seems to have been taken account of in the planning of the mission. The first referred to the very demanding flight from the *Nimitz* to Desert One. As the commander of the overall mission, Major-General James Vaught, said in the briefing to President Carter:

> The helicopters [are] ... not made for long-distance, heavy-duty flying at low altitudes with full loads. That's why we've added two extra choppers to give us a wide margin of safety. Our experts believe that we could lose a helicopter. (Jordan, 1982, p. 257)

For this reason, the SORG report concluded:

> An unconstrained planner would more than likely have initially required at least 10 helicopters under JTF [Joint Task Force] combat rules, 11 under the most likely case, and up to 12 using peacetime historical data ... In sum, aside from OPSEC, no operational or logistic factor prohibited launching 11 from Nimitz and continuing beyond the halfway point to Desert One with 10 helicopters. (SORG, 1980, p. 33)

Yet again OPSEC dominated military requirements. Gabriel comments that:

> Given the long distance that the machines would have to fly, the failure to anticipate mechanical breakdown and to compensate for it by using a

larger number of machines was a major error. The '100% Rule' – employing at least double the equipment needed in these types of unconventional operations – was ignored. (Gabriel, 1980–1, p. 8)

This very optimistic planning clearly did not take account of a second weakness in the helicopter force, namely, the well-known mechanical breakdowns that they suffered from. The RH-53 is, in normal operations, considered to be mission-capable only 47 per cent of the time; it is fully mission-capable only 17 per cent of the time! (US Congress, House of Representatives, Defense Appropriations Hearings, 1980, pp. 622–3). Although in later evidence to congressional hearings on the mission, the planners argued that the actual mission-capable figures were much higher for this type of role than these figures suggest, even their figure of 85 per cent still gives only 6:8 helicopters being mission-capable. There is very little in the way of a margin for error. Finally, it is crucial to note that the helicopters used in training suffered from precisely the same mechanical faults as occurred during the mission, namely, rotor-blade failure, and hydraulic-pump failure. What seems to be very evident is that the concern with OPSEC severely reduced any realistic planning as to the likely depletion rate of the helicopters. It was, of course, the size of the helicopter component of the rescue force that resulted in the cancellation of the mission; and the mission planners were aware that the helicopter component was the most vulnerable of the entire force. With the benefit of hindsight, it seems incredible that despite this only eight helicopters were sent for a mission that had to have six fully operational helicopters remaining after such a demanding flight from the *Nimitz*.

Operational Issues

ISSUE ONE

Essentially the cancellation of the mission followed the non-arrival at Desert One of one helicopter. Yet the evidence that has become available since the mission indicates that such a decision to abort could easily have been avoided. Aside from the possibility of proceeding with five helicopters had the plan been less rigid, there is the possibility that had OPSEC not been so overridingly important the non-arrival at Desert One of the helicopter that turned back could have been prevented. This is for the reason that the pilot thought he was in the middle of a large dust storm, whereas he was virtually at the edge of it. The pilot

> based his abort decision on instrument malfunctions exacerbated by the visibility conditions. The crew commander indicated later that he would have continued had he known that restricted visibility conditions did not prevail at destination ... [and] that one additional mission-capable aircraft would have permitted the entire mission to continue. (SORG, p. 30)

What prevented the pilot from knowing this was the ban on radio communication between the helicopters. Not only had some of the helicopters exited the dust storm, but the C-130s at Desert One knew that the area was free of such conditions. The SORG report concluded that

> the major factor in [the helicopter pilot's] abort decision was lack of readily available information on weather conditions further en route... Information on the number of mission-capable helicopters ... could have influenced his decision and should have been made known. Failure to pass this vital information back to the carrier and support bases and rebroadcast it via secure HF was the result of a very restrictive communications doctrine related to the overriding concern for OPSEC. However, there were ways to pass the information to C-130s and helicopters en route that would have small likelihood of compromising the mission. (ibid., p. 45)

In other words, had the pilot known that two helicopters were suffering from mechanical problems, and that he was some twenty-five minutes away from exiting the dust storm, he, by his own admission, would have continued. Then six mission-capable helicopters would have been in place at Desert One.

ISSUE TWO

As was pointed out above, the helicopters suffered from identical faults in practice as occurred during the mission itself. Aside from the question of whether the size of the force should have been increased accordingly or whether such mechanical failures could be repaired were they to occur on the mission, it is evident that the dust caused severe problems for the helicopters. Although the protective sand screens were removed from the air intakes of the engines, it was later said that this was not a cause of either of the two mechanical failures (US Congress, House of Representatives, Defense Appropriations Hearings, 1980, pp. 674–5). Nevertheless, the dust storm clearly led to one helicopter turning back. Yet SORG reported that the helicopter pilots 'were surprised when they encountered the dust, were unprepared to accurately assess its impact on their flight, and stated that they were not advised of the phenomenon' (SORG, 1980, p. 38). On the one hand, this reflects the overriding role of OPSEC, since the traditional contact between pilots and weather forecasters was severed. Information on the weather was not relayed directly to the pilots, but rather went through an organizational filter. On the other hand, despite the fact that the planners knew of the dust phenomenon and that it was very common over the helicopters' route, they did not plan contingencies should it occur, let alone inform the pilots. It would, of course, have been possible to send a C-130 on a weather reconnaissance mission ahead of the helicopters without jeopardizing OPSEC; this could have advised the pilots of the problem and indicated alternative routes or recommended delaying the mission.

ISSUE THREE

One of the most surprising aspects of the implementation of the plan was that there was no one, overall commander. As Gabriel comments:

> In typical 'systems' fashion the operation was conceived and assembled in components, each with its own commander. Thus, at Desert One, there were no less than four commanders: the rescue force commander, the air group commander, the on-site commander, and the helicopter force commander. In addition, the Joint Task Force Commander was not even on the ground with his staff; instead, he was located aboard ship in the Persian Gulf. Finally, there was a direct link back to the White House. (Gabriel, 1980–1, p. 9)

As the hearings on the rescue mission in the House of Representatives reveal, this meant that to get an alteration to the plan, the rescue force commander had to go through four levels. Thus it took twelve minutes for the recommendation of Beckwith that the mission be aborted to be confirmed by the President (US Congress, House of Representatives, Defense Appropriation Hearings, 1980, p. 630). More problematic was the fact that this split command resulted in a situation where no one on site had overall command. This meant that *no one* on site could improvise or try to alter the plan to changing circumstances (for instance, five helicopters); all they could do was assume responsibility for their own area of competence and follow prearranged plans and contingencies. In this light it is unsurprising that they recommended cancelling the mission as the lack of a sixth helicopter challenged each unit's planning assumptions, nor is it surprising that no one tried to assume control outside his area of competence. In the absence of any authority to alter the plan the inescapable logic of all the planning agreements as to force levels, and so on, resulted in the joint recommendation to cancel.

This problem was exacerbated by the serious conflict between Beckwith's rescue force and the Marine helicopter pilots and by the addition, late in the planning stage, of navy and Marine Corps teams into the original army–air force team. As a former Pentagon official remarked: 'On the basis of my experience ... each service would want a piece of the action, and simply settling who was to do what ... would be a major problem' (McFadden *et al.*, 1981, pp. 223–4). This was reflected in the composition of the helicopter crews, which was a mixture of navy and Marine Corps personnel.

The SORG report concluded that there were serious problems with the command structure: 'There was no identifiable command post for the on-scene commander; a staff and runners were not anticipated; backup rescue radios were not available – and, lastly, key personnel ... were not identified for ease of recognition' (SORG, 1980, p. 50). Thus helicopter pilots did not know who was giving orders, and questioned their authority to do so. The staggered arrival of the helicopters exacerbated this, as the commander did not arrive first as scheduled. Further, when the helicopters were abandoned after the fatal crash, no one thought to give orders to destroy classified material.

ISSUE FOUR

The horrendous accident that occurred at Desert One when a helicopter was manoeuvring to be refuelled illustrates a number of implementation problems. The C-130 from which it was supposed to be refuelled had been waiting at Desert One for over four hours, with all engines running to guard against the possibility of engine-stall; it was, therefore, very low on fuel. This necessitated the repositioning of the helicopter to another C-130. This was undertaken in total darkness, with no lights and with the engines of the C-130s creating dust storms as well as air turbulence. Yet this part of the plan was never rehearsed in full. Rather, a 'training exercise ... conducted on 13–14 April with two C-130s and four helicopters was used to validate the Desert One concept' (McFadden et al., 1981, p. 223).

ISSUE FIVE

When Desert One was evacuated, classified documents were left on the helicopters. These contained pictures and details of the subsequent operation, with the location given for the warehouse Richard Meadows had arranged as a staging-post. While the pilots surely had no need to know this location since their helicopters would not fly there, it gave all the information needed to compromise severely the CIA's operations in Iran. That they all managed to get out safely reflects the state of turmoil inside Iran. But the potential for damage occasioned by leaving the documents was sufficient to cause Beckwith to request an air strike to destroy the helicopters that had been left behind. This was refused by Washington in an attempt to preserve the image of the rescue as a bloodless, humanitarian mission (*Newsweek*, 12 July 1982, pp. 22–3).

Contingency Issues

In addition to the major issues raised above, there are four issues that could have had a significant impact on the implementation of the mission had it proceed as planned.

ISSUE ONE

It is rather surprising to learn that the rescue force only found out the precise location of the hostages in the US Embassy some four hours before the mission began. The team was ready to leave for Iran without a clear view of exactly where the hostages were, when they learned, by chance, their location. This occurred because the Iranians allowed the Embasssy's Pakistani cook to leave Iran three days before the rescue mission was to take place. The cook did not inform anyone of his release, and the CIA found out only because he sat next to a deep-cover agent on the plane from Iran. He was soon debriefed and was able to give the precise locations. Clearly, the mission would have entailed significant risks if it had involved the rescue team searching the four probable locations in the compound.

ISSUE TWO

The location of Desert One was chosen despite the fact that it was near a main road. Indeed, some forty Iranians had to be detained as they drove along in three vehicles as the rescue force assembled. Had the mission not been abandoned, their presence would have caused serious problems for the rescue force, especially since the actual assault on the Embassy was not due for over 24 hours after they were detained. Quite what would have happened to them is not known, but they would in all probability have been taken away by C-130s or by helicopters. Their non-appearance at their destinations *could* have caused problems for the mission's secrecy.

ISSUE THREE

The choice of Desert One nearly resulted in the mission being discovered, since a CIA plane flew to Iran to sample the landing conditions. As the agents took soil samples and installed remote-control beacons no fewer than six vehicles drove past. This did not compromise the mission, as no one appeared to take any notice. In a similar vein the preparations of the rescue force in Egypt had to be timed around the passage overhead of a Soviet satellite. When it was overhead, the 400 soldiers took cover in an aircraft hangar.

ISSUE FOUR

Finally, the mission was very nearly called off from the Tehran end, because two days before the raid the Iranian exile who had rented the warehouse on the outskirts of Tehran left the country without explanation. Then just thirty-six hours before the start of the mission, a group of Iranian workmen dug a trench across the front of the warehouse, cutting it off from the road. Despite the obvious concern that the mission was expected, and that the CIA group in Tehran was being set up, Meadows bribed the workmen to fill in the trench, and then sent Washington the all-clear to proceed.

Conclusion

In his analysis of the rescue mission Gabriel concludes that it

> seems an almost classic example of one planned and executed by a bureaucracy. It placed many military requirements secondary to others; it was over-officered but not focused in command responsibility; it was over-rehearsed in systems fashion to the point of inflexibility; there was no major dissent from within the military as a result of the planners'

cloak of secrecy which left no one who would subject the plan to a critique except for those who formulated it. (Gabriel, 1980-1, pp. 9-10)

It was, he feels, an operation almost predestined to fail. The SORG report concluded that the concept of the mission was valid and that the operation was feasible. They point out that it was the best plan available, and that it could not have been attempted at an earlier date. But the operation was not successful for a number of reasons: of these, the critical ones were the overriding importance of OPSEC; the fragile nature of command and control in the rescue forces; the lack of full-scale training; the lack of provisions for weather and dust contingencies; and the absence of sufficient in the way of backup helicopters (SORG, 1980, pp. 57-9).

While it is a matter of debate as to whether or not changing one of these factors would have allowed the mission to continue, and although there has been much in the way of discussion as to which implementation problem was the most serious, the overwhelming finding of this case study is that the implementation process severely influenced the actual behaviour. Those who took the decisions were very evidently expecting something far removed from what actually happened. While they expressed surprise and saw events as occurring because of unexpected accidents and bad luck, an analysis of the evidence suggests otherwise. The failure of the mission was not due to bad luck, but to systemic deficiencies in the implementation process. As has been argued above, had the mission not been aborted at Desert One, there are strong reasons to suggest that it would have run into further problems as the mission unfolded. But with reference to the actual cause of the failure of the mission, it is evident that the planners were so concerned with OPSEC that they simply did not follow through the logic of their own assumptions as to the likely depletion rate of the helicopters. In this regard much of the mission illustrates very well the phenomenon of groupthink (Janis, 1982) in that a small group of planners accepted very optimistic estimates as to the functioning of the units of the rescue force in order to be able to provide the mission that political leaders so clearly desired. For their part, the political decision-makers accepted the plan despite clear weaknesses (which they discussed) and some evidence that it would not be successful. Thus Cyrus Vance's doubts were dismissed, as he was seen as someone who was tired and who wanted to resign anyway (Carter, 1982, p. 510; Jordan, 1982, pp. 283-4; Brzezinski, 1983, p. 496). While from an implementation perspective it is possible to identify the ways in which that process affected the outcome in a way that was significantly at variance from that called for in the planning of the mission, from a political perspective it is equally evident that the political leaders wanted something to be done. Not only does this come across very clearly in the memoirs of those who took the decisions, but it also offers an explanation of why the plan was not subjected to the kind of critical analysis that possibly would have highlighted some of its weaknesses. Having said this, these weaknesses were so fundamental and so widespread that some would surely have slipped through tighter political scrutiny. It is exactly because of this that the rescue mission so vividly illustrates the ways in which implementation matters and, therefore, indicates the explanatory power of the implementation perspective.

Notes: Chapter 2

I would like to thank the research fund of the School of Economic and Social Studies of the University of East Anglia for providing me with financial support to carry out the research for this case study.

1   There are many studies of the main events of the hostage crisis. Of these, the most useful are House of Representatives Committee on Foreign Affairs, *The Iran Hostage Crisis: A Chronology of Daily Developments*, US Government Printing Office, Washington, DC, 1981; and Robert McFadden, *et al.*, *No Hiding Place*, New York Times Books, 1981.
2   For a detailed account of the intelligence operation in Tehran, see the lengthy special report by David Martin in *Newsweek*, 12 July 1982, pp. 16–25.
3   The military aspects of the training and the actual mission are discussed in detail in the *Rescue Mission Report* prepared by the Special Operations Review Group of the Joint Chiefs of Staff (SORG), published in Washington, August 1980.

3

Britain and the Implementation of Oil Sanctions against Rhodesia

Brian White

It was ironically the successful implementation of the Unilateral Declaration of Independence (UDI) by the Smith regime in Rhodesia on 11 November 1965 that led to the unsuccessful attempts over more than a decade by successive British governments to implement economic (including oil) sanctions against Rhodesia. Though Prime Minister Harold Wilson was convinced that UDI could be averted and claimed to have done everything possible to prevent it, the Wilson government was immediately faced with the problem of how to respond to this act in what was, in law at least, a British colony. Even before UDI, the British government had been aware of pressures upon it not to grant independence to Rhodesia until majority rule had been achieved for the black African population. After the Declaration of Independence in Salisbury, such pressures naturally intensified.

In Britain various groups including important sections of the labour Party, the Liberal Party and church organizations made their views clear. More significantly perhaps, international opinion on the matter was forcefully expressed and centred on the demand for military intervention in Rhodesia. The United Nations (UN), the Organization for African Unity (OAU) and the Commonwealth provided for both a collective condemnation of UDI and for the generation of pressure upon the British government to respond decisively. On 5 November the General Assembly of the UN passed a resolution calling upon Britain to take all necessary measures, including military force, to meet the threat to international peace and security arising from the Rhodesian situation. This was followed later that month by a Security Council resolution which reinforced the General Assembly resolution and also imposed voluntary economic sanctions on Rhodesia. The OAU met early in December at Addis Ababa and agreed that members should break off diplomatic relations with Britain if appropriate action to end UDI was not forthcoming. Ghana and Tanzania did, in fact, break off relations on 15 December and relations with Zambia were severely strained. Meanwhile growing concern within the Commonwealth as a whole led to the convening of a special Commonwealth conference at Lagos in January 1966, devoted specifically to Rhodesia.

Mr Wilson later recalled the pressure to which the government was subject in the period immediately after UDI, referring to the 'four constituencies' of Rhodesian, British, Commonwealth and world (UN) opinion. At the UN 'the Foreign Secretary was having the roughest possible ride – almost every non-aligned nation, headed by the Africans, and supported by the Soviet bloc, was pressing for immediate action'. As for the Commonwealth, 'there was the clear fact that if we failed to react strongly against UDI, the Commonwealth as we knew it, would break up or perhaps be reduced to a handful of the old dominions plus perhaps Malaysia and Malawi'. Eager to avoid a situation which could have been exploited by the USSR and China, he concluded that the strongest possible response to UDI was necessary. Wilson makes it clear that he regarded this as nothing less than part of a 'battle for the soul of Africa' (Wilson, 1971, pp. 234–7).

As there were evident pressures both inside and outside the country pushing the government towards the use of military force as the most (if not the only) effective way to end the rebellion, and given Wilson's perception of the significance of these demands, the decision to resist requires some explanation. In the context of this chapter the refusal to use military force crucially narrowed the options available to the government and some comment on this must necessarily precede an account of the decision to impose economic sanctions in general, and oil sanctions in particular.

It had been repeatedly asserted in the months before UDI that Britain 'would never use force either to prevent or to reverse an illegal seizure of independence' (Windrich, 1978, p. 58). If the use of force was considered after UDI, it was firmly ruled out. Both military and political factors have been advanced to explain the ruling out of this option. The military arguments turn around the logistics of deployment in Central Africa, the existing overcommitment of British troops 'east of Suez' and the possibility of significant resistance by Rhodesian forces. Harold Wilson has added some weight to these arguments by highlighting the 1963 agreement by which the previous Conservative government had transferred to Southern Rhodesia the military forces of the former Federation. Most commentators, it must be said, have questioned the validity and/or the relevance of these military factors, preferring to focus on the domestic political context. Wilson himself has stressed the weakness of his minority government, claiming that neither the Parliamentary Labour Party as a whole nor enough Conservatives would have supported the use of force: 'On the day UDI was declared our majority was one' (Wilson, 1971, p. 236). Others have pointed to residual memories of the Suez débâcle and the 'kith and kin' argument with its uncomfortable racial overtones given the deployment of British forces elsewhere, in order to explain the refusal to intervene militarily. What can be asserted is that the Wilson Cabinet was predisposed to believe that the most the domestic political situation would allow by way of a response was also the most that was needed (ibid., 1971; Wallace, 1975). Thus the strongest possible response to UDI could not include the use of military force.

The Decision to Impose Oil Sanctions on Rhodesia

More insight into the decision not to use force can be gleaned from the pattern of decision-making that followed. Throughout, the response to UDI was regarded by the government as essentially a 'damage limitation' exercise. The object of any response was to retain control of the situation and to do no more than was necessary to achieve that objective. H. R. Strack offers a useful summary of the government's position: 'Central to British policy after UDI were the objectives to secure universal acknowledgement of British responsibility for Rhodesia, to retain, at all times, the initiative in the UN regarding any action taken against Rhodesia, and to discourage the use of force' (Strack, 1978, p. 16). In an effort to divert the pressure for military intervention as well as to deter UDI, Wilson warned Ian Smith in their 8 October meeting of the possible use and the consequences of economic sanctions. Having presented draft regulations to the Cabinet that same day, the Prime Minister was in a position to announce to the House of Commons a series of economic and political measures as soon as UDI was declared. By early December up to 95 per cent of total Rhodesian exports to Britain had been banned. Sanctions were clearly regarded by the government as the most effective means available, short of military force, for compelling a return to legality in Rhodesia. What is interesting, however, about the first and the second round of sanctions measures announced is the important economic measures that were not taken: notably 'the most obvious omission from the list was oil, and on this product, so crucial to the survival of the Rhodesian economy, the government had no proposals to make' (Windrich, 1978, pp. 63-4).

The government nevertheless felt it necessary to demonstrate to world opinion that effective measures were being taken and Foreign Secretary Michael Stewart was dispatched to New York to present the British case to the UN Security Council. It was hoped that this would enable the government to retain the initiative and prevent 'excessive action'. But the very act of internationalizing the issue meant that the government had to sacrifice some ability at least to control the outcome. Though the British delegation refused to accept the Ivory Coast resolution calling for comprehensive economic sanctions, they were forced to compromise, not for the last time, by accepting a new resolution which included significantly a voluntary ban on the supply of oil to Rhodesia. The British fear, expressed then and more forcefully at later UN meetings, was that sanctions could escalate into a confrontation with third countries, a reference to South Africa and Portugal in this context. As a result of the Security Council resolution, though, the British government could not but proceed with the imposition of oil sanctions on Rhodesia in its own right. If the Prime Minister had any doubts on this score, they would have been removed by a strong attack by his own backbenchers in the House of Commons on 7 December, when the government was roundly criticized for failing to prevent BP tankers delivering oil to the Mozambique port of Beira destined for Rhodesia.

However reluctant it may have been, the government passed the Southern Rhodesia (Petroleum) Act by Order in Council on 17 December 1965. This Act prohibited the import of oil and oil products into Rhodesia and made it a criminal offence for British nationals to supply or transport oil for Rhodesian use. It called upon other states to take similar action, stating Britain's legal right to forbid the import of any product into Rhodesia. Now committed to an oil sanctions policy, the government was soon faced with the problem of maintaining at least publicly an effective policy. Reports of violations of oil sanctions in the spring of 1966 took the government back to the UN to get the legal authority to stop tankers unloading oil at Beira:

> Had we left matters where they were, sanctions would have become totally ineffective and our Rhodesia policy would have been destroyed. Pressure for the use of force would have become stronger and stronger, with incalculable results. (Wilson, 1971, p. 290)

Having secured this authorization, the government's attention turned, rather hastily in the view of many, to initiating talks with the Smith regime. A first round of negotiations began in May, and ended with the abortive meeting aboard HMS *Tiger* in December 1966.

Though the government implied that it was the impact of sanctions that was forcing Ian Smith to the conference table, it became increasingly clear to observers that sanctions were being viewed by the government essentially as an adjunct to a process of negotiation between Britain and Rhodesia. David Vital develops this point: sanctions were 'employed reluctantly and with the express and explicit desire to return to non-forcible methods of implementing policy as soon as possible'; Thus sanctions were primarily 'marginal supplements and reinforcements to overt diplomacy' (Vital, 1968, p. 14). With the failure of the *Tiger* talks, however, and with renewed Commonwealth pressure at the London Conference (September 1966), the government was again forced back to the UN. The Security Council resolution of 16 December, sponsored by Britain, outlined a new policy of selective mandatory sanctions. Despite British protests, oil was again included, though this time 'the British

delegation refused to accept responsibility for preventing "by all possible means" the transport of oil to Rhodesia' (Windrich, 1978, p. 106). Additional British legislation was now required to give effect to mandatory
sanctions and the Southern Rhodesia (Prohibited Trade and Dealings) Order was passed in February 1967. The process of setting up sanctions against Rhodesia was completed in May 1968, when the Security Council passed a resolution imposing comprehensive mandatory sanctions.

The Implementation of Oil Sanctions

This brief review of the pattern of decision-making shows that at one level the British decision to impose oil sanctions was consequent upon the rejection of the military option and the decision to take a number of economic and political measures against Rhodesia. As William Wallace puts it, 'no single decision determined the government's handling of UDI, but a number of earlier decisions had effectively foreclosed other options' (Wallace, 1975, p. 83). At another level the decision emerged as a rather reluctant response to a series of pressures and a set of interactions in a multilateral context that it could not wholly control. Having chosen to internationalize the issue, though that may have been unavoidable, the government could not unilaterally determine the outcome of that process even if it clearly had a preference for a non-coercive strategy.

The government did nevertheless give the impression that it believed an oil sanctions policy could be successfully implemented. Harold Wilson confidently told the House on 20 December 1965 that the ban on oil could be made effective. The Middle East oil-producing states would institute a boycott, other major trading countries would cooperate and the government had taken appropriate action with the oil-distributing companies under its control. The following month the Prime Minister made his famous speech to the Commonwealth Conference in which he said that the cumulative effects of economic and financial sanctions might well be to bring the rebellion to an end 'within a matter of weeks rather than months'. Certainly, some groundwork had been done. The Prime Minister personally consulted the Americans in Washington and soundings were taken in other capitals. The prospects looked promising, but as Mr Wilson later commented with reference to his Lagos speech, 'we were misled, but what I said to my colleagues at the time appeared to be a safe prophecy' (Wilson, 1971, p. 256). These optimistic predictions were justified on the basis of expert advice available to the government, even though different assessments were in fact received from different government departments, some much less optimistic than others. The government appears to have selected the more optimistic advice it received from the Department of Economic

Affairs. It is difficult to resist the conclusion that 'faced with varying advice from officials, ministers chose that which best fitted their preferred course of action' (Wallace, 1975, p. 84).

If the official optimism was misplaced, and the Bingham Report (1978) has since shown that oil was reaching Rhodesia in substantial quantities as early as February 1966, to what extent did the apparent failure of the oil sanctions policy stem from problems at the implementation stage of the policy process? Some analysis of the emergence of the policy at the decision stage has already been offered, but it is necessary to look again at the decision from an implementation perspective.

In order to establish the nature of a decision and therefore the implementation requirements that stem from it, the objectives or purposes of that decision must be clearly identified. In November 1965 the British government regarded sanctions as the most effective way of compelling the Smith regime to restore the rule of law in Rhodesia. While there was no question of immediate majority rule because, as Mr Wilson made clear, Rhodesia was not ready for it, once the illegal rebellion had been ended, independence could be discussed on the basis of the famous Five Principles. From the outset, however, there was ambiguity about the purposes to be served by sanctions and little thought appears to have been given to the precise methods by which the policy would be implemented: 'Although the government had got their oil measures approved, the means by which they intended to enforce them remained undefined' (Windrich, 1978, p. 71). While there had been some consideration of the problem of implementation as far as military force was concerned, and this contributed to the rejection of that option, it is curious that so little consideration was given to the implementation of sanctions. With regard to what sanctions were intended to achieve, it is clear, as indicated above, that they were also intended to serve purposes other than the ending of UDI. Being seen to act, retaining control of the situation and demonstrating strength of resolve were as important as the substance of the act itself. This helps to explain, for example, why Britain went back to the UN in April 1966 to get legal authorization to stop tankers unloading at Beira.

Initial ambiguity led to growing confusion over time as to the precise purposes of sanctions. A variety of political and economic justifications were advanced particularly when the annual renewal of the Sanctions Orders was debated in Parliament. The range of justifications included keeping settlement proposals on the table, discrediting Ian Smith, or alternatively strengthening Smith against his more obdurate colleagues, and securing a better deal for black Rhodesians. It was even suggested in 1973 that a major objective of sanctions was to safeguard British trade and investment in Black Africa. Increasingly the object of the policy was simply to keep the policy in existence. The mere existence of the policy itself became a justification for its continuation. Certainly by the early 1970s, 'the only relevant issue about sanctions was not whether they should be continued, since Britain could not opt out of an international obligation it had initiated, but how they could be tightened up and made more effective '(Windrich, 1978, p. 204).

From this it can be argued that the decision to impose sanctions on Rhodesia had two essential dimensions. At one level the decision can be labelled *strategic*, the object being to induce political change in Rhodesia. At another level the decision was *symbolic*, the object being to demonstrate or signal concern about and disapproval of UDI, to a domestic and especially to an international audience. This sort of analysis fits neatly into the existing literature on economic coercion which suggests that sanctions can serve broadly three functions: to secure compliance, to punish the target and to serve symbolic or expressive functions (Galtung, 1967; Wallensteen, 1968; Schreiber, 1973). As the British government consistently denied that it was seeking to use sanctions punitively against Rhodesia, and there is no apparent reason to question this, that leaves the compliance and symbolic functions as important here.

Whether the sanctions decision was strategic or symbolic (or perhaps both) is important in terms of evaluating the significance of the implementation process. To the extent that the decision was strategic and designed to secure compliance, then implementation was crucial. The policy that flows from the decision must be implemented if compliance is to be achieved. Though, of course, even the successful implementation of a policy is no guarantee of compliance. It might be regarded as a necessary but not a sufficient condition. On the other hand, to the extent that the decision was symbolic, the implementation process was much less significant. If a policy is essentially presentational, it merely needs to exist and to have a degree of credibility. This point will be taken up in the final section of this chapter.

Looked at in strategic terms, however, there can be little doubt that sanctions failed. Sanctions themselves were insufficient to stimulate the required political changes in Rhodesia until international and regional conditions changed quite dramatically in the mid-1970s, with the Portuguese revolution of April 1974 as the critical catalyst. The overthrow of Caetano was followed by a series of governments in Lisbon determined to end Portuguese military involvement in Africa. The important result here was that Mozambique became an independent Black African state in June 1975 and a radical shift of power in southern Africa had taken place.

The impact of an independent Mozambique was threefold. First, it facilitated an intensification of the guerrilla war against the Smith regime, with Mozambique providing sanctuaries and staging areas as well as moral support for the guerrillas. The escalation of a war which had begun in 1966 weakened the regime's ability to resist sanctions by increasing the demand on resources to finance the war effort and tying up growing numbers of skilled personnel in active service. Secondly, the Vorster government in South Africa now felt compelled to go through an agonizing reappraisal of its regional strategy and decided that a settlement of the Rhodesian issue was necessary to preserve the stability of the region. It, therefore, initiated a détente with its neighbouring Black African states and they collectively began to exert influence by putting pressure on the Smith regime to resolve the issue. Finally, the new Frelimo government was now in control of Rhodesian transit facilities through Mozambique. The closure of the border with Rhodesia in March 1976 cut the traffic from Lourenço Marques at a stroke and fundamentally changed the prospects of implementing sanctions. At the same time the world recession was beginning to have a devastating effect on the Rhodesian economy. Soaring oil prices and high rates of imported inflation produced severe balance-of-payments problems and increasing economic stagnation. By 1976 the writing was already on the wall, and in September of that year, nearly eleven years after sanctions had been established, Smith finally agreed in principle to end UDI and began the process of yielding power to the African nationalists.

Retracing the story from a British perspective, the Bingham Report shows in detail how sanctions could not have secured compliant behaviour because they were not effectively implemented. Leaving aside the question of whether compliance would have been achieved at an earlier stage if implementation had been successful, the failure of sanctions as a strategic policy can be usefully analysed as an implementation problem.

The analysis would start with the policy instrument to be implemented. Again the literature on sanctions and economic coercion in general is helpful. The history of sanctions applied elsewhere prior to 1965 would suggest that they were unlikely to be used successfully against Rhodesia. Wallensteen argues that 'sanctions are badly suited for influencing the receiver: they seem to contribute to the stability of the receiver and increase popular support for the receiver government' (Wallensteen, 1968, p. 265). Hoffmann makes the point that 'when sanctions are used, the manifest goal will probably not be attained, because the very decision to apply sanctions probably indicates that the motivation of the sanctioning country is relatively low' (Hoffmann, 1967, p. 156). In a major study of economic coercion as an instrument of foreign policy Schreiber concludes that the effectiveness of sanctions is strictly limited and 'may well depend on the support of diplomatic and military pressure' (Schreiber, 1973, p. 413). Finally, Strack suggests that there is a consensus among scholars to the effect that sanctions are 'not only an ineffective means to secure policy objectives, but may be dysfunctional or counterproductive, producing results opposite to those desired by the initiators of sanctions' (Strack, 1978, p. xii). Implementation problems began with the very policy instrument chosen by the government. If the implementation process is followed through for the purposes of analysis, further problems can be seen to have revolved around the implementation environment, and the ability and willingness of the government to control that environment.

The Implementation Environment

The environment in which implementation takes place can be divided broadly into what might be called *agents* and *targets*. Agents refers to those bodies whose co-operation is required by the policy-maker to implement policy. The lower the level of co-operation received from agents, the greater are the problems faced by the policy-maker in implementing policy. Targets refers to the body/bodies against whom the policy is directed. The greater the ability of the target to resist the policy, again the greater are the problems faced by the policy-maker. In this context agents refers to those transnational corporations and states with oil interests in Southern Africa, together with the UN. The British government as policy-maker required co-operation from all these bodies for the implementation of oil sanctions to be effective. Target here simply refers to Rhodesia and the ability of the Smith regime to frustrate the sanctions effort.

As indicated earlier, Harold Wilson was confident that the oil ban could be implemented. In December 1965 he took the view that at worst only 'seepages and leakages' of oil might get through to Rhodesia. If this occurred, he reserved the right to raise the matter again at the UN in order to co-ordinate international action more effectively. When the government (hereafter HMG) felt compelled to go to the UN in April 1966 to get legal authorization for the Beira patrol to intercept tankers, co-operation was forthcoming. As a result, supplies of crude oil to Rhodesia via Beira were effectively stopped. As Bingham notes rather sardonically, this was the 'first, perhaps the only, major victory won by the oil sanctions policy' (Bingham and Gray, 1978, p. 66). Though HMG was concerned at the escalation of sanctions, as enshrined in successive UN resolutions, it could not complain about the level of co-operation received. After May 1968, a Security Council committee was established to monitor the implementation of sanctions. The real problem here, as Cross points out, is that the world economy is simply too complex to be adequately policed by international agencies (Cross, 1981, p. 74).

If the UN was broadly supportive, the relationship between HMG and other agents was more problematic. This was particularly the case with the oil companies. At the time of UDI Shell and BP between them supplied approximately 50 per cent of Rhodesian oil. In December 1965 they were instructed by HMG to obey the Orders in Council and prevent supplies of oil reaching Rhodesia. The corporate structures of these companies, however, made it difficult for them to co-operate even with the best of intentions. They operate internationally 'through locally-incorporated subsidiaries where the subsidiaries enjoy a large measure of autonomy and seek to observe the laws of their place of incorporation' (Bingham and Gray, 1978, p. 46). The two oil companies marketed in Southern Africa through a separate company called the Consolidated Petroleum Co. which they jointly owned, though for historical reasons Shell tended to be the dominant partner. The practical effect of this was that BP was one step further removed than the Shell Group from direct involvement in the business operations of the local companies. Local Shell and BP companies in Southern Africa were subsidiaries of Consolidated at least until the mid-1970s. Corporate structures meant that day to day management, how much to sell, at what price and, significantly, to whom had become over the years local decisions. Bingham discovered that 'not only was there much less direct control of the subsidiaries than is frequently found, but also there was much less detailed knowledge of the subsidiaries' activities' (Bingham and Gray, 1978, p.11).

Clearly, the states that sought to control the activities of the other oil companies supplying Rhodesian oil faced similar layers of control problems, assuming that they wished to co-operate. Certainly the USA and France appeared to co-operate with HMG by asking their oil companies to comply with the ban. But even though Bingham received no information from the other companies (Mobil, Caltex, Total), there must be doubts about how effectively oil supplies from other sources were controlled. A major report, titled *The Oil Conspiracy*, published in the USA in 1976, documented the commercial success of the Mobil Co. in Southern Africa during the period of sanctions. The lukewarm French attitude was clearly indicated by the decisions to abstain in both the UN votes on a voluntary oil ban and mandatory sanctions. There is no evidence that the French government was seriously intent on seeking to control the Compagnie Française des Petroles which marketed in Southern Africa as Total.

While many states and companies were half-hearted at best in their compliance with sanctions, Portugal and South Africa were explicitly and actively opposed to sanctions until the mid-1970s:

> From a date well before UDI, the Portuguese policy was one of close cooperation with the Smith government in Rhodesia. After UDI it did all it could to ensure continued supplies of oil to that country (Bingham and Gray, 1978, p. 59)

Dr Nogueira, the Portuguese Foreign Minister, in a press conference in November 1967, made no secret of the fact that oil products were passing through Lourenço Marques in Southern Mozambique to Rhodesia, though he claimed that the products were the property of non-Portuguese firms and carried in non-Portuguese ships (Strack, 1978). Portugal and South Africa refused to end trade with Rhodesia and voted consistently against every UN resolution on sanctions.

Their role was significant, then, in helping Rhodesia, the target state, to resist sanctions. Rhodesia was part of a core of white states in Southern Africa that were sufficiently linked to provide an important regional base of moral and material support for Rhodesia. The volume of bilateral trade that was maintained between South Africa and Rhodesia was critical. The UN Sanctions Committee's figures for 1965–75 show that South Africa accounted for one-third of Rhodesian exports and nearly one-half of Rhodesian imports. Furthermore, South Africa helped to protect Rhodesian oil supplies by passing legislation which imposed secrecy on oil stocks and supplies and restricted the right of the vendor to sell. This meant that South African companies, and this included Consolidated were not allowed to make it a condition of sale to any South African buyer that the product should not be on-sold to Rhodesia.

Rhodesia itself had appeared to be highly vulnerable to economic and particularly oil sanctions in 1965. The economy as a whole was 'comparatively small and undeveloped with a fairly narrow base' (Cross, 1981, p. 70). There was a high level of dependence on the export of a narrow range of products (mainly tobacco and asbestos) to a small number of states. Imported products similarly originated from a few states, some 30 per cent from Britain alone. As far as oil was concerned, Rhodesia was landlocked, had no indigenous oil and was, therefore, wholly dependent on imported oil. Bingham took the view that 'denial of this oil [approx. 3·3 million barrels per annum] would gravely have damaged the economic and social life of Rhodesia' (Bingham and Gray, 1978, p. 2). An independent study prepared for the UN Secretary-General in February 1966 found that oil consumption was concentrated in road transportation where the possibility of substitution was minimal. Oil shortages could be expected to have a major impact on the Rhodesian economy and society directly affecting the mobility of people and goods. The report concluded that 'an oil embargo, therefore, would be the most direct and potent manifestation of sanctions' (Strack, 1978, p. 132).

Despite Rhodesia's apparent vulnerability to sanctions, the economy and the regime proved to be remarkably resilient. Admittedly the situation was helped by the slow escalation of sanctions which provided time to set up countermeasures. But the dysfunctional characteristics of sanctions became evident. In political terms the imposition of sanctions did appear to enhance the solidarity and cohesion of the regime. Sanctions reinforced a grim white Rhodesian determination to preserve supremacy at all costs. Their mission, as they saw it, was not only to save their community, but also the whole of Western civilization. They regarded themselves as nothing less than a bastion of anti-communism and an outpost of civilization in Africa (Strack, 1978). Strong ideological convictions, then, underpinned the regime's efforts to frustrate sanctions.

Sanctions did, of course, impose strains on the economy but not enough to cause a level of stagnation and recession that could of itself have induced the required political changes. Indeed, what Strack calls 'the sustained growth momentum of the Rhodesian economy' (ibid., p. 88) only came to an end in the mid-1970s when the worldwide economic recession, sparked by the oil price increases, began to bite. During the period 1967–74 GDP actually increased by more than 8 per cent in real terms and income per capita also rose considerably. Sanctions in fact served to stimulate a general diversification of the economy, particularly of manufacturing industry, which made Rhodesia more self-sufficient in a wide range of goods previously imported. Traditional patterns of trade were also changed with new markets either created or developed. As far as oil and petroleum products were concerned, emergency powers legislation was speedily passed, making local oil companies controlled industries. This meant that they were legally bound to continue the supply of oil and faced legal penalties if they attempted to implement a sanctions policy. A government agency called GENTA was set up specifically to procure and oversee oil supplies. Thus the Smith regime gave itself the means and the authority 'to impose its will on any recalcitrant organisation' (Bingham and Gray, 1978, p. 31). The overall result was that 'until 1974, the Rhodesian economy prospered in the face of UK and UN sanctions' (Strack, 1978, p. 237).

The Problem of Control

To control a complex implementation environment that consisted of transnational corporations, the UN, independent states and a target state for whom Britain had 'responsibility without adequate power' (Grieve, 1968, p. 442) would have been a daunting enough prospect without the constraints that were self-imposed by the British government. Had HMG bothered to consult Shell or BP at the outset concerning the efficacy or the likely results of oil sanctions, some apparent illusions might have been shattered. According to Bingham, Shell at least took the view 'from the start that sanctions against Rhodesia could not be effective unless South Africa also were blockaded and that implementation bristled with difficulties' (Bingham and Gray, 1978, p. 45).

The consistent line adopted by HMG, however, was that a confrontation with South Africa and Portugal was to be avoided at all costs. It was, of course, this fear of confrontation that explains the initial British opposition to the escalation of UN sanctions to include oil, and it put HMG in a weak position in terms of persuading these states to support sanctions. As Windrich puts it, 'since the Labour government had been concerned throughout with preventing the extension of any UN sanctions against either of these two countries, the pressure they were able to exert was minimal' (Windrich, 1978, p. 84). It is not difficult to explain this position, certainly as far as South Africa was concerned. While attitudes appeared to be coloured by the fact that Portugal was one of Britain's oldest allies, economic 'realities' rather than political nostalgia governed the relationship with South Africa. Quite simply, the economic ties with South Africa were considered too important to be put at risk. Windrich has estimated that trade was worth more than £265 million and investment approximately £1,000 million per annum (ibid., pp. 84–5). With the British economy facing mounting difficulties through 1966, culminating in the devaluation of November, 1967, it became all the more important not to endanger the relationship with South Africa. The political and economic unacceptability of risking a confrontation with two states whose links with the target state were so crucial is a major factor in explaining the failure of sanctions as an implementation problem.

The ability of HMG to control the activities of Shell and BP was constrained not only by the corporate nature of the companies, but also by the salience of sanctions as a political issue over time. Salience refers to the perceived significance of an issue compared to other issues, the amount of time and resources devoted to it, and the level of concern about and commitment to a policy. The salience of an issue, therefore, has an important impact on the monitoring of a policy and affects the whole implementation process. Shell and BP were, of course, commercial organizations with important interests in Southern Africa. Bingham's figures (Bingham and Gray, 1978, p. 2) show how healthy their economic position was at the time in terms of market shares, and naturally the companies were concerned to maintain that position and dissuade South Africa in particular from obtaining a higher proportion of oil supplies from other sources. For the implementation of sanctions to be successful, it was important for HMG to maintain over time a high level of monitoring to stand a chance of penetrating the layers of control in the corporate structures of the oil companies.

The information available suggests that the sanctions issue retained a high degree of salience until the end of 1967, signified by the setting up of an *ad hoc* Cabinet committee which monitored sanctions and the Rhodesian issue as a whole. In a series of meetings with the Shell and BP groups in London, HMG maintained pressure upon them by laying down a hard line. The groups were clearly instructed to obey the Sanctions Orders irrespective of any legal or practical difficulties involved. It was assumed by HMG, and it appears to have been the case, that this instruction was passed on to the Consolidated companies in Southern Africa. The relationship with the groups began to deteriorate, however, as reports from the spring of 1966 indicated not only that large quantities of oil were in fact reaching Rhodesia, but that a large proportion of it was British oil. Shell and BP consistently argued that, as far as they knew, no British oil was getting through. As Bingham notes, continual protestations of innocence by the companies led to a progressive worsening of relations with HMG through 1967 (Bingham and Gray, 1978, p. 105).

At the beginning of 1968, however, the situation changed dramatically. Shell and BP in London received information which confirmed that the Shell subsidiary in Mozambique (Shell Moçambique) was supplying oil through Lourenço Marques to a broker in South Africa who was reselling it to Rhodesia. HMG had already begun to suspect this, but by the time it was officially informed by the companies (either in February 1968 or later that year) Shell (South Africa) had negotiated a deal with Total (South Africa) whereby the French company took over that supply and was compensated for an equivalent amount in South Africa by Shell (South Africa). This swap arrangement had the effect of getting Shell Moçambique 'off the hook' as far as the Sanctions Orders were concerned, it being a UK registered company, though it left the Shell and BP groups vulnerable to the extent that they continued to supply oil to Shell (South Africa). The two groups apparently differed about whether to give HMG the information they now possessed; BP, with its large government shareholding, took the view that HMG must be informed and this view eventually prevailed.

HMG's reaction to this information is interesting. The concern now was less with stopping the flow of oil to Rhodesia and thereby with implementing the Sanctions Orders, and more with the political embarrassment arising from the alleged connection of British companies in the chain of supply. George Thompson, as Commonwealth Secretary and later as minister without portfolio, was the Labour minister most closely involved in the meetings with the groups in London. His evidence to Bingham, therefore, provides an important summary of HMG's position at this time: 'the more we went into the repeated problem of the allegations about oil from British companies reaching Rhodesia the more we came to the conclusion I think, that the best we could make of a bad job in this respect was to be in a position to say at least there was no oil from British oil companies reaching Rhodesia' (Bingham and Gray, 1978, p. 105).

The new HMG line was a result of two things. First, having considered and rejected for one reason or another a number of schemes through 1967 to make sanctions more effective, HMG was now far more aware of the practical difficulties involved. Given the initial optimism about sanctions, this must have been a painful learning process. HMG 'was driven to the conclusion that oil could not be prevented from reaching Rhodesia, at any rate without major international action which would involve South Africa' (ibid., p. 105). Thus HMG, like Shell and BP in London but for political rather than commercial reasons, condoned the essentially cosmetic swap arrangement. Equally important, however, was the fact that the sanctions issue was beginning to lose its salience. Other issues were competing for ministerial time and attention. In particular, severe economic problems which had beset the Wilson government through 1966 culminated in a 'period of acute crisis' (ibid., p. 104) at the end of 1967 with the devaluation of sterling. The pressure of concurrent problems on the policy-making machinery must have affected the close monitoring of sanctions. As Wallace notes, 'the Rhodesian question – shifted up and down from ministerial to senior and middle official levels as new developments loomed or stalemate returned' (Wallace, 1975, p. 17). George Thompson held his last major meeting with the oil companies in February 1969, when the swap arrangement was spelt out to him in some detail. There were no further meetings with the companies until 1976. After 1969, comments Bingham, 'the enforcement and monitoring of sanctions came to assume a lower governmental priority than they had previously done' (Bingham and Gray, 1978, p. 111). During the period 1969–76 HMG thought that the swap arrangement was still in existence. But as Bingham discovered, the companies had returned to the 'pre-cosmetic' situation. The arrangement with Total ended in 1971 and after that date Shell was again directly involved in the supply of oil to Rhodesia. By not holding meetings with the companies – imperfect a control mechanism though that was – HMG was not even seeking or receiving relevant and up-to-date information. If information did reach HMG informally, as seems likely, it was simply 'turning a blind eye'.

The importance of controlling the implementation environment can be shown by way of contrast. Strack reminds us that while economic sanctions against Rhodesia failed, political sanctions were much more successful. These included non-recognition of the Smith regime, withdrawal of consular facilities from Salisbury and the termination of Rhodesian membership of international organizations:

> International visibility of these sanctions is high and cost of implementation low. The degree of control is also high, because political recognition and the establishment of diplomatic relations are sole prerogatives of sovereign governments. (Strack,, 1978, p. 247 ff.)

The point is not simply that these were political rather than economic instruments. Cross makes the case that economic sanctions imposed by South Africa upon Rhodesia after 1975 were successfully implemented, though he perhaps overstates their overall significance: 'it can be argued that the key element in the process leading up to the successful Lancaster House talks and the subsequent transfer of power to "majority rule" and in due course to Robert Mugabe's government was South African economic sanctions against the Rhodesian government.' South African sanctions were successful, because South Africa 'had complete control over the economic and strategic existence of the Rhodesian government.' This example suggests that for economic sanctions to be effective, 'alternative sources of supply and outlets for export activities must be capable of physical control' (Cross, 1981, pp. 75–6). HMG never had and, arguably, never could have had this level of control, given the politico-economic constraints outlined above.

The Symbolic Function of Sanctions

It has been argued that economic sanctions as a strategic policy designed to bring down the Smith regime and return Rhodesia to the rule of law failed, and that this failure can usefully be analysed by looking at the implementation process. This has been attempted here by focusing in some detail on the problems of implementing oil sanctions. To put the problem of implementation into some sort of perspective, however, it is necessary to return to the idea introduced earlier that the decision to impose sanctions was symbolic as well as strategic. The issues to be dealt with in this final section can be put as a series of questions. Did HMG seriously believe that sanctions, even oil sanctions, would bring down the Smith regime? To what extent was the primary purpose and function of sanctions symbolic? Did sanctions as a symbolic act fail? How significant in this context was the implementation process?

The Bingham evidence suggests that early hopes and expectations about the efficacy of sanctions soon waned. Certainly by 1967, as George Thompson puts it,

> we [the government collectively] came increasingly to the conclusion that we couldn't bring the Rhodesian government to an end by sanctions, unless we were prepared to apply them to South Africa. We were under no circumstances prepared to do that. (Bingham and Gray, 1978, p. 105)

There must be doubts, however, about how serious HMG was about sanctions even before 1967. Indeed, Brown-John goes so far as to argue that 'it is doubtful whether Britain ever seriously believed that sanctions would bring the Smith regime down' (Brown-John, 1975, p. 342).

There are clear indications that the public statements of confidence in the ability of sanctions to bring down the regime and end UDI were significant as declaratory rather than substantive statements. Wilson's 'weeks rather then months' speech is a good example. This is understandable given HMG's prime concern to avoid the use of force and retain control of the Rhodesian situation. As we have seen, there were strong pressures on HMG to create the impression at least that it was responding positively and effectively to UDI. The actions, however, rather belied the rhetoric. The apparent unwillingness even to include oil on the list of sanctions against Rhodesia clearly shows a lack of serious intent to bring the economy and, therefore, the regime to its knees. The speed with which talks were initiated with Smith suggests that the real concern was to negotiate a settlement, perhaps at any price, rather than to implement sanctions effectively. Indeed, the way in which HMG sought to implement sanctions from the outset poses major problems for the idea that sanctions was a strategic decision. The condonation of the collusion between the oil companies in particular would have certainly given the companies the strong impression that HMG had no real commitment to implementing the Sanctions Orders. As Bingham notes, 'it induced among some of those most directly concerned [within the groups] a belief that compliance with the Sanctions Orders was to be regarded as a matter of form rather than substance, that it was the latter which mattered not the spirit' (Bingham and Gray, 1978, p. 221).

The condonation of the swap arrangement is but one example of a concern throughout with the presentational aspects of the sanctions policy. The use of the UN, particularly in December 1965 and April 1966, is interesting in this context. It served as a convenient forum to demonstrate to the widest possible audience Britain's strength of resolve and seriousness of intent. The highly publicized Beira blockade is perhaps the best example of this concern. British naval vessels were deployed in the Mozambique Channel from December 1965. By the spring of 1966 it had become clear that their mere presence was not sufficient to deter tankers unloading at Beira, and the Royal Navy had no authority physically to stop ships. Therefore, HMG very publicly took the matter to the UN in April, where the Security Council passed Resolution 221 giving Britain powers to stop 'by the use of force if necessary' vessels believed to be carrying oil to Beira. During 1966–75 as many as seventy-six ships including the aircraft-carriers *Ark Royal* and *Eagle*, twenty-eight auxiliaries and 24,000 men, costing many millions of pounds, were deployed. In addition, an air reconnaissance squadron of Shackletons was stationed at Majunga on Malagasy between 1966 and 1972, to assist in the surveillance of the sea approaches to Beira. Over the period the number of patrolling vessels was reduced and the number of tanker interceptions declined until the deployment was finally ended. Bingham concludes that the force 'had achieved its object of preventing crude supplies reaching Beira' (Bingham and Gray, 1978, p. 174). While this is not inaccurate, it rather misses the point. The Beira blockade was maintained by HMG as a highly visible symbol of action. The object was to give the impression that sanctions were being successfully implemented even when HMG knew that oil was reaching Rhodesia by other routes, notably by rail through Mozambique.

The essentially symbolic importance of the Beira force is shown by the unwillingness of HMG to tighten up the implementation of oil sanctions by extending the Beira patrol. In May 1972 Sir Alec Douglas-Home was bluntly asked in the House 'what vital British interest is served in having Rhodesian oil imported through Lourenço Marques instead of Beira?' (Strack, 1978, p. 135). Not surprisingly, the Foreign Secretary was rather stuck for an answer. In November of that same year James Callaghan specifically suggested that the Beira patrol should be extended 'to close up the obvious gap at Lourenço Marques'. Though it was common knowledge by this time that oil and other supplies were reaching Rhodesia from this port, the Conservative government like the Labour government before it was not prepared to take any action to prevent this violation of the sanctions effort (Windrich, 1978, p. 204). The general attitude to the infringement of sanctions was demonstrated by the frequent British votes against UN resolutions designed to tighten them up. As Strack comments, 'this is a good example of a government committed to a policy which proved to be unsuccessful but which had to be maintained for symbolic reasons' (Strack, 1978, p. 135). The symbolic nature of sanctions as an international action was finally admitted by a Labour minister in October 1975:

> The argument for sanctions is not simply economic. It is political and profoundly so. There is a symbolic significance about taking action that is in accordance with an international decision and with decisions taken by successive governments. (ibid., p. 81)

It would appear, then, that while there was a strategic dimension to the sanctions decision, the symbolic significance was important from the outset, and it can be argued that sanctions against Rhodesia very quickly came to serve primarily symbolic functions for the British government. This conclusion matches the findings of those who have investigated other examples of economic sanctions. On the basis of a comparative analysis of ten cases of sanctions Wallensteen concludes that sanctions are most useful as what he calls 'expressive acts'; they are 'often not intended to be more than acts of protest and condemnation' (Wallensteen, 1968, p. 267). Anna Schreiber's conclusions are particularly appropriate to the Rhodesian cases:

> It is mainly its symbolic function that makes economic coercion a tempting policy to governments. Regardless of its concrete impact on the target state a government may consider economic coercion useful if it serves to declare its position to internal and external publics, or helps to win support at home or abroad. (Schreiber, 1973, p. 413)

If the primary purpose of sanctions was symbolic, can they be judged to have failed? While it is difficult to establish criteria here, it can be argued that sanctions did serve useful functions for Britain. With regard to UDI, Britain was in what Hoffmann calls 'a political cross-pressure situation' (Hoffmann, 1967, p. 145). Having rejected the military force option, sanctions served to ease the tension and to some extent defuse the issue. In a 'damage limitation' context gestures were very important to avoid permanent political embarrassment. Sanctions enabled Britain to reassure Black Africa and avoid confrontation with South Africa. Given the initial concern with the possible break-up of the Commonwealth, and leaders like Nyerere were making scarcely veiled threats about seeking allies elsewhere, sanctions kept the Commonwealth in being, though many would argue that it has never been quite the same since. In a UN context Britain could be seen to be both supporting a collaborative international effort and paying lip-service at least to the idea that an international order can be maintained by mobilizing pressure without resorting to violence.

As far as the international community was concerned, sanctions kept the Rhodesian issue on the international agenda, maintaining concern and a level of hostility against the Smith regime. Rhodesia was virtually isolated diplomatically and states which continued to trade with Rhodesia were at least embarrassed by so doing. The regime itself was forced to struggle for survival at ever-increasing costs. Writing in 1975, Brown-John offers this interesting prognosis about sanctions:

> They have not succeeded in the short run because they were not decisively and effectively imposed. However, it would seem highly probable that they will ultimately succeed because they will provide a constant focus on Rhodesia and implicitly legitimise violent African attempts to overthrow racism in the country. (Brown-John, 1975, p. 368)

After international and regional conditions had changed in the mid-1970s, sanctions could be seen to have played a not insignificant role in ultimately producing political change in Rhodesia.

The importance of the implementation process is clearly dependent upon assumptions made about the nature of the initial decision and the ensuing policy. It has been argued here that the British decision to impose sanctions on Rhodesia had both strategic and symbolic dimensions. To the extent, however, that the policy served primarily symbolic functions non-implementation was not critical. The British government was able, though not without difficulty, to maintain a level of credibility for its policy that carried it through. Nevertheless, it is reasonable to conclude by suggesting that the problems of implementation, ill-considered at the outset and only apparent over time, would in pragmatic terms have served to reinforce the symbolic rather than the strategic functions of the sanctions policy.

4

The Foreign Policy System and the Vietnam War: Henry Kissinger as *Deus ex machina*

Walter Goldstein

The explanation of US foreign policy behaviour has engaged the energies of countless scholars. Fascinated, or in a few cases repelled, by the statecraft practised by a nuclear superpower, they set out conceptual theories, analytic models and (heaven help us!) 'macroheuristic paradigms' to explain *why* policy decisions were made and *how* they were implemented. Considerable attention has been given in the scholarly literature to the controversial lessons learned during the Vietnam War. Six presidential administrations drifted from one mistake to another in Indo-China for more than twenty years; millions of US servicemen and a succession of fact-finding missions were sent to Vietnam, at a cost exceeding $500 billion, to wind up or wind down a war that could be neither won nor ended. But the slide towards disaster could not be halted.

By 1975 the US position in Indo-China had collapsed, President Nixon had been driven from office, and the credibility of the foreign policy system had been gravely weakened. It appeared that the reputation of Henry Kissinger, the master tactician of the war, was the only one to survive the fiasco; and that too is now the subject of critical review. The generals in the field and in the Joint Chiefs of Staff had won little glory; and the Presidents they served were severely censured – ranging from Truman to Eisenhower, to Kennedy, to Johnson and, ultimately, to Nixon – for losing the first war in America's history. Mr Reagan referred to the Vietnam War as a 'noble cause' but his impromptu judgement was never explained. In fighting a losing war, the USA had rigidly steeped itself in errors of military strategy and hindered the operations of government. It had acted indecisively in Asia and in Washington, and no one could identify the lessons that ought to have been learned to correct future mistakes.

The academic literature on the Vietnam War has generated a considerable number of theoretical constructs and policy studies; its aim has been to explain the failures in strategic planning and political manoeuvre that pushed the war policy in Vietnam into an unending quagmire. A talented writer, and active policy-maker, Leslie Gelb, concluded that Vietnam policy had obviously failed but that the system had in fact worked well. As he writes: 'The paradox is that the *foreign policy* failed, but the *domestic decision-making system* worked' (Gelb with Betts, 1979, p. 2). Most scholarly writers emphatically disagreed. For differing reasons they concluded that policy had failed because the policy-making system had failed. Some found fault with the incremental compromising that beset the process of decision–making; as they put it, decisions were not made at any date, rather people slid into them. Others insisted that the political skirmishings and the 'bureaucratic politics' fought out in the Washington hierarchy had been decisive; they had distorted orderly procedures of policy perception and implementation (see Jensen, 1982; Bloomfield, 1982; Goldstein, 1971). Theodore Draper saw the Vietnam failure as the result of 'incrementalism' run rife; one miscalculation led to another, and instead of adapting to a deteriorating situation, as organizational theory would recommend, 'an enormous disproportionate military and political investment' was made simply to sustain an unwise commitment (Draper, 1967, p. 161). Ideologists of the right and left argued that the system had failed because the political leadership had lost its nerve to fight a major war, or because the 'national security managers' (as Richard Barnet put it) were corrupted by the exercise of power and by the imperialist values that had warped their tactical and technical judgement (Barnet, 1972; Stavins *et al,* 1971).

The literature on Vietnam can be segregated according to conflicting interpretations of political behaviour. A first set of theorists applied a 'rational actor' model of analysis to explain the defects in strategic planning; they found fault in the ideological dogmas and the containment doctrines of Cold War (Zagoria, 1968). Senator Fulbright criticized, in *The Arrogance of Power* (1966), the foolish notion that the USA could serve anywhere in the world as the policeman of a nuclear balance of power. As he put it: 'great nations [tend] to equate power with virtue and major responsibilities with a universal mission' (Fulbright, 1966, p.9). All six of the postwar Presidents had succumbed to the 'illusion of American omnipotence', unrealistically trying to shore up the ex-colonial and unstable regimes of the Third World that were caught in the global struggles between the superpowers. Hans Morgenthau pointed to a fundamental misperception of national interest: in trying to suppress national liberation forces in the monsoon jungles of Vietnam the USA had thrown energies into a peripheral war that strained the Western alliance structures and that failed to weaken its communist adversaries (Morgenthau, 1978).

As distinct from the 'rational actor' theorists, most writers concentrated on the weaknesses that had been revealed in the decision-making system in Washington. It was not the irrationality of policy choices that worried them and that confused other nations whether they were allies (especially in Saigon) or adversaries. It was the confusing behaviour of the policy-makers in the National Security Council which drew their criticism. As they put it: the Vietnam War was in fact fought between a succession of Presidents, their bureaucratic chieftains, the Congress and the leaders of public opinion. With such rivalry for power, one did not need an enemy. Hence, they concluded, it was the failure of political input (procedures) rather than of policy output (strategic doctrine) that explained the continuing débâcle in Vietnam. The choice of policy goals was relentlessly wrong, largely because the process of choosing and implementing policy was steeped in confusion. Two academic authors – one a radical, one a conservative – typify this argument: both had served in high office in Washington and then retired to write about their depressing experience in bureaucratic guerrilla war; both had been neutralized by the policy process (Ellsberg, 1972; Hilsman, 1967).

Morton Halperin and Graham Allison wrote at length about the secretive games and the jockeying for privilege that characterize the process of 'bureaucratic politics'. They examined the presidential preference to work with in-house loyalists, as in the National Security Council, and to disregard the technical advice of credentialed experts in the State and Defence agencies, the CIA and the Congress (Allison, 1971; Halperin with Hoffman, 1977). David Halberstam emphasized the simplicity practised by the military chain of command and the bureaucratic barons who manoeuvred for position and inside information through machiavellian power struggles in Washington (Halberstam, 1972). Others pointed to the catch-22 games and the 'effectiveness trap' that undermined the men who made the war; if key actors dared express their dissent to erroneous war policies they would forfeit their own influence, but if they held their tongues they would be rewarded for sidelining their scepticism (see Thomson, 1968). When prominent leaders spoke too freely – like Robert Macnamara, George Ball, Melvin Laird, or William Rodgers – they were eased out of policy positions and replaced by more pliable presidential loyalists. In his work on groupthink Irving Janis concluded that senior advisers preferred, on the whole, to retain their inside status on a decision team than to seek voluntary exile. As he noticed, not a single adviser chose to resign or publicly to expose the collective mistakes that had been programmed by their powerful colleagues and superiors (Janis, 1982). Radical critics commented on the cowardice of political and academic appointees to government who would rather surrender their conscience than their prospects for promotion (Chomsky, 1970).

Arthur Schlesinger Jr, a liberal defender of the Kennedy mystique of power and an ardent critic of the imperial presidency, insisted:

> The Vietnam story is a tragedy without villains ... Vietnam is a triumph of the politics of inadvertence ... Each step in the deepening of the American commitment was reasonably regarded at the time as the last that would be necessary ... until we found ourselves entrapped ... in a war which no President ... desired or intended. (Schlesinger, 1967, pp. 31–2)

Thus *unavoidable decisions* went awry, misguided beliefs about Vietnamese society and its war aims created an erroneous assessment of strategy, public opinion at home was mobilized with false hopes, and the checks and balances exercised by political debate were swept aside by the policy momentum (Fitzgerald, 1972; White, 1970). Leslie Gelb evaluated the major criticisms that had been articulated: the pragmatic managers of national security may have acted egotistically, the bureaucracy might have been trapped in its own falsehoods, and successive Presidents might have fooled the Congress and the electorate (if not themselves). But in the end these were all third-order issues because the US political-bureaucratic system did not fail; it worked (Gelb with Betts, 1979, p. 353).

From this brief survey, it is evident that three schools of thought emerged in the scholarly writing on the Vietnam War.[1] The first emphasized that the choice of policy goals was drastically limited but at all times realistic. The memoirs published by Johnson, Nixon and Kissinger argued that the goals in the superpower struggle were correctly designated but they were too difficult to implement in a messy ground war in Indo-China. Their critics disagreed and pointed to egregious mistakes in the choice of strategic objectives that were pursued. The second school of writers concentrated on the implementation of policy and the bureaucratic convulsions that weakened the procedures of decision-making. They noted that the military fed false reports from the field; that the White House staff consistently undermined executive hierarchies (at State, Defense and the CIA) who questioned its judgement; and that the Congress could not perform its constitutional task of mobilizing public opinion. Policy was inevitably warped because no outsider to the system could challenge the misuse of the President's war powers.

The third school was concerned neither with policy inputs (procedures) nor outputs (war-fighting strategies). These writers located the source of failure in the blinded values and the misused structures of the US political system. Vietnam-style wars would recur time and time again – said the left – if elitist politicians manipulated the resources of imperialist capitalism and bourgeois pluralism to suppress revolutionary forces in the Third World. Vietnam-style wars would always be lost –

judged the right – unless the USA geared up its military capabilities and its political institutions to fight – and win – a long, costly battle against the global encroachments of communist power. The ideological arguments of the left and the right are not at issue in this chapter. It is worth noting, however, that they have flourished anew in the contemporary debate over US military intervention in the insurrectionary wars that are escalating in Central America.

A Reappraisal of Henry Kissinger

Of all the actors in the Vietnam war, Kissinger emerged with the least sullied of reputations. He had been awarded a Nobel prize for his efforts to end the war; he had not fallen foul of the Watergate probe into illicit White House activities; he was the first, and the most indispensable, appointee to be brought into the caretaker administration of Gerald Ford; and his two hefty volumes of memoirs were compared to the work of Metternich and Bismarck, the two statesmen who served as his diplomatic role models. Kissinger played so many roles during the Vietnam years that his behaviour has been praised – or criticized – by each of the three schools of critics. The ideologists of the left and right were determined to block his appointment to the Reagan administration. The 'rational actor' theorists invoked his record in office in order to condemn the behaviour of his successors: the Carter staff had dithered and vacillated, General Haig had blustered from one crisis move to the next and George Schultz showed none of the global historic vision that had informed Kissinger's masterly statecraft. The third school invokes his record, too. President Carter had failed to resolve the squabbles of 'bureaucratic politics' between Secretary Vance, Zbigniew Brzezinski and Andrew Young; and, for their part, Secretaries Haig and Schultz never learned to work with the White House staff in the manner that Kissinger had uniquely perfected. To extend the proverb of Machiavelli, Kissinger appeared to perpetrate evil, but he was an effective actor in an evil world who managed to change the course of events.

The publication of a 650-page blockbuster by Seymour Hersh, *The Price of Power: Kissinger in the Nixon White House* (Hersh, 1983), has revived the academic argument about how policy was made in the Vietnam years. The book is filled with telling anecdotes and appalling revelations. Future scholars will have to regard it as a serious source when they come to revise their theoretical explanations of US foreign policy behaviour. Admittedly the author is passionate in his denunciation of Kissinger as a mean-spirited manipulator of diplomatic behaviour. Hersh chronicles a succession of mistakes and misleading interpretations in Kissinger's memoirs; and he dwells vehemently on incidents of duplicity and misperception that distorted the first four years of Nixon-Kissinger diplomacy. To be fair, he has worked thoroughly with his source material. He notes critical discrepancies between the extensive and self-serving memoirs that were published by Nixon and his national security adviser. He cites copiously from official records, from classified documents that he obtained under the Freedom of Information Act, from the works of leading authors and members of the Nixon administration, and from the thousand or more interviews that he pursued (and which he lists in countless footnotes).

The specific veracity of his reporting may be questioned one day; but for the time being the Hersh book can be viewed as a critical document. An awesome amount of detail has been marshalled to support his exposure of Kissinger's performance and it is likely to disturb the theories built by political scientists as they argue a central question: was it the implementation of foreign policy or the choice of strategic plans that was most at fault in prolonging the painful débâcle of Vietnam?

The sensational stories in the book were seized upon by reviewers for the Sunday and monthly papers, but they deserve only the briefest of summary. Hersh carefully notes the dates on which Kissinger proferred his services to *both* contenders for the presidency in 1968. He used top-level contacts in the Johnson administration to brief the Nixon campaign with classified information about the Vietnam peace talks that were being held in Paris. But he also denounced Nixon, and his fear that peace might suddenly break out, to the Hubert Humphrey people who wanted him to play a leading role in the next Democratic regime. He told Brzezinski that 'I've hated Nixon for years' and would pass him the 'shit files' on Nixon compiled for Nelson Rockefeller (Hersh, 1983, p. 30).

More salacious are the revelations about the secret US bombing of Cambodia initiated early in 1969 (Hersh, 1983, pp. 54–62, 122, 180–2); 3,695 sorties by B-52 bombers dropped 105,837 tons of bombs on Cambodia in thirteen months, but not a word was reported to the press, the Congress, or even to the Secretary of Defense. Another 8,944 bombing missions concentrated on Laos, and 160,000 tons of bombs were dropped on the Ho Chi Minh trail (Hersh, 1983, p. 55). A far larger tonnage was dropped in the next four years on North and South Vietnam. The most amazing stories concern the vicious scrambling for power among the White House staff and the National Security Council. Kissinger had the FBI tap the telephones of top aides in his own office and in the Pentagon, but his own conversations with the press were monitored by Alexander Haig and Bob Haldeman (Hersh, 1983, pp. 91, 182, 193, 314, 465). At the Watergate inquiry Kissinger swore that he knew nothing about the illicit phone taps or Nixon's private recording system – which later produced the 'smoking-gun' evidence of the cover-up of the Watergate crimes for the impeachment committee of the Congress; Hersh gives the exact dates and some of the transcripts of the tapping that Kissinger had personally ordered from the FBI (Hersh, 1983, pp. 400, 477). To a certain extent it even became necessary to conceal the undeclared war on Cambodia because the discovery would reveal the dimensions of the espionage system that the White House staff had used to intimidate and to spy on the closest of presidential advisers. Kissinger tapped the phones of his own staff, of the personal aides to Secretaries Rodgers and Laird, the Thieu government in Saigon and a number of embassies in Washington. These taps led to the firing of 'disloyal' people in top places, and scared others away from talking to their friends or to the press (Hersh, 1983, pp. 314–17).

Leaving aside the pornography of power that Hersh richly details, it is useful to concentrate on just one aspect of the book: his documented and inside reporting on the Vietnam War. Hersh allows barely a single illusion about responsible or constitutional government to remain intact. At each turn the Secretaries of State of Defense – two personal friends and political allies of Nixon – were cut out of the cable traffic and systematically undermined (Hersh, 1983, pp. 232, 444, 590). The top military received similar treatment; in order to catch up with the clandestine planning exercises held in the White House basement the Chairman of the Joint Chiefs of Staff authorized a navy signal clerk to pilfer Kissinger's briefcase on his secret trip to China and to photocopy thousands of 'Eyes only' reports that had been kept from Cabinet and military leaders (Hersh, 1983, p. 465).

Hersh described two important devices of power with considerable detail. First, the clever development of 'back-channel reporting', coded messages telexed to key subordinates through the CIA networks, to change strategic policy and to communicate secretly with Moscow, Hanoi, Peking and Bonn. The top leadership charged with the implementation of policy in Vietnam, NATO, the Middle East and the SALT talks were thus left helpless and cut out of command links. Laird and Rodgers were told next to nothing as policy commitments were abruptly switched in the SALT talks, the Middle East, the 'tilt' to Pakistan in its war with India, the bombing halt and the 'peace offensive' in Vietnam, and the decision to send first Kissinger, then Nixon, to Peking.

Secondly, Hersh reveals the extent to which policy was defined and changed by a frequent, furtive leaking of information to favoured journalists and trusted lobbyists. Kissinger outmanoeuvred his superiors, including the President, by planting stories with journalists of the highest reputation in the nation's leading newspapers. When his own position in the White House was threatened, he gave 'background briefings' day after day to exonerate himself at the expense of his enemies (Hersh, 1983, pp. 135, 255, 314, 402, 604–7, 618, 631). Kissinger established his power base by confiding, improperly, to the press as each new crisis emerged. Indeed, the great diplomatic breakthrough of the Nixon visit to Peking was not so much a triumph of diplomacy, but of subterfuge and of public relations. Using back-channel traffic and contrived 'background briefings' for the media, Kissinger and Nixon competed to secure their own place in history. They needed to score a personal success prior to the 1972 election and they disregarded basic questions about national security – such as the future status of Taiwan or Bangladesh – to fulfil their political ambitions. Peking saw the advantage of working with the 'back-channel' and the press-release form of government practised in the White House, and agreed to provide live TV coverage for Nixon's visit to build up the prestige of the President prior to the 1972 election. This allowed attention to be deflected from questions about the agreements reached – that were *never* published – concerning the ousting of Taiwan from the UN, the use of China's influence in Pakistan and in Hanoi, and the provision of US satellite data concerning Soviet military deployments on the Chinese frontier (Hersh, 1983, p. 469 ff.).

From the 'Decent Delay' to the 'Madman Theory'

The question posed in this chapter can now be narrowly defined: was the behaviour of the White House Staff more significant than any other factor in formulating and implementing foreign policy during the Vietnam years?

Obviously a simple answer cannot be given. But a surprising number of writers have firmly said no. They admit, necessarily, that demogogic leaders or wily Presidents could delay or deflect the course of debate. And yet they argue that, by and large, the parameters of policy are inflexible; the 'objective definition' of the national interest cannot be trifled with (Morgenthau, 1978), and the voting public insists that political leaders ensure that commitments will be honourably fulfilled (Gelb, 1979). These parameters are of transcending importance. Vietnam policy was not made by caprice or mistake. Personality struggles in the Johnson and Nixon administrations played a major role in shaping Vietnam strategy, but these were overshadowed by the *doctrinal* necessities of pursuing the war to the bitter end. Ravenal rejects the conventional explanations about the war. It was, he argues, not a mindless or inadvertent slide into a quagmire, as Schlesinger argues; it was not a systematic 'mistake' in perception and bureaucratic synergy, as Gelb insists; nor was it an act of criminality and immorality, as Ellsberg contends. Rather he emphasizes the erroneous doctrines of militant, anti-communist strategy that prompted Cold War passions in Washington (Ravenal, 1978, pp. 38–52). Between 1962 and 1974 the US electorate voted in six presidential or mid-term elections. On each occasion a resounding majority endorsed three basic axioms:

(1) *The prestige of the USA* as a superpower must be strongly demonstrated; the forces of communism must therefore be contained and their insidious proxies, the Vietcong and the NLF,

must be decisively suppressed. As Arendt argued, the war was fought to strengthen the reputation of the USA as a world police force.

(2)   *The escalation of the war effort* and the tactics of Vietnamization were neither popular nor effective, but there was *no alternative* available; the electorate was not ready to concede military defeat, the abrupt withdrawal of US forces, or a political compromise that left the NLF intact in South Vietnam; it was imperative that the war should go on.

(3)   Somehow *the rate of US combat fatalities* had to be reduced and the drafting of middle-class youth to Vietnam had to be ended; if these adjustments could be effected, the duty of the President was to hold on – rather than to win – in Vietnam until the next election.

The above axioms appear to be irrational, and possibly cynical, but there was no group in the electorate (excepting a minority 'peace' fringe) that clamoured for a radical change in doctrine. Indeed, as polling studies have shown, in the 1960s the peace dissenters tended to antagonize majority opinion and to reinforce its support of the war (Rosenberg *et al.* 1970). Presidents were forced to do the best job they could manage, even if US war aims became evermore unrealistic. The electorate would not be moved, the adversaries were not pliant and the goals of final victory receded further from attainment. Given these formidable constraints, the Washington system hammered out a viable mode of operation. As Kissinger had noted in 1955, 'Americans are pragmatically and empirically oriented', responding strongly, but doggedly, in response to crisis situations (Kissinger, 1955, p. 286). The administration resolved to fight the enemy to a stalemate, though it recognized at every stage that it would *never* succeed in imposing an unconditional surrender on its opponents. It used the 'Nixon Doctrine' to remove US troops from the fighting zones but it massively increased US bombing all over Indo-China to punish its implacable adversaries. Hersh describes the 'Götterdämmerung' and 'madman' strategies that were designed to correct the pessimistic projections that were held at State and Defense (Hersh, 1983, pp. 118–30).

A contrary position has been argued by writers who answered yes. They concede that the three axioms together formed a mind-set that could be neither abandoned nor ignored. But there was still ample room to manoeuvre, they argued, and to shift policy priorities. Given the concentration of military and political power that the President constitutionally enjoys, and the dominant command of the war powers entrusted to the chief executive, he could have chosen a different timing schedule to implement his policy objectives and a different choice of tactics to modify his strategic options. Berman found a similar pattern in the Johnson administration. Johnson considered a few alternative options to escalating the war but quickly dismissed them, using his personality, position and advisers to forge ahead with his own war-fighting enthusiasms (Berman, 1982). The thrust of this argument can be clearly stated: if the President had selected policy advisers and Cabinet leaders who were willing to support cautious but innovative efforts to wind down the war, rather than to excalate its intensity, a plausible and realistic peace could have been negotiated between 1969 and 1972. The personality fixation of the President, and of the bellicose advisers with whom he surrounded himself, made the critical difference in the conduct of foreign policy. After all, Eisenhower had applied himself to break the log-jam that Truman had created and had thus ended the war in Korea, and Nixon could have followed his stern example (Hersh, 1983, pp. 51-4).

So the counterargument was made. If the policy system had worked as the writers of the Constitution had intended, a President driving onwards into the Vietnam quagmire would have been halted by the countervailing powers exercised by the Congress, the 'out' political party, the mass media and the electorate. Indeed, Johnson's escalation of the war succeeded largely because the countervailing powers failed. Congressional opponents were ineffective (until 1973), the political parties declined to campaign on the war issue, the mass media refrained from criticism and public opinion was neither questioning nor resistant (Goldstein, 1971, 1970). Instead of resorting to executive subterfuge and *raison d'état*, the White House staff would have been forced into open debate and into political compromise. But so long as debate was stalled or misled, there was no possible alternative or restraint, and the administration blindly pushed forward towards the disaster that came in the humiliating collapse of Saigon in 1975.

The theoretical assumptions in this controversy can be clarified by restating the argument in empirical terms. When Nixon and Kissinger entered office in 1969, they acknowledged, but only to themselves, that it was no longer realistic to plan for 'total victory'. There were three reasons for this:

(1) *The forces of South Vietnam* were too weak, and those of North Vietnam (and the NLF) too strong, to allow a decisive military triumph in the field. Hersh cites National Security Memorandum No. 1, which had been compiled from a questionnaire answered by the Pentagon, State and the CIA: the efficiency of the aerial bombing and the military pacification of Vietnam was strongly doubted and it would take anywhere from 8·3 to 13·4 years for an American army to regain and control the areas of South Vietnam held by the NLF (see Hersh, 1983, p. 50).

(2) *There were limited costs* that the USA could pay to sustain, let alone escalate, the war effort. Though Mr Nixon was to rally 'the silent

majority' to support his *announced* programme, tactics had to be fundamentally changed. The criticisms of the peace movement had to be answered; the scepticism of the Congress had to be allayed before it cut off further funding (as it voted to do in 1973); combat fatalities had to be reduced – by Vietnamizing the ground action; and the President needed to score successes at home and in Vietnam if he was to avoid the dithering and defeat of the Johnson administration.

(3) *The underlying strategy* was to hold the fort (now massively financed) in Indo-China and to impose painful retribution on the adversaries. Attempts were made to cajole or bribe Moscow and Peking to exercise influence in Hanoi; while they did so, the USA would bomb the North Vietnamese to the bargaining table, where they would be forced to negotiate a compromise favourable to the corrupt and incompetent authorities in Saigon. On the basis of this strategy the evaluation of military intelligence and diplomatic manoeuvres was distorted by frightened and thwarted bureaucrats who were too inhibited to dissent from the formulation of policy as the war rolled onward (see Gallucci, 1975).

The situation in 1969 was, by official admission, desperate and chaotic. Before entering office, Kissinger had written that a superpower would be defeated, and an insurrectionary power would be victorious, if the war were to be concluded in stalemate. His conclusion, therefore, was that the best possible outcome was simple: the USA should secure *a decent interval* between the negotiation of a truce, the gradual withdrawal of its forces and the inevitable collapse of its partner's authority in South Vietnam. Stark realism dictated that the conflict should be gradually phased down and that the US electorate should be firmly led towards the acceptance of a 'no win' solution (Hersh, 1983, p. 46).

On entering office, however, Nixon and Kissinger abandoned the reasonable strategy of securing 'a decent interval' to negotiate a compromise peace. Instead they harnessed the formidable might of the US military to embark in full secrecy on a contrary campaign. The bombing halt ordered by Johnson just before the 1968 election was terminated and North Vietnam was threatened with aerial annihilation. The rolling thunder of a new bombing assault was extended to Laos and Cambodia – two countries on which the USA had never declared war. A strong signal was sent to the USSR, threatening the suspension of trade and of the SALT talks unless it persuaded its allies in Hanoi to concede to US demands. A stronger signal was sent to the junta in Saigon: it would be directly punished unless it stepped up the combat effectiveness of its bedraggled forces, which the USA had lavishly armed and financed[2].

There were two critical elements in the Nixon–Kissinger resort to force. Both involved systematic duplicity and the selective filtering of communications. The first was to control the politics of the war, especially at home, by broadcasting one set of signals of *announced* intentions to the world while communicating a different and covert set of messages to the adversary. Nixon advertised his resolute and pacific intentions by cutting down, stage by stage, the enormous US troop formations in Vietnam. At the same time the clandestine air bombardment was massively escalated, and Haldeman wrote that Nixon planned to end the war in his first year in office (Hersh, 1983, p. 50). Nixon's show of toughness appealed to the silent majority and Middle America, the Congress muted its criticisms and the peace movement remained ineffectual in its protests. But no one knew that the de-escalation was symbolic or that the stepping up of the war effort had been surreptitiously programmed. Hersh demonstrates how the press was cleverly, and willingly, misled with frequent and 'not for attribution' briefings (ibid. pp. 132, 255, 604–7). Yet he omits one crucial actor – the members of Congress who knew that a smokescreen had been laid to conceal new plans to escalate the war. Hersh never mentions them.

The second element of strategy was to mount a campaign that the public did not know about until years later. Kissinger began a series of furtive meetings with North Vietnamese delegates in Paris which were to be hidden from view for nearly four years. He intimated to them that Nixon's patience could not be tried indefinitely and that the level of violence would shortly be raised. American voters might be impressed by the 'Nixon Doctrine' to reduce US garrisons and to Vietnamize the ground war; but other plans were going forward, under deep cover, to deliver punishing blows against Haiphong and Hanoi, to devastate the North and pacify the South with considerable ferocity. They were known as the Duck Hook Plans, and Hersh reveals how, through back-channel reporting, they were kept even from the eyes of the Secretary of Defense, Melvin Laird (ibid., pp. 120, 130). Nixon enunciated the theory (that he had held back from the electorate during the 1968 elections) of how he was going to resolve the impossible war that he had pledged to end in one year. He told Haldeman: 'I call it the madman theory, Bob . . . I want the North Vietnamese to believe I've reached the point where I might do *anything* to stop the war' (ibid., p. 53). He explicitly referred to Eisenhower's threat to use nuclear weapons in 1953 if the Koreans refused to sign an armistice. He now proposed to act like a maddened and nuclear-armed autocrat. Hersh gives a startling portrayal of Nixon's mentality. Nixon scorned his friends and allies, and was frequently drunk; he saw the movie *Patton* over and over again to bolster his personal courage and determination; and he planned some of the military campaign while drinking heavily on the presidential yacht with trusted intimates such as Rebozo, Mitchell, Colson and Kissinger (ibid., pp. 88, 184, 191).

From their first days in office, therefore, the Nixon people chose to pursue a war strategy that was *not* the only single option available. It was their choice to widen the war, covertly, and not to close it down. The delegates from North Vietnam had proved themselves to be amenable to working out a compromise of the basic military and political issues in 1969. They were ready to discuss peace terms until late in 1972, when Kissinger revealed that he had won his renowned peace formula (on the latter date, unfortunately, his move was premature; Nixon wanted to end the war after the 1972 election, not before it, and Kissinger was forced to retreat humbly from his own diplomatic victory). But the top staff in the White House were swept away in a newly found euphoria of power; they savoured the pleasures of tapping phones, outwitting the leadership at State and Defense and ordering up cataclysmic bombing assaults all over Indo-China. Secrecy was the vital factor in their operation. Coded messages in the back-channel communication net went through the Digital Information Relay Center in the Pentagon and an armed guard was posted at the door to keep out any unauthorized entrants – including the Secretary of Defense. Military officers were instructed to keep back intelligence reports from their superiors or from US embassies – especially in Saigon. Phone taps were placed in homes of top officials to catch them leaking privileged information to one another or to the press. Many of them learned about basic policy switches only after they had been publicly announced: no wonder that euphoria prevailed in the Oval Office (ibid., pp. 88, 91, 182, 193, 314). They felt that their omnipotence and their duplicity were beyond challenge. They saw no reason to resign themselves to the tortuous and glamourless bargaining needed to thrash out a peace settlement with the delegates of Hanoi – who kept returning to the sessions in Paris. Moreover, they had learned how to master the subtle techniques of public relations. Thus trusted columnists in the world's press were ready to publish every hint or nuance that they cared to drop; and even the Hanoi delegates were prepared to maintain their silence about the secretive, double-track programme of war-and-peace. There was no point in abandoning ingenious power games when all the world believed in the announced intentions of the White House; and no one dared publicly to expose the escalation strategies that had been secretly started (ibid., pp. 54–63).

'Peace with Honour' ... but not too soon

The thrust of the argument so far is that the policy system was basically subverted during the Vietnam War. That policy itself failed is beyond dispute, since the war terminated in ignominious defeat. Of central concern here is the process of making disastrous policy choices. Although Krasner has argued that a better definition of policy objectives, not better control of the bureaucracy, is needed (Krasner, 1972), it is argued here that the imperfect and unauthorized working of the policy system was the root cause. There would have been a different outcome, and a more rational deliberation of policy, if the extensive misuse of war powers had been checked and balanced by congressional questioning, mass media inquiries and public debate. In short, if the Constitution had been properly utilized, it is likely that countervailing powers would have halted the abuse of authority by executive fiat and diplomatic duplicity. But the countervailing powers had not been wheeled into use – at least not before 1973. The senior staff in the White House had become remarkably adept in imposing their own will on the policy process. The fallible mechanism that is responsible for the implementation of US foreign policy had been captured and systematically subverted.[3]

Hersh illustrates these points with hundreds of pages of document citations and cross-checked interviews. He reveals the extent to which senior appointees in the Pentagon, State and the US embassies overseas were shut out of the cable traffic when Kissinger insisted on formulating his own, headstrong initiatives. The stories of reckless intrigue and diplomatic manoeuvre are manifold and sensational. No one, it seemed, had survived after trying to block his wilful initiatives, his constant stumbling into error or his artful dissembling. He ordered a sharp switch of policy in order to support the colonels's junta in Greece (Hersh, 1983, p. 139) and the Nigerians' starvation of Biafra (ibid. p. 141); to overthrow the Allende regime in Chile and the Soviet hold on Cuba (ibid., p. 211 ff.); to demolish the Rodgers plan in the Middle East and the administration's carefully prepared positions in the SALT talks and in the complex negotiations over Berlin (ibid., pp. 232, 334, 416, 529). His notorious 'tilt' to Pakistan during the war in Bangladesh was inhumane and disastrous; it was dictated, like the bombing of Cambodia, not by the statecraft but by the sinuous secrecies that characterized Kissinger's style of leadership. How reminiscent of Bismarck's convoluted reinsurance treaties in the 1870s were the pledges given to Pakistan largely to conceal his hushed-up communications with Peking (ibid., p. 368). As a consequence of his manipulation, India was forced into a closer rapport with the USSR, Pakistan stupidly declared war on India and no one bothered to tell the Japanese that their future nuclear armaments were being discussed with Peking (ibid., pp. 450-63).

The chronicle of Kissinger's mistakes and intrigues can be set aside in these bungled crises in order to return to his record on Vietnam. Two prolonged assaults by B-52 bombers on North Vietnam were ordered in 1972, the first in the early spring and the second in the 'carpet bombing' raids that extended through Christmas and the New Year. The press faithfully reported his argument, that the saturation bombing had been provoked by the aggressive and menacing behaviour of the North Vietnamese. In the first instance Hanoi had launched a successful land attack into South Vietnam; it was supposed to be stopped by the USA smashing into its source, the supply depots in the North. In the second case he intimated that the Hanoi delegates had refused to accept the peace settlement offered by the USA in the Paris discussions and they once again had to be bombed back to a reasonable position.

Hersh is at his most compelling in demolishing the justification that has been made for both sets of bombing raids; he draws his best ammunition from the conflicting accounts that appear in the Nixon and Kissinger memoirs. In the earliest of the two events it was recognized that the round-the-clock bombing could not possibly halt the spring offensive which had been unleashed by the North Vietnamese in the South. Laird and Rodgers insisted that aerial interdiction had not succeeded in the past and it was not likely in 1972 to seal off the supplies coming down the multiple capillaries of the Ho Chi Minh trails (ibid., pp. 504, 520). But they were trapped, without knowing it, in a *fait accompli*. The principal objective held by the White House was not to interdict the supply lines, but to teach a lesson to the Soviets and the Chinese. Nixon had already returned from Peking and he was about to set off for his summit conference in Moscow – a symbolic ritual that an incumbent President should stage six months before his second-term election falls due. Nixon gambled, recklessly, that the Soviets would not call off the summit talks (on arms control and trade) in Moscow, even though he had ordered the mining of Haiphong Harbour and the strafing of downtown Hanoi. The risk, he calculated, was worth taking. Nixon's aim was not so much to halt the North Vietnamese assault in the South, but to demonstrate to the American electorate that he was the only leader who could outwit the Soviet demons in their own den; and he would prove it too on prime-time TV direct from the Kremlin. To his surprise, his gamble succeeded. he co-opted the Russians, like the Chinese, into supporting his ruse of replacing diplomatic negotiation with political advertising (ibid., pp. 523–6) and he enjoyed their support in the years ahead as he fought off the Watergate inquiries.

The second incident was more important and more revealing than the first. In the middle of October the Hanoi delegates in Paris accepted Kissinger's formula to settle the outstanding issues that had blocked a settlement of the war. He assured them, on Nixon's direct authority, that the bombing would stop on the day before the treaty was initialled, and that a cease-fire would be called on 31 October. It was exactly at this point that Nixon changed his mind (ibid., pp. 591–7). He cancelled the agreement and left Kissinger dangling in the worst predicament of his career. Kissinger had triumphantly told the press that 'peace is at hand'. Now he had to explain a *volte face*. Ironically it was his turn to be mauled by the decision system that he had himself created in the National Security Council in the White House basement. Haig, Colson and Haldeman had set out to ruin him and to prevent his eagerly solicited appointment as Secretary of State in 1973. Nixon refused to talk to him for weeks on end; the American allies in Saigon denounced his peace settlement as a manipulative fraud; and worse yet, the Hanoi delegates confirmed to the world that he had put in writing his serious intention to initial the treaty. As he sheepishly noted in his memoirs: 'Nixon was right ... I had overreached' (ibid., p. 601).

What had happened? Nixon had consulted the pollsters who were favoured by the White House. They had convinced him that he would win millions more votes if he continued the war and the bombing than if he climbed down from his belligerent position and signed a cease-fire immediately prior to the election. As the election date drew close Nixon disavowed his 'good faith' message to the Hanoi peace negotiators, claiming that the Saigon regime had not been fairly consulted. He also began to talk about firing Kissinger, Rodgers and Laird. Kissinger struck back with vigour and good timing. He urged that Haig be promoted from a two to a four star general to get him out of his eyrie in the National Security Council; he endorsed all of General Thieu's objections to the peace settlement, though he had previously dismissed them as absurd obstacles that Saigon threw forward in order to derail his peace plan; and he became the most strident advocate of the Christmas 'carpet bombing' of North Vietnam (ibid., pp. 609–23).

Kissinger turned around the press with his customary mastery. He placed the blame squarely on Hanoi for refusing to initial the peace treaty, even though their acceptance of its basic clauses had been fully publicised. In briefing the nation's top editorial writers, he once again became the superhawk. Two hundred planes, including half of the B-52 fleet of SAC, were dispatched to plaster Hanoi; the losses were enormous but they were calculated as America's 'last roll of the dice'. The aim was *not* to change opinion in Hanoi, but in Saigon. General Thieu had to be convinced that the USA now wanted to end the war. He had to be reassured that the USA was still seriously committed to the indefinite survival of his regime, and that it would re-enter the war at any point that his fall appeared imminent. This latter promise was never published. It created a storm of fury when Kissinger revealed it three years later as the last defences of Saigon were crumbling before the NLF sweep to victory (ibid., pp. 624–8).

The ending of the charade came suddenly in the first few days of 1973. An overwhelming majority of the Democrats, who controlled both the Senate and the House, voted to cut off all funds for the war as soon as the orderly withdrawal of US forces and prisoners of war had been arranged. Nixon gave his personal pledge to General Thieu that further assistance would be furnished after the bombing had stopped and the treaty had been initialled in Paris. The American's war was finished.

The truth began to emerge that the war had been not only ruinous, but futile. No new concession had been won from the North as a result of the extensive US bombing raids. More significantly, no genuine commitments had been won to secure a cease-fire in place, to remove NLF cadres from the South, to neutralize the DMZ as a permanent frontier, to administer free elections, or to partition the country between the Saigon and NLF authorities. A better version of this 'no win' outcome could have been concluded in 1969 or 1971, if the White House had been so minded. Four more years of war had done little to improve Saigon's strength or US bargaining power. But the cardinal principal remained: wars can be terminated after an election, not before it. If incumbent Presidents find themselves committed to fighting the wrong war in the wrong place, they must hang on for the right time – after an election. Truman had been impelled to drag on the war in Korea until the 1952 election; Nixon had relentlessly bombed Vietnam until 1973; and Carter had fought the Iranians (over the US Embassy hostages in Tehran) until the last hour, literally, that he held to office. In each case, if the President had exercised his leadership to sway public opinion and his own administrative staff in the years before an election, he might have secured a better policy outcome, with a loss of thousands of fewer lives. Hersh notes the striking fact that on not one page of Nixon's or Kissinger's memoirs is regret expressed for the millions of lives lost as a consequence of their calculations of *machtpolitik*. Indeed, Kissinger even suggested that if Thieu interfered with his negotiating intrigues, 'We'll kill the son-of-a-bitch if we have to' (ibid., p. 617).

Epilogue

Ten years after the Americans walked away from the war, the question has surfaced once again over the execution of foreign policy: are the goals of diplomacy that the USA pursues so badly chosen or is it the decision process that systematically perpetrates error?

The partisan advocacy on either side of the argument has not changed since the 1970s. The powerful men of decision insist that their perceptions and goal selection were fundamentally correct; unfortunately they were let down by the 'fatigued' state of public opinion and stymied by political bickering in Congress. Their opponents disagree; they still argue that the policies chosen were wrong because the decision system has been abused. The argument came to a head over three crises that were poorly handled:

(1)   In 1975 Kissinger urged that US troops should be rushed back into Vietnam and hastily inserted into Angola but Congress baulked; relying on their newly found activism and the War Powers Act, Congress delayed impetuous action that could have led only further to disaster.

(2)   *Kissinger's successor*, Brzezinski, defended plans to deploy the CIA and US military forces to shore up the Iranian generals and the Shah against his rebelling subjects in Iran. Once again it was the

probing inquiries of the press and the delaying tactics in Congress that foiled precipitous action.

(3)   *The wars in Central America and the Lebanon* (in 1983) are tempting 'targets of opportunity' to the Reagan staff who yearn for military intervention. But their plans are not likely to succeed. There are too many rival actors who have set out on fact-finding missions, who have blocked military appropriation bills, or who have questioned the fragile excuses manufactured by the White House.

Two factors have changed the operational rules since the Kissinger years but one has remained the same. The constant factor is the secretive, manipulative power that is still concentrated in the hands of the White House staff. Brzezinski succeeded in forcing out Vance as Secretary of State, and 'Judge' Clark later undermined Haig (and probably Schultz too). High-level missionaries were sent by the President to the Middle East and Central America; they bypassed ambassadors and expert staff overseas and the Washington bureaucrats at home, as they began to negotiate deals directly for their boss with the head of state in Beirut, El Salvador, or Guatemala. The trend towards implementing policy by executive fiat did not disappear when Kissinger departed from government. Not a single Cabinet officer has succeeded in asserting his independence or his policy leadership in recent years. The power to initiate and execute policy has been tightly held by the White House staff. Though the present incumbents – Reagan, Meese, Baker, Deaver and, especially, Clark – had little knowledge and no experience in foreign policy, they firmly restricted the operational discretion of senior echelon appointees to State, Defense and the CIA. Yet political scientists allow little room for the executive cabal that has come to dominate the control of foreign policy: Waltz, for example, contrasts the secrecy enjoyed by authoritarian regimes to the 'widely debated ... content of policy' in a democracy (Waltz, 1967, p. 311).

But two significant changes have occurred. After many years of a 'supine' acquiescence to the Cold War initiatives waged by Presidents prior to Vietnam, Congress has begun to assert itself as the monitor and watchdog over foreign policy decisions. It no longer defers to the professional judgements and the urgent calls for action that the executive agencies send to Capitol Hill. Further funding for Vietnam was cut off in 1973; military aid to client states was stopped or cut back; and the War Powers Act was invoked to limit the discretionary authority of the Chief Executive. These countervailing tactics could not correct fundamental errors in defining policy objectives, but they curbed the excesses of covert action planning in which Kissinger excelled. They have also called into doubt the assurances given by presidential loyalists – such as Ambassador Kirkpatrick at the UN, Defense Secretary Weinberger and CIA chief Casey – that the dispatch of US troops to 'grey zones' of confrontation in the Third World would not build up the momentum to start another Vietnam-style war.

Secondly, public opinion grew more wary and sceptical. There was little popularity to arm dubious client regimes (as the USA had done so lavishly in Saigon) or to garrison American troops and advisers in disputed war zones. More important, the media and public opinion became sceptical of the notion that executive secrecy is the first prerequisite of effective statecraft. Doubts were expressed, as they never had been during the long years of the Vietnam War, about the wisdom of presidential decisions; secret pledges to aid client regimes were challenged, and executive agreements to sell them sophisticated weaponry were put to the vote – as in the case of the AWACS planes sold to the Saudis. The results of this awakening are difficult to judge. If inadvertent and 'quagmire' wars are to be fought in the 1980s, in Nicaragua or the Arabian Gulf, it is less likely that the national security managers will enjoy the free rein that Kissinger once commanded. It is more likely that *both* elements in foreign policy – the process of decision-making and the policies selected – will be exposed to political inquiry and debate. Of all people, it was Zbigniew Brzezinski who had claimed that only serious discrepancy between democratic expectations and external behaviour would be 'exposed and undercut' by the mass media of communications (Brzezinski, 1970, p. 255).

Of course, the activism of Congress and the scepticism of public opinion will not work marvels. Exposure alone will not curb the defects of the policy process or correct the poor selection of strategic goals. But it will force leading actors to reveal more of their hidden agendas and to contend openly with the force of criticism. In the last resort the Vietnam War provided a triumph for executive dominance and back-channel conspiracies over constitutional safeguards. In the next Vietnam War, or in its careful planning stages, the Chief Executive will not be able to shrug aside the countervailing powers of the legislature or to play on the gullibilities of the press. The political deference that characterized the Cold War era has been eroded. It was Kissinger' masterful control of peace-in-war diplomacy that undermined the bureaucracy and the opposition to the war. But today there are counteracting interests, whether conservative or liberal, that concur on at least one point of *procedural* emphasis: Vietnam, never again.

Notes Chapter 4

1   An extensive survey of the literature on Vietnam policy is given in Gelb, with Betts, 1979. They list hundreds of books written by soldiers in the field, by leading apologists and critics of the war, and by academic analysts.
2   No accurate count has been made of the costs of fighting the war and of equipping South Vietnam with the fourth largest airforce in the world. An attempt to calculate

actual US outlays and opportunity costs (as in the GNP that was forfeited) appears in Stevens, 1976).

3   Strangely little consideration is given in the academic literature to the stratagems pursued by the President and his staff to outwit the checks and balances that should have arrested headstrong Chief Executive. For a discussion of this, see George, 1980; Destler, 1972; and Johnson, 1974.

5

'Diamonds and Impotence': the Implementation of Giscard d'Estaing's African Policies

Christopher Farrands

When President Giscard d' Estaing lost the French elections of March 1981, his African policies had come to be seen as an unprincipled comedy of errors. While no doubt his management of the economy and the standing of rival parties mattered more to voters, the failure of his foreign policy in Africa played an important part in shaping a public image of his presidency (Crandall Hollick, 1981; Frears, 1981). Between 1974 and 1981 Giscard and his advisers had sought to evolve new policies on Africa. Yet they ended up, after some embarrassing and humiliating difficulties, roughly where they started out. Critics could allege that there was little originality in Giscard's policies except the extent of their failure. This chapter focuses on the implementation of some of the key policies involved. It looks especially at French problems in Chad, Zaire and the Central African Republic (CAR), and discusses briefly policy towards Angola in 1976, and the problems of Mauritania and the western Sahara.

Most studies of policy implementation have looked primarily at policies handled within the distinctive environment of the state. Only a few of these studies take seriously the broader environments in which policy must be sustained (Kress for example, *et al.*, 1981). Even in the foreign policy literature, where the environment of policy is clearly more ambiguous and where authority and power are equally more uncertain, writers have tended to focus on problems of bureaucratic control and co-ordination (Rosenau, 1980). Now while bureaucratic difficulties can be a major headache for policy implementation, the central focus of this chapter is on the way in which the international environment of policy distorts, obstructs, or confounds decisions, even when they are taken by a relatively powerful and cohesive foreign policy machine in which bureaucratic conflict, disobedience, or misunderstanding are very limited (see Clarke, 1979).

This chapter looks, first, at the French system of decision-making, and then at Giscard's initial approach to African policy. This was intended to be a global, coherent approach, but it was never implementable as such. Liberal rhetoric reflected a genuine aspiration held in Paris, but it also masked the growing importance of African policy, and a shift away from a liberal military-security policy. In any case, by 1976 it was clear that the pressures of particular issues had made a nonsense of the aspirations either to liberalism or to any cohesive strategy in Africa. Subsequent sections look at policy in Chad, Zaire and the CAR. The chapter concludes with an attempt to assess the implications of these discussions for a study of foreign policy implementation.

The Context of Policy

Wallace has argued that the American model of 'bureaucratic politics' as developed by Graham Allison (1971) does not really fit the French experience (Wallace, 1978b). He argues that the complex of internal debate between institutions and committees of government which Allison describes do not occur, or occur in a different way in France. This is broadly supported by other writers on French foreign policy. Hayward (1973), for example, has argued that the constitutional position of the President guarantees him a special personal role in policy supervision.

In maintaining his control the President has in his *cabinet* in the Elysée an African adviser. From 1960 this office was held by a close confidant of General de Gaulle, M. Foccart, who, for the most part, shared de Gaulle's view of the world. In the President's absence he chaired key co-ordinating committees on Africa, dealt directly with African leaders and liaised with the various government ministries involved.

But it was not Foccart, despite his awesome reputation, nor any other individual, that guaranteed the relative cohesion of French policy. It was the institutional and ideological cohesion of the French foreign policy system. Tint (1972) has argued that French policy in the Third World, in particular, reflects strong organization, which would only work if based on an ideological consensus. Charlot (1971) emphasizes the extent to which Gaullism was a popular reflection of generally held French attitudes and not simply the invention of Gaullist politicians. Waites (1983) has shown that although the constitutional position of the President allows great personal latitude, there has been great continuity in French policy both because of continuities of external pressures and because of ideological cohesion. And while Giscard sought a new role in international politics, he had great difficulty elaborating and implementing anything very new (Serfati, 1976; Frears, 1981). If there was something new about Giscard's approach to foreign policy, it lay in aspects of style, and perhaps in the greater domestic insecurity of Giscard, rather than in substance.

The President is constitutionally central to foreign policy in the Fifth Republic. He is commander-in-chief, appoints the Prime Minister and Foreign Secretary, has a wide range of emergency or special powers, and direct control over security and intelligence services. On Africa, in particular, key decisions are made in the Elysée. The Foreign Ministry may be useful, and is an important source of communications, but it can be cut out of policy-making in a crisis. The Finance Ministry may also be involved (and has a higher status), but Giscard, as a former Finance Minister, exercised close supervision over the ministry that helped supply very large sums to maintain his African policy. The Co-operation Ministry was upgraded in Giscard's early years in office, but Giscard appeared to have no major problems in controlling it. These separate arms of bureaucracy were, in any case, co-ordinated through a committee system controlled from the Elysée, which was designed to minimize conflicts or contradictions in approach. The evidence seems to be that this system worked well (Tint, 1972; Wallace, in Cerny and Schain, 1980; Hayward, 1973; Crandall Hollick, 1981).

The military played a major role in French African policy. There is almost certainly more to be learnt about the relations between the military and the Elysée over African intervention in the 1970s, but the evidence available to this writer suggests that, at least until 1979, military objections to government policy were confined to arguments within the relevant committees, and to a number of evident, but in themselves not very serious, leaks to the press. Again the strength of ideological solidarity and a broad sense of common purpose in forces which had an intimate role in the determination of their mission seems to have overcome any temptation to Pentagon-style political infighting.

French policy towards Africa, therefore, does not exhibit major features of 'bureaucratic politics'. It does reveal some problems in the implementation of standing procedures in day to day policy (for example, over the CAR), and some mindbending improvisation (for example, the Zairean parachutes: see p. 85). But the main problems the French government faced were in carrying out policy in the African context, and in reconciling decisions which sooner or later contradicted each other. African affairs were traditionally seen as separate from other aspects of French foreign policy, and of relatively minor importance (Ullmann, 1973). The President had always enjoyed a high standing among France's African clients, although this was not true in Pompidou's last months in office. African policy was very largely free from public or parliamentary scrutiny, being treated as a largely private domain of the Elysée. Giscard was to lose these advantages, and this loss cost him dearly.

French interests in Africa were primarily economic and security ones. France gained an increasing proportion of its raw materials from Africa, and raw materials policy had become crucial by 1973 (Wigg, 1975). but

France's interests also hinged on prestige, on its putative independent standing and on its self-appointed special cultural mission. The economic interests were especially in minerals. France imports most of its uranium and copper, and some of its iron, diamonds, manganese and other special ores, from countries involved in African conflicts. Many of the companies (and their employees) are French. But France also had economic interests in African markets and investment, and hoped to develop energy supplies which it alone would control in Africa. Security interests include the security of supply of these minerals, and the protection of these investments, but they hinge more around the balance of power in Central and Western Africa. This has been shifting because of the growing Soviet and Cuban involvement in parts of the continent, the unsure approach of the USA to Africa, Britain's withdrawal, and the rise, after 1970, of Nigerian oil and military power. But the most potent issues for French security policy came from three other sources: the Libyan revolution of 1970 and the interest of President Qaddafi in his neighbours; the spread, and changing nature, of Islam in the 1970s; and the instability of colonies cobbled together (by France, Britain and Belgium) to create states of dubious viability.

The Decline of French Institutions

French institutions in Africa were in serious decline by 1974. Regional organizations set up to handle economic, financial and cultural co-operation were either abandoned or simply faded away. African leaders became suspicious of France's often blatant use of these institutions and, faced with growing pressure at home, could no longer afford to accept them so easily. Legum (1975) lists a series of institutional failings, while a number of commentators were to note the inadequacy or unacceptability of Franco-African institutional arrangements (see Maurice Duverger in *Le Monde*, 28 December 1977; *Le Monde*, 20 May 1979). These failures to maintain a multilateral system led to an increasing reliance on bilateral agreements, which were more *ad hoc*. They included military assistance and arms supply deals as well as economic arrangements (Lellouche and Moisi, 1979).

The absence of reliable institutions for economic and military co-operation called for improvisation. The wide range of institutions that remained were seen as ineffectual, or were not trusted by the African leaders who dealt with them. This institutional instability is one reason why French decision-makers found themselves subsequently resorting to force. But the economic weakness and political intractability of the countries concerned was the fundamental cause of the rash of French military interventions (see Wodie, 1970).

Giscard's Assumption of Office

Giscard sought to present himself as a liberal, and argued that French diplomacy needed a 'new liberalism': 'la diplomatie a cessé de se presenter en termes de conflits' (Giscard d'Estaing, 1976, p. 163). Co-operation was to become 'more meaningful'. Foccart was dismissed, and a new and genuinely liberal Co-operation Minister, M. Pierre Abelin, was appointed (*Le* Monde, 29 September 1974). The technical and financial aspects of co-operation were liberalized, and more aid money was allocated (*Le Monde*, 14 January 1975).

There was a genuine aspiration in the first eighteen months of the new administration to change French policy. It aroused new expectations among African leaders (Legume, 1975, A34, A49), it had support from Giscard's liberal UDR supporters and it earned Gaullist criticism for its woolly-headed softness (*Le Figaro*, 9 July 1974). Yet the government in Paris, in 1974, had a number of serious problems: the oil crisis, its relations with the USA and with the European Community, and the future of détente were the most pressing. Thus African policy was conducted in the light of events elsewhere. It had three faces: liberalism, economic self-interest and strategic insecurity. Each of these was a 'rational' response, given France's history and perceived situation. But these did not add up to an implementable policy programme even where the separate elements could be pursued.

The Policy: Three Phases

French policy towards Africa can be seen as falling into three broad phases. The first is the 'liberal' phase, running from 1974 to the spring of 1976. It is followed by a much more active and interventionist stage, when the liberal motives and cautious economic activities of the earlier phase were seen to have failed. Yet French interventions from 1976 to 1979 were more haphazard responses to the pressures which overwhelmed the 'liberal' phase than a systematic new plan of approach. While it is sometimes forgotten that some of France's interventions in Africa were, at least in the short term, important successes, the difficulties of maintaining an active, wide-ranging role in Africa led to a third phase. In this phase, sapped by the size of the problems, distracted by events in the Middle East and under strong domestic attack, the Giscard government gave up the attempt to intervene widely and alone in African politics. This third stage lasted from 1979 to the end of Giscard's *septennat* in March 1981.

Implementing the 'Liberal' Phase

The 'new look' that Giscard and his advisers sought to give to French policy in Africa was marked by a series of internal institutional changes already mentioned. While accompanying these changes were a decreasing emphasis on military instruments, and an assertion of the importance of the independence of the francophone states, the main instrument of the 'new look' was economic: more aid, more financial support on softer terms, and more technical training and assistance.

The Ministry of Co-operation was allowed a budget of 2·163 million francs, a 9 per cent cash increase over the previous year. Abelin visited Africa in January 1975 and sought to increase the scope of technical assistance, while increasing the French aid programme to 0·7 per cent of GNP. The Franc Zone was liberalized in order to help the borrowing and trading position of the francophone states, although even at the time this was not thought to amount to very much (*Le Monde*, 19 November 1974). The number of French teachers in Africa was increased to 30,000 under the co-operation programme. French military presences were run down and, following the withdrawal from Nigeria after the coup in 1974, France had a military presence only in Senegal, Gabon, Chad and the Ivory Coast (although there were French military advisers and delegations on training and evaluation missions elsewhere).

Giscard also sought a *rapprochement* with Guinea, a former francophone state which had fallen out with de Gaulle on independence. Relations between France and Guinea had alternated between frosty accommodation and cold war since the early 1960s, and the government in Guinea had become firmly Moscow-oriented. The President sent a deputy of his own party, M. Bettencourt, to settle some of the outstanding issues, which included the question of compensation payments to French interests for the nationalization of assets and the back payment of pensions and allowances to Guinean veterans of the French services. It is significant that Giscard d'Estaing chose a politician well known in Africa for his liberal views rather than professional diplomats whose integrity the Guinean regime would doubt. Normalization of Franco-Guinean relations in July 1975 was the main achievement of this phase.

This range of measures led up to a presidential visit to Africa in March 1975. Giscard chaired a conference of leaders of the francophone group at Bangui. The previous Franco-African Summit, held in November 1973, had marked a low point in French policy in Africa, with Pompidou finding himself having no control of events and being much criticized for the failings of French aid, and the arrogance and neo-colonialism of its policies. Giscard hoped that the Bangui Summit would change all that (*Le Monde*, 28 February 1975).

The summit was successful in helping the French government restore prestige among its traditional African clients. The discussion of financial questions was seen as especially useful. Giscard's argument that France could offer unique support in an increasingly difficult world environment struck a welcome note, according to accounts at the time (*Le Monde* and *International Herald Tribune*, 2 March 1975). Giscard was able to develop personal contacts with traditional French-oriented elites, especially those in Ivory Coast, Niger, Mali and Senegal.

Yet all the French government's efforts in economic and financial support in this early period were severely weakened, and eventually undone, by two sets of problems in the international and domestic economic environments. Inflation in France cut the real purchasing power of the French co-operation budget to the level it had stood at in 1956 (Legum, 1976). Yet the developing economies this budget was designed to help were suffering evermore acute difficulties because of the effects of the oil crisis on their balance of payments.

If in the economic sphere where the 'liberal impulse' of French policy was more genuine, there were growing doubts, there were even more serious doubts about the 'liberalism' of Giscard's policies in other areas. While he had indeed replaced Foccart, his action was largely symbolic, as Giscard appointed as African adviser René Jourmiac, Foccart's former deputy and close confidant from the 1960s. The great emphasis on cultural contact and education in Giscard's policy was a continuation of a policy which had always put great stress on the cultural dimensions of control (Thompson, 1974; Tint, 1972, pp. 165–75). Only a little later *Le Figaro* observed that 'the importance of French language and culture in diplomacy are that they remain ... [the best index] of *the reliability* of the former colonies' (25 June 1977; emphasis added).

The 'liberal impulse' was already under stress in the spring of 1975. French policy in Giscard's first year was marked by an uneasy mixture of a genuine desire for a more liberal relationship with the ex-colonies, traditional attitudes of paternalism and cultural superiority, and commercial exploitation. All of these were heavily coloured by the considerable uncertainty about raw material supplies, and monetary and strategic instability, which characterized the environment of world politics after the oil crisis (Wigg, 1975).

The Bangui Summit was seen at the time as a qualified success, politically important but hedged with economic doubts (*Le Monde*, 5 March 1975; *The Times* and *International Herald Tribune*, 6 March 1975). A month later the delicate political situation in Chad exploded. In a military coup President Tombalbaye, a firmly reliable French client over fifteen years, was killed. He was replaced by a military government which could not contain a bitter civil war. The main cause of the coup was a worsening economic situation which resulted from growing import costs (especially oil and goods imported from France), and the long-term expansion of the Sahara desert into the populated areas to its south. What had been seen as a secure French ally became an arena of 'complete insecurity' (Legum, 1975, p. B563).

The main line of French policy at this time was described by Giscard as 'globalism'. Frears has argued that this represented no more than the old Gaullist pursuit of prestige, 'grandeur' and independence of both superpowers in disguise (Frears, 1981, p. 96; cf. also Cerny, 1980). But from 1975 on a new element is evident in French policy which does make Giscard's *mondialisme* distinct from de Gaulle's 'policy of grandeur'. That is, that while de Gaulle and Pompidou were able to keep their African policy separate from their broader policies on Southern Africa and the Arab World, Giscard was unable to maintain the separation of issues. He was forced to recognise powerful forces which created new linkages between the three issue-areas which his predecessors had largely been able to separate. The Chad war, in which French troops and prestige were involved from the start, linked the Arab and African worlds geographically and politically. The interest shown by African leaders (including those like President Senghar normally most compliant to French policies) in Giscard's extension of arms sales to South Africa in 1975 was further unwelcome evidence of the difficulty of isolating policy on francophone Africa from other policy areas. *Mondialisme* is an unwitting recognition of French inability to keep separate major issues on its foreign policy agenda, although it appears in Giscardian rhetoric as a claim to an independent world role.

French Arab policy and the initiation of two sets of talks, the Euro-Arab Dialogue and the North-South Summit talks designed to produce a New International Economic Order (NIEO), form part of the response to the interlocking of previously separate policy areas. Both provided an institutional framework of talks in which France could play a leading role, and both were major diversions from France's traditional partners in Africa. These partners were aware of the diversion – and were unhappy with it. Golan has concluded that French policy in the Third World had become a wrapped-up Arab policy leaving the francophone countries (and their ruling elites) searching for crumbs of support: '1975 was not a happy year for the francophone family – this can be blamed on France even more than at any time in the past' (Legum, 1976, p. A96).

During the Angolan civil war France began by supporting the FNLA, which was more pro-Western and run from Zaire, a country where Giscard sought more influence. He opposed the MPLA, which was more pro-Soviet and had gained the support of a large (and very effective) Cuban force. In opposing the MPLA, however, Giscard offended the government of the Congo (formerly French Equatorial Africa) and divided the francophone bloc. Only when the Paris government had reached a *modus vivendi* with President Mobutu of Zaire, and when the MPLA were clearly winning, did France switch allegiance and recognize the MPLA government in Launda. This remarkably open piece of machiavellism demonstrated to even the most francophile the declining level of French concern for francophone interests, and the priorities of resource diplomacy, meeting a Soviet challenge and undermining US influence, which together informed French policy. But just to say that is to suggest a degree of cohesion which was simply absent. The policy of the mid-1970s became increasingly unco-ordinated, and increasingly uncertain of purposes.

The implementation problems which emerge from a survey of French policy during 1974–6 are numerous. They rest in large part on the deteriorating economies of the areas of Africa which France sought to influence. The 1973 oil crisis, the expansion of the Sahara desert and a decline in demand in the European economy for African products had profound political effects. Economic means of handling these problems in order to maintain 'stability', to keep out Libyan influence, control tribal divisions, or keep in power favoured clients were insufficient. But the main alternative, military intervention, was unlikely to produce effective results. Indeed, the effects of prolonged fighting on the economies of countries like Chad were to increase fragmentation and instability. French policy in Africa was, in economic terms, wildly overstretched by 1976. A drought affected three-fifths of Mali and cut food production in Mauritania by 60 per cent (Legum, 1976). A change of French economic policy was also unlikely to help; the size and direction of French aid played a major part in distorting these economies in the first place (Thompson, 1974, passim). French aid and loans for balance-of-payments deficits and budget shortfalls alone sustained the economies (and governments) of Niger, Upper Volta, Mali and the CAR. But they helped to make them more divided, less self-supporting and more unstable in the longer run.

The political consequences of economic decline were exacerbated by growing tribal and religious differences. The development of a more militant force in Islam throughout North Africa was a major part of this, but even in the non-Islamic communities (for example, in the CAR and in southern Chad) serious conflicts between Christian sects or shamanist cults undermined what political cohesion may have existed before. National governments were often incompetent or severely repressive in dealing with these. If we add to this the increasing interest of Libya in her neighbours' affairs, it is clear that the French government faced a set of severe problems.

French officials in Paris and in Africa were, of course, aware of these increasing pressures. If they had had time to develop a 'long-term' response to them, they might have handled them better; or they might have suffered from 'groupthink' and misled themselves in their response. An attempt to develop a long-range approach is evident in repeated assertions of French independence and self-sufficiency (see, for instance, Le Monde, 11 March 1976), and in declarations by Co-operation Minister Lipkowski and Foreign Minister Sauvagnargues that France would act militarily to prevent destabilization of its allies. But this was hardly new; and it is hardly a policy. The main pressure which evoked the fragmented responses of 1976–9 was time. The Paris government found itself confronting grave and increasing problems. It couched its responses in military terms because no other measures seemed to offer any chance of success. But the root of the problems was not military security, and the urgency of particular issues led to ill-coordinated, *ad hoc* responses. These attempts to implement a defence of French interests need closer, case-by-case analysis to explore how these environmental and political factors affected French behaviour.

Phase Two: Intervention in Chad

The civil war in Chad had begun in 1965. It involved two major 'sides': one was northern, Arab, Muslim and backed from 1970 by the revolutionary government of Libya; the other was based in the richer African south of the country (which included the capital Ndjamena), a mixture of Muslim, Christian and traditional shamanist peoples. But both sides of the dispute reflected personal allegiances, groups changed sides with frequency and both sides had a tendency to fracture. The French government was consistent in supporting the group that controlled Ndjamena, but also sought to eliminate Libyan influence and to ensure that Libyan-backed forces did not penetrate to the southern side of the Sahara. Military successes in the early 1970s failed to prevent a steady growth of power for the main opposition, FROLINAT (Buijtenhuis, 1978, *passim* and p. 239).

French troops were officially withdrawn in 1972, when the war quietened down. In fact a number remained covertly until the coup of 13 April 1975 when they helped to support a new regime led by Felix Malloum. With the help of pro-government groups, French troops were able to contain the Libyan-backed invasion which followed the coup. They were then largely withdrawn, to be recommitted again in 1978, when it became clear that Malloum had lost control. Turning to negotiation, in August the French government arranged a conference of the various parties at Tripoli. There Giscard switched horses. The new government was a coalition of Malloum and the FROLINAT leader, Hissan Habré, but Habré was in effective control (*International Herald Tribune*, 9 May 1975; *Guardian*, 8 September 1975; *The Times*, 3 June 1978; *Le Monde*, 4 July 1978; *Le Monde* and *The Times*, 30 August 1978).

The French with their experienced troops and air support were able to win any major encounter. But in the classic problem of guerrilla warfare they had enormous difficulty turning their victories in the field into lasting gains. Furthermore, Chadian politics fractured around them. By 1979 Chad's tortured polity had fragmented into more than a dozen elements.

French policy was also constrained by a major propaganda and military factor. In early 1974 Habré had captured a French anthropologist, Mlle Françoise Claustre. She remained his prisoner until late 1977. The threat to her life restrained French forces from attacking Habrés bases in the north. And while rescue missions failed to find her, Western journalists were able to do so with embarrassing frequency. Her plight was never out of the French papers, and sometimes even found a way on to TV screens. This was public evidence of the apparent impotence of French military power and marked the first of a number of African impacts on French domestic politics which broke down that traditional lack of interest in government policy in Africa which had been a major governmental resource since the end of the Algerian problem in 1962.

The Chad settlement of August 1978 lasted three months. Fighting was renewed in November, this time with Libyan support for dissident Christian groups in the south as well as for various tribal factions in the north. French chances of maintaining the government, described as 'very slim' in January (*Le Monde*, 21 January 1979), worsened when fighting broke out between factions led by Habré and by Malloum in the capital Ndjamena itself. The civil war continued, fought on three sides. By April it was estimated that over 10,000 had been killed in five years of inconclusive warring (*International Herald Tribune*, 10 April 1979). The very high financial and prestige costs of the war had become a serious concern to allies in London and Washington (*New York Times*, 25 March 1979). But by this stage French decision-makers had also recognized the limits of French powers and a new diplomatic solution was sought.

The first French efforts to negotiate a way out of Chad was an approach to Nigeria to have a new conference. A number of bilateral cease-fires and armistices were made to allow a meeting to take place. This produced the Kano Agreement by which French troops were replaced by an African peace-keeping force dominated by a large Nigerian army contingent. The agreement was rejected by Libya, which supported a new offensive in May. Meanwhile the Nigerians made themselves very unpopular and were asked to withdraw by Chad leaders (the only thing they could agree on). France was asked to commit more troops again, while the Organization of African Unity (OAU) tried to negotiate a new peace. In November eleven factions met round a table. By this time the French government had virtually given up any hope of influencing the outcome, and agreed to support any new government. French support continued to maintain the Chadian economy, at great expense, with little reward and with massive arms flows irrelevant to the economic problems which the war itself had worsened (*Financial Times*, 21 March 1979; *New York Times*, 25 March and 21 April 1979; *Le Monde*, 25 February, 6 June, 6 September, 7 and 13 November 1979).

To the extent that French policy was concerned to contain Libya it succeeded. But it was equally concerned to stabilize Chad, and here it was unsuccessful. French policy might have made more headway if Chad had been a state with a recognizable community, a measure of cohesion and the symbols and institutions of statehood which could be fought for and won. But Chad was (and is) no more a 'state' than Lebanon. The divisions of culture and society are as great, but Chad is far less economically developed. Politics grouped around armed factions, which identified with individuals and with family feuds as much as with ideologies or religions. Military gains in this situation are very hard to relate to tangible political effects. Chad had in any case been created out of a chunk of the French empire: it lacked any 'natural' identity, and French policy had never succeeded in synthesizing one. Furthermore, Chad is a very large country, four times the size of France. Even at the peak of her involvement, with over 5,000 men there, French influence only applied to part of the country. The war, and the diversion of aid into military effort or political bribery, undermined what economic progress might have survived the Sahel drought. Through the 1970s the Chadian economy contracted on average by 2 per cent a year.

The civil war in Chad broke out again following a further division of the government agreed under OAU auspices in May 1980. In September the President, Goukouni Ouddei, made an agreement with Colonel Qaddafi under which Libyan troops invaded and this time seized Ndjamena and most of the country. French forces, under pressure to leave from Nigeria and other West African countries, and having recognized the limits to their power, had been withdrawn earlier and did not return. The Libyans had control of the country.

Yet Qaddafi's forces could control Chad no better than could the Foreign Legion. The Libyan leader made the mistake of announcing the merger of Libya and Chad. His allies revolted at this and the war began again – and has continued ever since. After Giscard's electoral defeat, Mitterrand involved France again from the autumn of 1981 (Crandall Hollick, 1982).

The further details of the Chad conflict can be left aside for present purposes. French efforts began confidently before 1977, won an uncertain victory and returned with confidence in 1975. By 1979 it was clear that French policy had failed. Only later, when Nigerian arms and diplomacy, the efforts of the OAU, the Libyan military, as well as Hissan Habré (the most able of Chad's leaders) had all failed to do any better, did the French failure in Chad stand in perspective.

It is hard to argue that French decision-makers mistook the importance of Chad. For its uranium, its geographic position on the frontier of Black Africa and Islam, its importance to Nigeria, Sudan and Libya, it is what in geopolitics would be known as a 'heartland'. But the political and economic environment in Chad (not to mention the geography) made success elusive. Involvement and withdrawal were forced in turn on Giscard's government. African countries demanded that France should look for African solutions, but when pressed to help were ineffective or worse. Yet it is hard to quarrel with Thompson and Adloff's judgement that 'France's vacillations and conspicuous diplomatic and political failures in Chad were transforming the image it had long sought to maintain into that [of an] ineffectual gendarme' (Thompson and Adloff, p. 140).

Lellouche and Moisi argue that French policy in Africa was designed to maintain only a limited commitment (Lellouche and Moisi, 1979, p.122). Yet even an operation on a considerable scale was ineffective and eventually, in 1980, the government in Paris seems to have made a deal with the Libyans, only to find that that too was unacceptable to the fragmented groups in Chad (Crandall Hollick, 1982). The experience in Chad reveals four main kinds of implementation problem: first, the problem of maintaining Chad's increasingly divided political elite, which military action further divided. Secondly, the nature of the fighting in a country of this size and terrain did not allow for decisive action. The French military have great experience of such 'low-intensity operations', but such operations hinge on there being clear and achievable political goals which they support. The French government wobbled between political goals in Chad, committed and withdrew itself alternately to different sides, and recognized its failure by its effective pull-out by 1980. Thirdly, the government in Paris was evidently pursuing goals that were incompatible, and failed in any case to maintain some sort of political consensus among major groups in Ndjamena which would have achieved them. Fourthly, the domestic context changed. Increasing criticism at home, culminating in the collapse of policy over the CAR in autumn 1979, forced a general reversal of African policy. The Paris government was by early 1980 merely an impotent observer in Chad.

Zaire, Limited and Effective Intervention

In contrast to the problems in Chad, French military actions in Zaire were more limited in scope. But one main reason why they succeeded was precisely because they had a limited, defined objective. The Zairean economic and political situation had become desperate by early 1977. The government's corruption, incompetence and weakness was well known. The mineral wealth which alone sustained President Mobutu declined as world prices fell. On 10 March 1977 a force of mercenaries and ex-Katangese secessionists from the Congo War of the early 1960s invaded Zaire from Angola.

American aid to Zaire was promised almost immediately, but the promise was equally quickly qualified. It was recognized that direct American intervention would be barred by Congress and that, in any case, the administration lacked the experience and immediate military means to act on any scale. The Carter administration was appalled at the prospect of getting bogged down in open-ended commitment to support

Mobutu (*Financial Times* and *International Herald Tribune*, 17 March 1977).

French interests in Zaire included investments worth 87·4 million francs. More to the point, one-third of French copper came from the invaded Shaba (formerly Katanga) province. The government in Paris recognized from the start that these interests were under threat. It was also concerned for the lives of several hundred mining engineers and their families in the area. Its growing economic and diplomatic interests in Zaire were creating a conflict with the Belgian government, which claimed a special interest in its former colony.

It quickly became clear that the invasion was essentially a revival of Katangese secessionism, not a Cuban or Angolan invasion. While the French Cabinet had prepared for intervention, there was increasing pressure from francophone and other states (led by Nigeria) for an African solution rather than a European invasion. This was arranged in secret talks between the Moroccan, Senegalese and French governments. Using French support, and with some French back-up and air support, Moroccan troops were flown into Zaire on 11 April 1977 (*Le Monde*, 12 April 1977). France sponsored and supplied the operation, but was thus able to claim that it had encouraged a multinational, African operation. The issue of presentation of policy was important both to Giscard and to Mobutu. The invading force was successfully repelled. The French action was a short-range, specific application of force, a 'punctual operation' after which the French military presence was reduced (until 1978) to a force of seventy advisers (Lellouche and Moisi, 1979, pp. 109, 122).

It is not clear what King Hassan of Morocco gained beyond the moral satisfaction of having helped a neighbour. But it is reasonable to suppose that there is a relationship between his support of the Zaire action and the increasing scope of French support for his claims in the western Sahara. There, frontier and tribal conflict had become the cause of serious fighting between a nationalist group, Polisario, and various other groups backed by Morocco, Algeria and Mauritania. The western Sahara, and conflict in Mauritania itself, became another arena of conflict which France was drawn into with uncertain objectives and little success. There, a limited diplomatic settlement only followed a withdrawal of French direct involvement later.

In May 1978 the fighting in Zaire flared up again. Again President Mobutu proved incapable of protecting his regime. But this time French troops intervened directly. Belgian troops supported them, but the French went in first, encouraging Belgian suspicions of French motives. The French force borrowed US transport planes for the action, as well as Zaire airforce parachutes. This was taken at the time as an index of the lack of preparedness.

The urgency was caused by the Kolwezi massacre on 19–20 May when several hundred French and Belgian civilians were killed. The effectiveness of the action saved more lives, resulted in the evacuation of other European civilians and led to the invaders being pushed back. This time the Foreign Legion paratroops involved were calculatingly ruthless in their pursuit of the invaders. President Mobutu's troops were able to join in the victory, restoring some of their confidence and creating the impression again of an African involvement in the solution of an African problem.

The French action won a great deal of support abroad, especially in the USA, in Britain and in the Middle East, where French efficiency and strength were advertised (*International Herald Tribune*, 25 May 1978; *The Times*, 24 May and 12 June 1978). The Saudis clearly were especially impressed (Frears, 1981, p. 116) and increased their arms purchases from France as well as using French troops to clear a large group of Islamic fundamentalists who seized the Grand Mosque at Mecca.

Although the operation was a major success militarily, it provoked a sharp reaction in Paris, being followed by the largest demonstration against French foreign policy of any kind since the Algerian War. The demonstration concentrated on the growth of French military involvement in the continent. French troop commitments had risen from about 2,500 in 1975 to something nearer 14,000, We can conclude that the Zaire action was the occasion for this public revulsion rather than the cause of it. In Zaire 'policy drift', which *was* a feature of French involvement in Chad and the western Sahara, was absent. France increased its role in Zaire in terms of economic aid. Its raw materials problem was helped, a group of its civilians saved and new arms orders won. The objectives of the mission were defined and controlled. Whether the longer-term effects of the operations helped the people of Zaire is another question, but the Mobutu regime was saved. The longer-term spin-off of the 1977 involvement, France's greater commitment to support King Hassan, in the Sahara, led to serious difficulties and, eventually, to defeat. The longer-term spinoff of the 1978 operation was certainly seen in Paris (as in London, Washington and Tehran) as a valuable bonus for France in one arena that had high priority, Saudi Arabia.

Phase Three: France and the Central African Dictator

When Giscard came to office in 1974, French relations with the Central African Republic were not good, mainly because of attacks in the French press on the CAR's leader, President Bokassa. His extremely authoritarian police state, his suppression of any opposition and especially of minority tribal groups were one set of causes for these attacks. But many African leaders displayed these traits, including some of the closest francophone allies. What seemed to create a special fascination for the French media were the personal habits Bokassa

advertised to his own people: he was proud of his status as a tribal
witchdoctor, and never tried to refute allegations of cannibalism; he kept
many wives; and he took personal interest in his prison service, especially
on execution days. He was portrayed as a francophone combination of
Papa Doc and Idi Amin. But he was Giscard's friend.

One potential disadvantage of the presidential position in French
foreign policy is that the Elysée takes an unavoidably high profile in
foreign affairs. While in Zaire and Chad it was the President's political
and strategic judgement which were at issue, over the CAR the issue was
more personal. In the long run it was more damaging to Giscard's
personal standing than anything else that happened in his presidency,
although it was of lesser significance for France than many issues. At the
1975 Banui Summit of francophone states (held in the CAR in the first
place, in recognition of a special relationship) Giscard went out of his
way to give approval and support to Bokassa against his media critics (*Le
Monde*, 5 March 1975). Giscard's cousin was chairman of the largest
mining company – and the largest business concern – in the CAR, and
Giscard had a holiday home in the CAR, which he often visited. These
personal interests became important, and help to explain why Giscard,
the self-professed liberal, went so radically out of his way to defend
Bokassa later.

France also had important public interests in the CAR. It provided an
airbase for French forces, and a military training depot. The CAR was
seen as especially important because of its geographic position. Lying at
the heart of Africa, it offered secure access to the north to Chad and to
the Sahara region, to the south to Zaire and to the east to Sudan. It
formed an intended stronghold against Islam behind the relatively weak
Chadian front line. Economically it was even more important, as a source
of minerals, especially diamonds and uranium.

The first form of French support for Bokassa was economic. The
CAR's economy was in the most desperate situation throughout the
1970s. For the budget year 1975-6, the CAR government raised only
3,700 million CFA francs to cover expenditure of 19,000 million CFA
francs. The rest of this budget was payed for by the French taxpayer. In
addition, France supplied a balance-of-payments subsidy of 2,000
million CFA francs, and French military support, including gifts of arms,
was free. The French press were entitled to ask what was gained for this
outlay.

But a second line of government support for Bokassa was censorship in
France itself. The government-run radio and TV networks were
instructed to speak of the CAR as little as possible, and to be favourable
in any mentions. Where newspaper stories were concerned, direct
censorship was impossible, but the government spokesmen devoted
special time to attacking stories critical of Bokassa. For example, the
President has powers under the French Constitution to stifle stories

defaming himself, and while de Gaulle and Pompidou had both used these powers (and on African issues at times), Giscard made a special effort to use them to muzzle critical comment on him and his links with the CAR. This tactic worked quite well until 1979. CAR opposition leaders in France could also be muzzled, since their books on the CAR could be banned (French press laws apply differently to books and newspapers). On a number of occasions books published in France were immediately censored under broad 'national security' provisions in order to avoid offending Bokassa. In the short run this technique of foreign policy management was effective as the means were directly under the government's control. But in the longer run it had the effect of drawing further attention to Bokassa's tyranny and the links Giscard had with it. When the crisis finally broke, almost all sections of the French press were fiercely antagonistic to government policy. When *Le Canard enchaîné* refused to be muzzled, and published material while daring Giscard to take legal action in October 1979, his bluff, was called. Press management can be valuable instruments of foreign policy, but in this case it proved a weak one because the crisis was seen not as an issue of state security, but as one of personal failure by the President, so media chiefs refused to co-operate. Giscard either had to face this or take extraordinarily totalitarian control of the media.

In 1976 Bokassa was suddenly apparently converted to Islam. This must have caused alarm in Paris, where he was seen as a bulwark against Islamic radicalism. But before Paris could recover from the shock, he disappeared. The CAR leader turned up in Peking. There he assumed as equally violent revolutionary posture, denouncing Moscow as well as Washington, and attacking all forms of neo-colonialism. The Chinese leaders, embarrassed and appalled by his arrival sent him home. After five weeks of continuing pseudo-Maoist rhetoric, Bokassa found a new idol. At a carefully staged news event he assumed the mantle of Napoleon, renamed his country the Central African Empire and named himself its emperor. The imperial consort was chosen from among his wives, the prisons were cleared in honour (by a round of mass executions) and a date for the coronation was fixed for December 1977 (Legum, 1977).

This series of events reverberated through the French media. But it also had serious implications for policy. Foreign Ministry staff, embarrassed and forbidden to comment, made it plain that policy towards the CAR was strictly for the Elysée. While it is clear that there was already in 1977 serious doubt about Bokassa in Paris, this was stifled by the President and his immediate staff. Indeed, France funded the coronation of Bokassa, treated the affair as a vital matter of state, providing £25 million for the coronation regalia alone.

In 1977 and 1978 Giscard had sought to develop a number of institutional arrangements which would create in Africa a permanent joint 'peace-keeping' force of francophone states. He raised this proposal at the francophone summit held in Paris, in May 1978 (*Financial Times*, 23 May 1978), and then got US approval for the scheme in a visit to Washington mainly for this purpose (*Le Monde*, 29 May 1978). He seemed to be on the threshold of an agreement which, at the expense of linking France more closely with the USA, would develop a permanent force of intervention in Africa, and would enable France to withdraw a part of her own forces. In all of these moves Bokassa remained loyal to Paris. When the proposals for a joint force fell through, Bokassa remained on Giscard's side (*Observer News Agency* and *Guardian*, 24 May 1978; *International Herald Tribune*, 25 May 1978). His value to Giscard was significant.

But the cost of Bokassa's allegiance to the French government grew. Opposition groups and Amnesty International produced well-authenticated stories of new tyrannies. Bokassa meanwhile gave France directly military support as well as bases in the new phase of the war in Chad in 1979 (*Le Monde*, 8 March 1979, 29 May 1979; *New York Times*, 19 August 1979).

On the 15 May 1979 Amnesty International released a story of a massacre of demonstrating schoolchildren in Bangui. Those who had not been shot in the street had been imprisoned, and a number of those had been appallingly tortured. The massacre had happened on 18 April, and had allegedly been known to the French authorities and concealed. As the scale of the massacre was confirmed the press declared open season on Bokassa and Giscard. The torrent of criticism surprised and wounded Giscard. Slowly the government found it had to shift positions. Even the French TV services began to criticize Bokassa (*Le Monde* and *Guardian*, 16 May 1979). The French government cut off military aid to Bokassa, at first thinking this could be a short-term response before a return to 'normality' (*Le Monde*, 24 May 1979). It was a 'pseudo-crisis' a spokesman said. But the criticism continued, French credibility was further undermined and economic assistance was cut off in August (*Le Monde*, 18 August 1979).

By this time the French government had resolved that Bokassa was a dangerous menace to French policy. René Journiac made a tour of francophone states to explain France's position and improve France's image with her friends. He also, presumably, got their support for what followed. On the 25 September 1979, in a quiet, well-planned and very popular move, French troops of the newly streamlined African force moved into Bangui. The force had been designed to stabilize African friends against outside attack. Its first use was to overthrow Giscard's most loyal supporter. Bokassa, stunned and disbelieving, flew in his presidential plane to Evreux in Normandy to seek French help against what he believed was a foreign-inspired coup. Giscard shuttled him off to house arrest in the Ivory Coast.

It is fair to say that Giscard had no choice but to oust Bokassa, but this was a direct result of the conduct of French policy in the previous five years. Yet the coup was no solution to Giscard's own problems. The major impact of these events made a nonsense of the attempt to set up a new co-operation secretariat in Niamey (Niger), and made a mockery of Giscard's repeated claims that 'France does not seek influence in Africa' and even 'France does not seek economic advantage in Africa' (*Le Monde* 18 and 19 May 1979). Such patent untruth only further damaged his standing at home and abroad. Statements like 'Europeans might misunderstand the significance of cannibalism' made by a French spokesman to European journalists in defence of the 'customs' of Bokassa's Empire, speak for themselves: the French government was getting desperate to the point of idiocy. The African consequences of Bokassa were overwhelmed by their European and domestic implications.

When in October 1979 *Le Canard enchaîné* published a story that Giscard had received a secret gift of diamonds worth nearly 1 million francs in 1973, public opinion was very receptive (*Le Canard enchaîné*, 10 October 1979). *Le Monde* (11 October 1979) commented, with a rather short memory, that there had 'never been such a scandal'. Conservative and liberal papers abroad joined in a wave of criticism which Giscard did not try to stem by a denial. When he finally defended himself on the ground that the 'diamonds were only little ones', he was clearly flustered and in grave difficulty (*Guardian* and *Daily Telegraph*, 10 October 1979; *Guardian*, 29 November 1979) and simply seemed to confirm the cupidity of Giscard's policy. Incompetence, greed, personal interest and bad judgement were taken as the hallmarks of Giscard's African policy. On 21 December the Assemblée Nationale debated this policy. Government and party spokesmen stumbled and blushed their way through a defence of Giscard's record, which the opposition reduced to shreds. The independence of action on Africa, and the capability to keep domestic and African policy separate, which had been one of the greatest assets of the presidency, had evaporated. From December 1979 on, Giscard was to be seen not as the defender of the honour and prestige of France, but as the incompetent manager of a 'policy of diamonds and impotence'. However just or unjust the image may be for this African policy as a whole, it stuck. Giscard's team staggered on in parts of Africa, but there were no new decisions and an embarrassed withdrawal diplomatically into the less sharply critical family of francophone countries. Policy on the CAR was a disaster for French prestige as well as for Giscard personally.

Assessing French Policy Implementation in Africa

Policy implementation hinges not simply on having the 'right' decision and the 'right' instruments, it rests also on a continuing process of the management of issues in the light of a learning process of what can work and what fails, what Berman (1978) has called 'adaptive implementation'. French policy-makers in the 1970s were neither the fools nor the rogues they came to appear in 1979. What went wrong?

First of all, we must admit that some bad decisions were made. Policy on Chad floundered. Support for Bokassa may have been necessary on strategic grounds up to April 1979, but the decision to do nothing about the school massacre, to treat it as a 'pseudo-crisis', was a grave error. However, while these errors were important, they do not account for French problems on their own. The range of difficulties decision-makers experienced included major problems of implementation.

Secondly, the geographical and economic factors which conditioned policy were not constant: the African economies as a whole were deteriorating through the 1970s, producing a growing instability which French policy confronted. But the French economy itself was in deepening trouble, especially in 1974–8.

Thirdly, there were a series of linkages which became progressively harder to handle. Policies devised in Paris helped to link domestic and African policy; but as African policy touch more and more on Arab policy it inevitably assumed a higher salience anyway. Further linkages between different aspects of African policy became very difficult to deal with. Here the problem is not primarily one of bad decision-making, since the consequences of the linkages between Nigerian interests in Chad or Zaire and French action, or the tangle of Moroccan, Algerian, Libyan, French, Tunisian and US interests in the western Sahara, were not easily predictable. It is indeed a characteristic of foreign policy reality familiar enough to diplomats, but often lost on decision-making theorists, that policy will have implications for the future, although it is hard to be confident about what that future will entail.

Fourthly, and following from the previous point, the nature of the issues under discussion changed as they were being handled. Over Angola, Zaire, in 1977 and 1978 and, above all, in Chad policies were devised in circumstances which were very unstable. The Zaire operations met with success because they were essentially short term. But French policy on the whole could not be maintained on a short-term basis. Even the Zaire operations had unforeseen, and probably unforeseeable, effects. Bad luck was not a major factor in French policy. Bad judgement was, yet, at times, decision-makers knew that they had taken a bad decision as a necessary alternative to taking no decision at all. Chad seems to be a clear example of this.

The introductory chapter to this volume has suggested a number of more specific ideas about policy implementation. It is argued that foreign policy is managed by coalitions which have to be maintained if policy is to succeed. This is directly relevant to this case in two senses. In a formal sense Giscard was in coalition with Gaullists who were prepared to back him when things went well (Zaire) but happy to turn on him as soon as he got in trouble. In a second, less formal sense Giscard's policy depended on a wider coalition. Would influential African states support him? The vulnerability of French policy to the withdrawal of Nigerian support over Chad, and over Zaire in 1978, is significant. So too is the alternatively close and bitter relationship between France and Algeria through the 1970s. The domestic coalition of bureaucrats, military and advisers held together reasonably well until 1979. Then, for example, the Foreign Ministry was forbidden to speak on the CAR, while Gaullist-oriented leaks from the military to *Le Figaro* and other conservative journals show an increasing dissatisfaction with policy. But it was the wider international coalition of Western-inclined states which limited French freedom of movement more, the ideology of 'independence' notwith-standing (c.f. Cerny, 1980; Waites, 1983).

Failures in foreign policy can none the less establish commitments. The more France intervened in Chad, the more Chadian politics depended on France. This was so regardless of the long-term failure of French intervention in Chad to maintain French objectives. The eventual cost of pulling out – a (short-lived) Libyan victory – damaged French standing, but did not produce greater stability. It was the highly dependent nature of the state of Chad, and the intractability of geographical, economic and political environments, which undermined French efforts.

Each case taken here involved a military intervention. Together they form a series of studies which shed light on the place of military action in policy implementation. Military action is inevitably emotional: it involves loss of life and the standing of a major national symbol, the armed forces. The piecemeal expansion of the military role in Africa from a force of 2,500 to a force of around 14,000 between 1975 and 1979 had a strategic justification (Lellouche and Moisi, 1979). But that justification looked rational and clear only in a Paris office. On the ground it looked messier, and French troops in Chad could be forgiven for wondering which of the groups they met really were on their side. In the haste of the 1978 Shaba operation French forces on several occasions found themselves fighting pro-government troops (interview evidence). The use of troops can create commitments; it is harder to justify mistakes when lives are lost, and more may be taken on to retrieve such losses. However, the main lesson of the three case studies is an old one: force is most effective when it is used for limited and defined objectives; but the use of force is in any case easier to begin than it is to control.

The implementation perspective on foreign policy draws our attention to the way policy is presented. Presentation is a part of policy, not simply a passing consequence. The presentation of French policy in Africa was handled by a variety of agencies, but above all by the Elysée itself. This chapter has referred repeatedly to 'Giscard's policy'. Although the Foreign and Co-operation Ministries did have a role, and although committees met and task forces planned contingencies, policy was very much a personal matter. It has been said that Giscard went a long way beyond his predecessors in his personal role in foreign policy (Frears, 1981; Crandall Hollick, 1981). This did not prove to be a source of strength. When Giscard presented French policy to Africa as his own, he committed his office and its standing to that policy. When the policy failed, the blame was directly attributed to him.

The most important issue of implementation was, however, the way in which policy led to decision, and decisions led to behaviour. French style in foreign policy-making hinges on the President, on secrecy and on the cohesion of the policy-making elite (Richardson, 1982; see also Cerny, 1980; Wallace, in Cerny and Schain, 1980; Hayward; 1973). Giscard was able, from 1974, to put forward broad policies which made sense in domestic political terms (liberalism, economic gain and strategic security), and which met the domestic and African client demands on him. But these aims were not consistent and could *never* be operationalized as decisions. The decisions which followed were selective. There was some effort to be 'liberal', above all in economic terms. But more and more, economic instruments took second place to 'la coopération militaire', arms sales and direct intervention. The attempt to control that intervention was made, but failed. In the CAR the eventual French-backed coup against Bokassa was not sufficient to save Giscard's position (it is certainly arguable that an ouster of 'Papa Bok' a year earlier might have helped but this raised great problems of unforeseen effects). The fabric of decisions which France pursued were incompatible. It is, therefore, a direct result of French policy that decision seemed ill-directed and that French behaviour was seen as highly ambiguous. The implementation of French policy effected the division of France's potential allies, although the policy goal was to unite and combine French efforts with those of friendly states. Communications broke down. Policy-makers resorted to bilateral deals and summits as the regular multilateral institutions of francophone declined. French intentions were increasingly misunderstood.

In 1979 French policy in Africa stood at a low point. Politically attacked, economically overstretched, Giscard's image at home was the target of very widespread attack. The machinery of government was in decay and the attempt to replace it with military power was in ruins. Until Mitterrand's victory French policy in Africa lay broken and becalmed. A focus on implementation is not a substitute for a focus on decision-making, but both are necessary to the understanding of foreign·

policy. 'Diamonds and impotence' was a media image, one part of a more complex truth. To get nearer that truth we can look at decisions, but we must also explore their implementation. And such a study has wide implications for any study of policy, especially where governments seek to make their will effective in the intractable, uncertainly changing policy environments of international relations.

6

Implementation in a Complex Arena: International Economic Policy in a World Political Economy

Roger Tooze

This chapter explores the implications of adopting an implementation perspective for the study of international economic policy. It does so in the belief that the contemporary arena of international economic policy, a world political economy, is highly complex and full of uncertainties. Given this, policy implementation is also full of uncertainty and increasing degrees of risk not only in regard to each individual state, but also to the present system as a whole. Some see this 'system risk' as a major problem, standing in the way of renewed growth: 'The main threat to the world economy ... is the gradual erosion of the fabric of international cooperation and of the institutional "architecture" on which it rests' (Bressand, 1982, p. xviii). The risk of the erosion of such 'architecture' is clearly central to the strategies and possibilities of implementation as much of it was originally set up to facilitate the international co-operation necessary for a successful foreign policy process in a complex international system. But 'system risk' is viewed here as only one, albeit an important one, of a range of developments which have transformed the arena of international economic policy and in doing so have increased the already formidable difficulties and problems of policy implementation.

The discussion is not a case study in the conventional sense, for two reasons. First, the application of an implementation perspective assumes available and reliable knowledge of the total policy process, as outlined in the introductory chapter to this book. For many OECD states, and certainly for the majority of non-industrialized states, this knowledge is simply not in existence: the initial research either has not been done or, as is more likely, cannot and will not be done for a variety of reasons. The exception, by and large, is the USA, where the Freedom of Information Act and the desire of those involved in the process to explain (and sometimes justify) themselves to their respective constituencies contrast greatly with the situation in, say, Britain where secrecy is the rule rather than the exception (Cohen, 1977; Wallace, 1977; Wallace, 1975).

Secondly, from what knowledge we do have of the relevant policy processes a precise implementation analysis in the form of identifying a decision and following through its implementation tends to miss the point of much of the politics of international economic policy. International economic policy is commonly a curious mixture of the external manifestation and/or consequences of domestic policy, the policy output demands of membership of international organizations and 'regimes', and *ad hoc* policies and implementation arrangements of a short-term and, usually, 'damage-limiting' nature. Major shifts in policy are rarely a product of an open, developed, coherent and single policy 'decision', and even if they are, rarely give explicit consideration to the enormous uncertainties and problems of implementation. David Calleo brilliantly explores the initial links between domestic and international policy, the policy contradictions and the essential *post hoc* nature of US international economic policy, and suggests that: 'In retrospect, a good part of American foreign economic policy seems the attempt to make an international system out of the consequences of the economic policies pursued at home' (Calleo, 1982, p. 5). With allowance for different positions and priorities within the structure of the world political economy, this characterization probably holds good for the majority of states.

A focus upon implementation is welcome, then, because it highlights the uncertainties of the arena of policy. It is also welcome in its demand for the recognition and analysis of the politics of implementation itself. However, the outline of an implementation framework appropriate to international economic policy is almost certainly not precisely that suggested in Chapter 1. Hence modifications to this conceptual framework will be suggested as a result of the present analysis. Accordingly this chapter attempts three related analyses. First, the world political economy is analysed as the arena of policy, and recent changes in the structure of the world political economy are assessed as to their policy implications. This is followed by an empirical and conceptual analysis of the implementation of international economic policy based on a variety of policies and implementation strategies, or as is often the case, non-strategies. The final and third part of the chapter is an evaluation of the implementation framework suggested in this book, and identifies a series of problems created by the present historical conjuncture of the state and the structure of the world political economy.

A final introductory point is that the term 'international economic policy' is deliberately used instead of 'foreign economic policy' because, as is demonstrated in the following pages, both in their making and in their implementation foreign policy and domestic policy are very much intertwined. In his pioneering study of the making of US international economic policy Stephen Cohen puts the point thus:

In today's world, policy making in this area must take account of too many questions of domestic economic and political policy to be considered 'foreign'. Moreover, the term 'foreign economic policy' usually connotes a subdivision of foreign policy as a whole and is therefore an oversimplification. (Cohen, 1977, p. xvii)

This is the case too for policy implementation. The implementation process, although nominally the job of one particular agency, usually depends on the co-ordination of a number of other agencies, both foreign and domestic. For instance, in most OECD countries the central banks are charged with the implementation of exchange rate policy through market operations and policy co-ordination at the international level. Hence policy implementation is directly linked with and effects implementation of domestic monetary policy. Moreover, in this case the actual *process* of implementation influences the *arena* of implementation and can, therefore, affect the chances of its own success by adding to the extent of uncertainty and risk prevailing in the exchanges at any one time. Similarly, in commercial and trade policy, implementation procedures nominally involve an external trade ministry or department but must, given level of trade interdependence, continually be linked to other 'non-foreign' agencies. Although, in the case of international trade policy, output may be more easily implemented than in areas such as monetary policy (see the third part of this chapter).

International economic policy is, therefore, atypical of foreign policy as characterized in the introductory chapter (the very nature of foreign policy being its distinctiveness from domestic policy-making). Hence much of what is said in this chapter may not apply to areas of 'pure' foreign policy as defined in the book. Manifestly the making and (successful) implementation of international economic policy require recognition of the multi-levelled interpenetration of domestic and foreign affairs plus a coherent policy content, process and output appropriate to these conditions. In this situation the 'distinctiveness' of the foreign policy process from the domestic policy process means that either foreign policy becomes more and more narrow as the concerns of the state widen and/or that foreign policy processes are increasingly bypassed in the making and implementation of relevant and important policy. Given the facts of contemporary international economic life, most foreign policy processes have adapted (or have been forced to adapt) to change, but many uneasy intragovernmental relationships have resulted from the blurring of boundaries. Nevertheless, despite much organizational change and critical policy reviews, it is clear that international economic policy is proving the most problematic of policies in its content, process and implementation. Much of the difficulty derives from the highly complex and uncertain nature of the world political economy as an arena of policy implementation.

A World Political Economy as the Arena of Policy

'World political economy' (WPE) is both a focus of investigation and a way of thinking about political economy. World political economy is used in preference to the usual term 'international political economy' because the latter is limited to a specific form of political economy which, as will be shown, is an inaccurate model of the arena of contemporary international economic policy. As a focus of investigation it is concerned with a wide and seemingly ever-increasing range of theoretical problems and policy issues, the majority of which relate at some stage to foreign policy behaviour: from the arcane matters of international monetary regulation to the everyday problems of tourism. Common to many of these phenomena is the fact that they cannot be understood (or effected) either as purely international or as purely domestic. Nor can they be seen as purely economic or purely political. This fact is an essential starting-point in the analysis of world political economy.

The breakdown of the traditional fourfold distinction which separated domains of activity (and their academic study) into politics, economics, international economics and international politics was, in fact, the breakdown of the myth of the 'liberal' state: a state in which economics is divorced from politics, government is *laissez-faire*, and the international involvement of the state is limited to defence and war in a world composed of similar independent states. Of course, this stereotype never really existed, but its ideology formed the basis for the development of the 'macro-social sciences' and ensured an economics which treated politics as an exogenous variable or ignored it altogether (and vice versa) and a study of international relations divorced not only from international economics, but also from the mainstream of political thought, yet copying it (and economics) in its adoption of 'scientific' method (Maclean, 1981; Strange and Tooze, 1981). And this ideology still informs much policy theory and actual policy-making and implementation today.

The failure of Keynesian-based national economic policies to avert recession in the past ten years stems partly from their 'liberal' assumptions, in the sense used here, and partly from the fact of their implementation by national authorities and agencies within a largely national environment despite attempts at international co-ordination and policy harmonization. The replacement of *laissez-faire* policy by Keynesian policies was predicated on a belief in the essential 'controllability' of the national economy, that is, the ability of national governments to initiate and direct economic change within their own territorial boundaries. All sorts of developments have challenged this presumed ability not the least being the extent to which, in the OECD countries, the state itself has become (and some say always has been) a major part of the economy.

The net result of these developments is to produce a policy crisis for the state: 'we are no longer living in a government managed economy and I do not think we will be living under one for the next twenty years' (Cripps, 1983). This conclusion was drawn on the economy of Britain, but it seems appropriate for the majority of national economies given the evidence of the last decade.

For our specific purposes, the most relevant developments are the increasing interpenetration of national economies and the widening of the agenda of politics consequent on the breakdown of the *laissez-faire* state. The implications of what has been called 'modernization' have been successfully analysed elsewhere (Morse, 1976), but in the rush for policy relevance writers on foreign policy seem to have forgotten that 'modernization' (or whatever we choose to call change) has not stopped, and that there is a possibility of fundamental change in the substance and analysis of policy.

The problem of adapting to change is further compounded by the understandable resistance of national institutions not only to adapt themselves, but also to accept the consequences of change in the world structure as a whole. In most of the industrialized states policy formulation and implementation is still institutionalized and co-ordinated on the basis of the separation of domestic from international affairs, if no longer on the separation of economics from politics. If foreign policy is all those 'decisions and actions which involve to some appreciable extent relations between one state and another' (Frankel, 1963, p. 1), then clearly many issues formerly domestic (or inter-national) are now in both arenas. In the case of Britain, 'The spread of traditional domestic issues which have gradually been drawn into international negotiations – agricultural, industrial, and now increasingly also environmental and social – has drawn more and more home civil servants into diplomacy, alongside their traditionally diplomatic colleagues' (Wallace, 1978a, p. 226). This development produces many problems not the least being (again for Britain) that policy 'has not always been well directed or co-ordinated and the administrative divisions appropriate to policy making within a national framework have not always proved appropriate to policy making and implementation at an international level' (Wallace, 1978a, p. 227). And studies of the US foreign policy process seem to confirm that this is a problem common to most OECD states, with the possible exception of Japan's MITI (Destler, 1980; Cohen, 1977).

There is, however, a more complex and far-reaching policy problem: that concerning the nature of the 'international' policy arena. The discussion so far has focused on the growth in importance of the international economy to most industrial states. The economic growth of the 1950s and 1960s was predicated on a stable monetary structure and a relatively open international trading and capital movement order. The maintenance of this order entailed, among many other factors, participation and negotiation over a wide range of issues (Keohane and Nye, 1977) and brought many benefits to its participants, although these were not equally shared. It was, and is, however, an order composed of the external relations of national economies. In this context, the 'problem' for foreign policy in general, and international economic policy in particular, is primarily one of formulating appropriate policy in line with broad objectives, and implementing it through a range of international and domestic agencies. This is a formidable enough problem. The international economic order necessarily rests more upon the world power structure than the rational optimization of economic processes and the maintenance of this order, in a form compatible with a broad range of nation state interests, is increasingly difficult, particularly as the order itself is now at risk (Bressand, 1982). But whatever the present difficulties, the underlying assumption in the policy process is the validity of the model of international economy itself and the logical distinction between domestic and foreign affairs (and for that matter, between economic and political/strategic). Yet this assumption is itself questionable.

An economy made up of the external economic relations of states is the traditional model of international economy: the state is the unit and international economy is the sum of all economic interactions between states. This model assumes a relative congruence between the political and economic boundaries of the state (Schmitt, 1972) and hence a fair degree of state control over these activities (or at least the potential for control). It also assumes that if the 'economic' boundary expands, through trade and capital movements, control can be (partially) exercised and policy implementation achieved through the creation of some kind of international structure, negotiated or imposed. Current academic and policy concern in the USA over 'regime' formation and change is symptomatic of the way of thinking (Krasner 1982; Strange, 1982). And because of the specific historical link between the American state and economy within the context of the present world economy the overwhelming US concern with regimes may well be justified. It does, however, serve to obscure the possibility that the structure of the international economy itself may have changed.

An economy of the external exchange relations of states is also consistent with the perspectives of national policy-makers, who see the state as the unit of the international economy and thus 'traditional' model. However, it can be argued that this economy of exchange relations between national economies has now been joined, and in some senses has been superseded, by a world economy of production and service structures which are not territorially bounded (Michalet, 1976, 1982). The world economy, in this sense, has been created by the internationalization of production and what Michalet (1982) calls the 'transnationalisation of monetary and financial circulation' (through the multinationalization of banks particularly) where the two processes are now contingent upon each other. The resulting configuration, that is, the present dynamic coexistence of the two forms of economy, is highly complex and in parts obscure, although its general characteristics can be outlined (Michalet, 1976; Cox, 1981).

The conceptual and policy implications of this analysis are significant, and one does not have to subscribe fully to the argument to suspect that present problems may not be appropriately addressed using national economy-based models of international relations. Research on the management of surplus industrial capacity by OECD states lends support to the conclusion that, with the possible exception of 'strategic' industries, more and more sectors of individual national economies are becoming incorporated into the world economy (Strange and Tooze, 1981). Not surprisingly, those sectors incorporated into the world economy prove even more difficult for the state to manage as they effectively have a different political economy from other sectors which are still based largely within an 'international' economy (Tooze, 1983). The differential extent of integration into world economy by sector serves to complicate the implementation of policy as well as disaggregating the arena of policy.

Now if it is the case, as Michalet suggests, that 'ideas of national and international, of domestic and foreign, of exterior and interior, and of frontier limits that used to define the existence of an international economy are losing their validity', and therefore that the 'outline of nation-states is becoming blurred and the power of the state over economic activity is lessened' (Michalet, 1982, p. 43), then our conceptions of the arena of policy implementation must now be changed. Clearly, on this argument, policies formulated purely on a national economy based 'international economy' model are conceptually flawed. As a result, their implementation cannot achieve the required objectives because both policy and implementation strategies are inappropriate to the conditions of the world economy. So what does the arena of international economic policy now look like? And how should national policy-making and implementation reflect this changed structure?

The arena of international economic policy is a complex structure, which for shorthand we have called 'world political economy'. It can only be described and understood by moving away from a reliance on concepts that take the present 'international economy' as the context for policy. Clearly, we need both a historical view of how the present has evolved and a set of concepts that enable us to describe that present; in other words, we need a critical theory as developed by Robert Cox, 'critical in the sense that it stands apart from the prevailing order of the world and asks how that order came about' (Cox, 1981, p. 129). We need, then, to understand the 'continuing process of historical change' rather than locate our understanding within a fixed and given set of political, social and economic relations, called by Cox 'problem-solving theory'. The distinction between 'problem-solving theory' and 'critical theory' (even if we do not wholly accept Cox's argument) forces us to look at the broad assumptions of our descriptions of the world.

Furthermore, we need to examine the framework of action that is constituted by the world political economy. Two related aspects are pertinent here. First, and relatively straightforward, is our conception of politics and political economy (this analysis is developed from Tooze, 1984). Present concepts of political economy impede analysis of the conditions of world political economy. In the majority of non-Marxist analyses politics is conceptualized in a particular way – politics is concerned with government as an organization, following from Max Weber's conception of politics. David Sylvan has shown that this conception and Weber's analysis gives rise to a particular notion of political – economic relations:

> From a theoretical standpoint economic activities are linked to politics in so far as they involve the government as actor or object of action. From a methodological standpoint, then, the way to study political–economic relations is by looking at actions. (Sylvan, 1981, pp. 388–9)

In this prevailing conception political economy is defined as government economic activity, and international political economy as the attempt by governments to regulate and manage international economic relations. It has been argued that this conception is too narrow; it precludes understanding of historical change in the world economy and skews the overall description of the world political economy (WPE) towards government activity and policy rather than the totality of political-economic relationships.

However, the concept of a totality of political–economic relationships is obscured by the second aspect: the conception of politics as action. Traditional models conceive of international relations as constituted of entities (primarily states) that act and interact within a framework of other similar entities. The whole vocabulary of international relations and much policy analysis is replete with references to this conception of international politics. But politics as action takes no account of the broader framework within which action takes place. This framework is rarely institutionalized, particularly at the international and world levels, but encompasses a wide range of social relationships which set the parameters for action and inaction. Again Robert Cox puts this succinctly: 'action is never absolutely free but takes place within a framework', and this framework has the form of a historical structure. Th concept of structure is thus central to any description of the world political economy and needs careful consideration. For Cox, a structure which can only exist historically is

> a particular combination of thought patterns, material conditions and human institutions which has a certain coherence among its elements. These structures do not determine people's actions in any mechanical sense but constitute the context of habits, pressures, expectations and constraints within which action takes place. (Cox, 1981, p. 135)

This particular conception of structure, among many others (see Kurzweil, 1980), is highly appropriate for our purposes.

Hence action, to be understood, must be placed in the context of structure. Only in this context can action be properly related to outcomes. This approach is in line with recent developments in thinking about international relations, specifically Kenneth Waltz's (1979) influential and important *Theory of International Politics* (but also see Ruggie, 1983). Waltz argues strongly for explaining variations in international outcomes through international structure. Structural analyses are not, of course, new – critical Marxism, as for instance manifested in critiques of 'liberal' development theory, has developed a structural explanation of development (Furtado, 1971; Cardoso and Faletto, 1978). And in the past few years the writings of Immanuel Wallerstein have given rise to a 'world system' approach that is unreservedly structuralist (this is best illustrated in Wallerstein, 1979; Bergesen, 1980). But what is new is the recent convergence of diverse approaches on the necessity of taking a historical, structural view, albeit with differing conceptions of the components of structure.

As we have seen, it is not necessary to adopt a particular structural explanation to utilize structural thinking in the study of international economic policy implementation (but for an example applied to policy, see Chase-Dunn, 1982). If 'structure depicts the organisation of a system, or the laws of association by which units are combined to form the systemic totality', and 'Processes are simply the patterned relations among units that go on within a system – relations that reflect in varying degrees the constraints imposed by the system's structure' (Ruggie, 1983, p. 264), then policy implementation must take account of such structure. It is important to note that, in this chapter, we are not in search of 'generative' structure, that is, 'the underlying principles that govern the patterning of interactions' (Ruggie, 1983, p. 266, n. 16), as this goes beyond our brief. What we identify and evaluate here are nearer to 'descriptive' structures, which are abstractions of 'patterned interactions within a system'. It may be that within the context of a specific approach a 'descriptive' structure, such as 'world economy', can become 'generative', but it is sufficient for our purposes to remain 'descriptive', and use structures as analytical frameworks.

A structural view of the WP E as the arena of international economic policy implementation differs substantially from the state-based 'international economy' view in its complexity and implications. First, as previously discussed, we have the existence of a world economy, which can be understood as a historical structure produced by the dynamics of capitalism. The problem lies in the dual existence of two types of economy. If we start from the point of view of an 'international economy' of nation states, then it is clear that:

> It is the world economic system that would determine the relative position of states ... the world economy could no longer be defined as the sum of the nation-states. As a whole, it is different from the sum of its component parts. *Taking national units as a basis does not allow for understanding the actual structure that is being developed.* On the other hand, taking the world economy, which is still a developing system, as a point of departure makes what happens at state level unintelligible ... Affirming the greater importance of the world economic system over that of the nation-states should not be interpreted as showing that the latter are eclipsed: they continue to exist, but their structure and their relations are determined by the whole of which they are part. (Michalet, 1982, pp. 49–50; emphasis added).

Unlike liberal 'transnationalists' (Keohane and Nye, 1972) and functional thought, this approach recognizes and confirms the existence and importance of the state. For all practical purposes it is unrealistic to talk of the 'withering away' or 'eventual demise' of the state. It is also inappropriate to treat the modern state purely as a manifestation of economic forces, with little or no autonomy from these forces. For all practical purposes the state is here to stay, as is the interstate system (although both may undergo severe crises). What is important is that the development of a 'world economy' has produced a configuration of structures that can only be analysed and effected through an understanding of the whole: this means that the state and interstate structures must be located within a broader framework of political economy. Consequently policy must also be formulated and implemented within this framework. Failure to account for structural influences on outcomes increasingly risks exacerbating the existing 'crisis' of the state.

So states exist within an international economy which is, in theory, amenable to some form of guidance or control, and within a world economy not necessarily amenable to control, or at least not with the same policy instruments and implementation strategies. However, the policy problem is compounded because as well as these two structures (emerging into one) there are other structures formed by the processes of specialization and consequential functional disaggregation within the whole. We have already considered sectoral frameworks and the problems resulting from differentiated integration of sectors of national economies into the world economy. Each sector has a particular set of processes and is more or less amenable to national control according to the extent of integration and the degree of political (that is, strategic) salience accorded to the sector by the state. Integrated sectors, in this sense, are conduits from one economy (national/international) to another (world), while sectors of high strategic salience (steel, shipbuilding and now, increasingly, microelectronics) are kept largely within a national/international framework. These sectors are, again in theory, more appropriate for state and interstate policy, but the 'international economy', as opposed to 'world', also means an international market because price control and planning are not really possible under the conditions of 'international economy'. And the consequence of the international market is to drive out the least efficient and/or the least 'subsidized'. Here the experience of implementing steel policy on both sides of the Atlantic is illuminating (see the third part of this chapter).

Specialization at the world level has generated another process of disaggregation and has produced worldwide functional structures, analytically and empirically distinct from one another, but together forming a mutually reinforced overall structure of multiple functions (Strange and Tooze, 1981; Strange, 1983). Examples include the security structure, the monetary structure, or the knowledge structure. Each structural whole constitutes the context for particular activities carried out by particular sets of actors. The same actors can be powerful (that is, control outcomes) in one structure, but not in another. Switzerland, for example, is a major actor in the monetary structure but figures very insignificantly in the international security structure. Issue analysis has also made the point of differential power according to issue (Keohane and Nye, 1977), but issue analysis tells us little of how issues actually *become* issues, and this is the impact of structure.

World political economy, then, is a nest of structures, and sometimes it is necessary to disaggregate the whole into functional and sectoral. But WPE can only be understood as a whole through an understanding of the process of historical change, and is not reducible to its constituent parts. The implications of WPE on external state policy are clear: new policies are frustrated, old policies that used to work do so no longer, implementation strategies fail and outcomes are not those desired by policy-makers. Celso Furtado has cogently summarized the policy problem:

Everything happens as if a new dimension had appeared which escapes the forms of action codified by governments on the national or international levels. In short, within the present institutional framework, governments do not have the possibility of coordinating the activity in which a whole agglomeration of powerful agents are engaged in the capitalist system. (Furtado, 1975, quoted in Sales, 1982, p. 2)

In the face of such structural incapability policy implementation assumes an even greater importance for the continued efficacy of governments. However, the policy problem has created a potential internal crises of legitimacy for contemporary states: the state can no longer achieve its 'mandated' objectives because it is not in control of the environments which produce political and economic goods (Wallace, 1975, p. 160; Anell, 1981). The situation is neatly summarized in an OECD report, originally quoted by Lars Anell (1981):

> The international economy, manipulated by its members, operates as a constant but unpredictable system of double distribution – of incomes, jobs, status within nations, and wealth and power among nations. But the domestic victims of this redistribution do not acknowledge the legitimacy of a haphazard or shifty mechanism that is external to the nation and competes or conflicts with the internal redistribution schemes that have been legitimately, authoritatively, or imperatively set up within the confines of the nation. (OECD, 1978, p. 195)

The potential threat to internal legitimacy is indeed real, and considering the developments of the past few years, as yet shows no sign of abating.

Implementation of International Economic Policy in a World Political Economy

Implementation is the process of using policy to act on an environment in order to achieve specified objectives. It has been clear for some time now that, in the area of international economic policy, the relationship between policy (content and output) and actual outcomes has become increasingly tenuous. We have argued that the tentuity of the relationship between policy and outcomes is partly attributable to the complexity of the arena of international economic policy, but it is also partly attributable to the difficulties within, and the politics of, the process of implementation. The policy-making process leads to policy output and, conceptually, implementation is thus a variable in the transformation of output into policy impact; that is, the actual (rather than the intended) effect of the policy on the environment. It is not the only variable but it is an important one, vastly overlooked in the extant literature on international economic policy.

In his study of US international economic policy Stephen Cohen identifies four major categories of policy output and these are useful and relevant here (Cohen, 1977, p. xx):

(1)   actions;
(2)   postures;
(3)   negotiating positions;
(4)   programmes.

Each of these four outputs poses particular problems for implementation. Actions are clearly the most important policy output: the other three outputs form the context for eventual action or inaction, though it must be stressed that a decision to do nothing – not to respond, not to change existing policy, and so on – is just as important as an action. Action/inaction is the conventional 'hard' language of international economic policy, but it is sometimes not the most successful means of achieving policy goals. Actions are formulated and implemented within a particular 'world view', which reflects prevailing notions of what is right and what is appropriate: the Nixon initiative of 15 August 1971, derived from the Peterson report, was clearly formulated and implemented by an administration that perceived the behaviour of other nations as the root cause of domestic problems. But world views also reflect a deeper level of assumption, which forms the structure of, and is normally institutionalized into, the policy-making and implementing process. These assumptions reflect basic approaches to understanding policy and are called 'decision-making epistemologies' by Miriam Steiner (1983). Most 'decision-making epistemologies' are based on the assumption of rationality – in the formulation and implementation of policy and in the response by other actors to that policy. Steiner demonstrates, quite rightly, of course, that these are inadequate. Policy at the international level is neither made nor implemented in a rational ordered world. Ambiguity and paradox are 'in the nature of things' and cannot, therefore, be understood in a wholly rational manner or successfully acted upon by a rationally constituted policy system. The world political economy presents many instances of ambiguity and paradox in its evolution, and perhaps one of the greatest ambiguities, from the point of view of the structure as a whole, is the present position of the state.

Instances of ambiguity, intended and unintended, colour the political economy of the relationship between the USA, as a hegemonic power, and Europe. A supposedly unambiguous action, such as Nixon's 'New Economic Policy' in 1971, seen by the then US administration as a firm, action-based statement, certainly achieved a response (but not necessarily that which was desired). The European responses were conditioned by the apparent unilateralism in the implementation of policies on matters which affected all major participants in the world economic structure – the effective devaluation of the dollar (the 'key currency') and the imposition of an import surcharge (affecting trading conditions with the world's largest integrated market). Had the same policies been implemented in a different fashion, over a longer period of time, in consultation with other leading members, then responses to the actions might have been quite different. As it was, not only the policies but their manner of implementation produced unintended responses, and probably contributed towards the later failure of that administration's 'Year of Europe' in 1973 (Hudson, 1977, Calleo, 1982).

Postures are both indicative of potential action and important outputs in their own right and, with negotiating positions, form the 'soft' language of policy. Negotiating positions are specified and 'firmed-up' postures, but both ultimately depend for their impact upon the nature of their implementation. As both are essentially expressions of intent/interest/status quo/dissatisfaction, they hinge on the efficiency and subtlety of the communication process and the extent of shared intersubjective meaning between policy-implementing agencies and policy 'targets'. Some postures clearly do not require implementation – a statement by the US President or Secretary of State, or the British Minister for Trade and Industry normally constitutes the basis of such an output and requires no further elaboration; the positional authority of the personnel involved makes the posture self-implementing. The majority of negotiating positions do, however, require extensive implementation as they are rarely 'negotiated' by the decision-makers themselves. The degree of interpretation available to the negotiators, the salience of the issues, the extent to which negotiators are subject to continuous political direction and the authority and status of the negotiators themselves are all elements to be considered. Finally, programmes entail commitments to action over time, normally within budget constraints, and as such they generally require a review of their implementation as part of the policy process itself. Aid programmes are the archetypal case: elapsed time, long distances, bad communications, idiosyncratic organization, strong ideologies and different values all contribute to what is sometimes a completely unrecognizable policy impact from that originally intended. It may be apocryphal, but the story of the (nameless) aid agency that spent so much of its budget on 'appraising' and planning how best to help a small township in Africa that it eventually had very little resources left with which to help, is a salutary tale of the consequence of neglecting implementation.

Each type of international economic policy output, then, poses different problems and presents different patterns of implementation. We shall now move to consider specific policies.

International Financial and Monetary Policy

International financial and monetary policy cannot be separated from domestic policy in this field, both in its formulation and implementation. The change from a fixed-parities international system, under Bretton Woods, to a floating system 'has not liberated domestic economic policy from all external constraints' (Emminger, 1979, p. 10); it seems in fact to have reinforced the linkage between domestic and international by stressing the consequences of both the 'openness' of national economies and the structural interdependence so created. In 'an "open" economy the scope for achieving major economic objectives – such as permanently low rate of inflation and a high level of employment – by means of an *independent* macroeconomic policy are extremely limited' (Panić, 1982, p. 37; emphasis added). The emphasis in policy has undergone a shift, as a result of the transition to floating rates which was itself no more than a response by governments to changes in the structure of the WPE over which they had little control. In its evidence to the House of Commons Treasury and Civil Service Committee the British Treasury stated: 'Against this world background [the breakdown of a fixed-rate system] it has been necessary, in this country and elsewhere, to shift the emphasis to the domestic discipline of monetary targets rather than the external discipline of an exchange rate objective' (HC (82–83) 21-II, p. 5, para. 6). But such is the structure of the WPE that states integrated into the world economy will not be able to avoid the consequences of this integration (Strange, 1976; Bryant, 1981; as well as Panić, 1982).

Part of the consequence is the perceived need to set up international rules in the face of interdependence: 'the whole point of contemplating international rules is to bring the general international interest to bear on the policy-making process in individual countries, so as to limit actions that have harmful spillover effects abroad' (HC (82–83) 385, p. xxiv, paras 4–5). We have argued earlier that international economy based policies and implementing strategies are insufficient. Nevertheless, given the great emphasis on them by states, international co-ordination within existing institutions is important in assessing policy implementation.

Clearly, a full discussion of the implementation of international monetary policy is outside the purview of this chapter, but some general points will be made and we shall look briefly at British international monetary policy as indicative of the conceptual and analytical problems.

The implementation of financial and monetary policy poses particular problems not faced in, say, the implementation of trade policy. Trade concerns generally, and the effect of low-cost imported goods specifically, are more easily and widely perceived and acted upon than matters of international finance and money. This is partly the result of a domestic political structure that enables the 'injured' group to transform their grievances directly into political action, and partly because the effects of monetary policy are generally spread throughout the economy so as not to engender group action (Odell, 1982, p. 347). International trade measures are also more straightforward in their implementation, at least until we come to non-tariff barriers and national government procurement codes. International financial and monetary policy, however, is viewed as an arcane, highly technical area by the majority in most democratic polities, and the formulation and implementation of such policy are thus not only 'elite' activities, but also only of elite concern. Academic and professional analysis of monetary policy is technical, complex and highly contentious, reinforcing its distance from the 'realities' of everyday life. Moreover, again unlike trade policy where implementation, possibly requiring complex international co-ordination, normally takes some time and only brings about the desired changes over time (if at all), the implementation of monetary policy can bring almost instantaneous responses, such are the speed and sophistication of the exchange markets.

The study of international policy implementation in this area is particularly subject to the constraints discussed in the first part of this chapter. First, the implementation process is largely hidden. It is, in Roger Williams's phrase, a 'closed-policy subsystem' within the overall policy process (Williams, 1980, *passim*). If not actually secret, it is the responsibility of a few 'professionals' who do not actively promote knowledge of what they do (sometimes for good reasons). Secrecy appears endemic in this field, and the veil is only partly lifted by 'official' and legislative investigations and reports (for Britain, see, for example, HC (82–83) 385).

Secrecy is not only an overwhelming factor in the process leading to policy output, it is part of policy implementation. Now the arena of international monetary policy does have certain characteristics that may justify secrecy is some cases. Agencies are implementing policy in the context of a complex, integrated and worldwide market structure based on a highly sophisticated communication system. If the precise details of policy implementation, say, central bank intervention in the exchange market, were known in advance (exchange rate targets, intervention points), this may alter the behaviour of the market. But notwithstanding these arguments the prevailing secrecy makes 'outsider' analysis extremely difficult, and perhaps even more necessary. Even the British Parliament is prevented from gaining full information on the implementation of exchange rate policy, as this is governed by the British Official Secrets Act (HC (82–83) 21-II, paras 207–11).

The second constraint on studying the implementation of policy in this area is that implementation has not yet fully entered into thinking about the policy process. Previous analyses have either ignored implementation altogether or have referred to it obliquely. Of course, the reason may be that analysts have chosen to focus on policy content or output: John Odell's excellent recent analysis of US international monetary policy focuses (deliberately) almost exclusively on policy content, with a few tantalizing glimpses of implementation. If we choose, however, to understand the whole monetary process, then we have no option but to engage in the analysis of implementation. Monetary policy outputs, both domestic and international, do not normally implement themselves (although in the past we have had the example of exchange rates being 'talked up' or 'talked down' – this is the exception). Given the nature of the arena of international monetary policy, its complexity and (increasing) uncertainty, we cannot assume that output means impact or outcomes and the policy process must therefore include implementation.

British international monetary policy is probably untypical of state policy in the sense of Britain's history of hegemony in monetary affairs, which has contributed to the current eminence of the City of London and the Bank of England in the world monetary structure. However, British policy does present most of the major characteristics and problems of implementation, although it may be the case that with the experience and knowledge of its implementing agencies and their power within the monetary structure, British policy is implemented with less formal effort than most other countries.

A tentative conceptual representation of British international monetary policy implementation is attempted in Table 6.1, as this seems the clearest way to illustrate the complexity of the process. The process is, of course, non-linear, is ambiguous, is one of constant movement and feedback, and is certainly not as clear-cut as any representation necessarily makes it. As William Wallace argues, even when we can identify a 'final decision', this is 'only the beginning of another series of consequential decisions and consequential consideration of further alternatives' (Wallace, 1975, p. 7). Many of the implementing agencies are also part of the policy-making process and hence implementation is also subject to the kinds of political processes that characterize policy-making. In Britain this involves not so much the kind of bureaucratic struggle of US policy, but a less obvious rivalry between and among departments concerned with variable status, the pre-eminence of the Treasury, the power of acknowledged 'seniority' and expertise, and the lack of a strong and effective legislative role. And no conceptual representation can do justice to the fact that, at least since 1972, when sterling was allowed to float, British international monetary policy (IMP), in common with many other states, has largely been reactive: a response to evolutionary pressures in the world monetary structure.

The objectives of current British IMP are summarized by the Treasury, the principal policy-making department, as the achievement of 'a system which produces greater stability [than the present] of exchange rates and also greater stability of all currencies in terms of goods, that is to say, the rate of inflation' (HC (82–83) 21-II, p. 32, para. 71). Stability and the

Table 6.1 The Implementation of British International Monetary Policy: A Tentative Conceptual Representation

I Policy content	II Policy output	III Policy implementation Agencies	Strategies (potential rather that actual)	IV Outcomes
Taken here as given, for objectives see text	Action, posture, negotiating position, programme	Government: Prime Minister, Chancellor, Foreign Secretary, Treasury, Foreign Office, Department of Trade and Industry and smaller agencies, e.g. Export Credit Guarantee Department Non-government: Bank of England, commercial banks and 'City' resources International: IMF (Group of Ten) (Group of Five) IBRD BIS EC(EMS) OECD (Working Party Three)	(1) UNILATERAL (a) Influence arena directly, e.g. intervention, exchange controls (b) Influence arena indirectly, e.g. protection, fiscal policy, monetary policy (c) Influence policies and behaviour of other states, i.e. targeted implementation – e.g. USA (d) Influence in structure – international and world (2) MULTILATERAL (a) international co-ordination, to enable states to achieve strategies 1(a),(b),(c),(d) (b) international rule establishment, to make strategies 1(a),(b),(c),(d) authoritative at international level (c) system, structure and process: resistance and change	Impact on arena of international economic policy, i.e. world monetary structure (which includes foreign exchange market) within WPE

control of inflation are both aimed at the reduction of uncertainty in the world monetary structure through the establishment of an international system in which long-term considerations dominate. As Tumlir (1983) well demonstrates, the present financial structures are extremely 'precarious' because of the preoccupation with short-term contingencies. Here we are not concerned with the process whereby objectives become specific policy content, suffice to say that interpreting the present situation is fraught with difficulty.

The major agencies of IMP implementation can be divided into government, non-government and international, but the dividing line is very fudged in places. Within the government category are the 'political' agents – the Prime Minister, Chancellor and Foreign Secretary predominantly, who, through their positional authority, act as distinct implementing agencies. A 'bullish' speech by the PM or Chancellor can have a stabilizing (or destabilizing) effect on the market according to the situation, and the presence of Cabinet ministers of high rank at events, discussions, or conferences lends authoritative weight to any proceedings. One particularly salient point is the ability/inability of certain key individuals in government (and central banks) to 'talk up' or 'talk down' the exchange rate of their currency. At various times in the past we have seen that certain statements, by those who are regarded by the exchange market as key personnel, have had a short-term impact on exchange rates. This is not, however, generally viable as an implementation strategy without the back-up of appropriate domestic policy, although the markets can and do respond to political statements in times of uncertainty (HC (82–83) 21-II, pp. 29, 71). The Treasury, and its financial divisions, acts as the co-ordinating centre for IMP implementation, sometimes through other government departments, such as the Export Credit Guarantee Department. However, the major implementing agency is the Bank of England, and the key implementation relationship is between the Treasury and the Bank.

In 1975 William Wallace wrote: 'The exact nature of the relationship between the Treasury and the Bank of England is one of the cardinal mysteries of British government' (Wallace, 1975, p. 164), and it still is despite the efforts of the members of the House of Commons Treasury and Civil Service Committee. Formally the Bank acts as agent for the Treasury, as the funds the Bank utilizes are 'owned' by the Treasury. In this sense it is a bank–client relationship. But it is also more than this and can be a highly ambiguous relationship. The Bank commands greater resources than the Treasury for research, information and expertise and it occupies a unique position within the international financial structure. As a major European central bank it is part of a very close central bank network, which involves almost constant communication, discussion and reflection on the state of the 'system' and individual problems within it (see, particularly, Strange, 1976) and this has implications for implementation. Nominally the Bank works within a set of guidelines:

> The Bank's activities are those of an agent operating to a strategic judgement of the Ministers of the day. The way it operates in practice is clearly that the day to day management will be in the hands of the Bank dealers with whatever additional strategic guidance may be found necessary in relation to particular occasions. (Treasury, HC (82–83) 21-II, p. 26, para. 31)

Clearly, the Bank does have, as is suggested, 'a very wide operational role', particularly as neither the Treasury nor the Bank could define what would constitute a 'particular occasion' in the above statement, although on something like market intervention to smooth variations the Bank 'will normally be the people making a judgement on an ordinary day' (HC (82–83) 21-II, p. 28, para. 42). The fact that both the Treasury and the Bank feel the implementation relationship works well is not necessarily encouraging, given the Bank's known disposition to identify itself with positions not necessarily supportive of government policy, or supportive of any 'narrow' definition of British interests.

Given the Bank's position and influence in the national and international financial structure, other institutions are sometimes involved as implementing agents, directly or indirectly according to the strategy being used. These are predominantly the clearing banks as well as other institutions within the City financial community, and that community as a whole. The Bank can do this not only because of its formal position, which if emphasized could sometimes prove counter-productive, but because of its informal structural authority.

International implementation agencies are important because of the highly integrated, worldwide nature of the financial and monetary structure. Most of these (see Table 6.1) are agencies for the co-ordination of policy and together have produced common (or as common as politically possible) approaches to current problems and an understanding of, if not sympathy towards, national positions. In this sense, they are mainly educative, and no less important because of it, although they are, in certain defined areas such as the liberalization of capital movements (Bertrand, 1981), important and necessary implementing agents in their own right. The International Monetary Fund (IMF) is distinctive, largely because of its formal position in the international structure and its resource base, both material and intellectual. It possesses, in certain circumstances, authority and direct economic power over national governments (and hence national policy), particularly, but not only, through the 'conditionality' process attached to its loan operations – as the British government itself found out. In this sense the IMF implements the policy built into its international 'role' in a way that no purely national institution could. It acts broadly for the structure as a whole, reinforcing the norms and processes of that whole. This does not mean, of course, that all governments at all times support this role, but that support is generally forthcoming.

The conceptual representation (Table 6.1) also indicates the range of implementation strategies available. This range is potential, rather than actual, because, as we shall see, some strategies are discounted or not attempted because of the limited and narrow self-reinforcing conceptualization of the structure that national policies work within. Clearly, the choice of strategies of implementation should determine the agencies of implementation. Whether this is the case in British IMP is difficult to judge, given prevailing levels of secrecy. It might be the case that the influence of the Bank of England is so strong that implementation strategies not involving the bank, or in accord with its conceptions, are eschewed or at least not given the prominence they deserve.

Strategies can be unilateral or multilateral depending on a particular state's importance in the world monetary structure and its resources (material, organizational and intellectual). Because of the predominance of the USA and of the dollar as a key currency, its monetary authorities have certain power within the structure and decisions/non-decisions concerning US monetary policy have consequences for the whole monetary system. The present (late 1983) US policy of non-intervention in the exchange market may change, and although it is economically justifiable and 'traditional', it has the result of making the implementation of the intervention policies adopted by other states more hesitant as their impact is not always effective in achieving policy goals. In the British case we would have to investigate the place of the monetary authorities (the Bank of England and, informally, the collectivity of the 'City') within the world monetary structure in much greater detail than is possible here. The formal/informal network of relationships, norms and expectations which constitute the context for action by the Bank will clearly influence its ability to implement monetary policy and the timeframe within which implementation occurs.

Unilateral strategies of implementation can be divided into those that are carried out within the framework of legislative and executive authority (protection, fiscal and monetary policy, exchange controls) and those that are non-coercive attempts to alter the behaviour of other entities (the market, monetary authorities, states). In as much as the implementing strategies carried out by legislative and executive authority are ultimately coercive IMP implementation breaks down into two of the categories suggested in the introductory chapter to this volume – coercive and non-coercive implementation. But this distinction, although technically correct, does not really help us to understand the process of the successful implementation of IMP. Coercive implementation is possible only within the territorial confines of the state or as the introduction of coercive measures into international monetary relations.

Policies implemented within the territory of the state and by the state are of limited effect (for a given level of 'cost'). The introduction of coercion into international monetary relations would change the present nature of those relations, and would not be a productive strategy. The point is that, given the structure of the world monetary system, traditional methods of policy implementation are not necessarily appropriate to IMP. As a further complexity, the implementation of IMP reinforces the problems of distinguishing between domestic and external policy. One of the major implementation strategies of IMP, for instance (and one of the most problematic policy areas), is through the use of domestic monetary policy, with its subsequent implications for the national economy.

The first two groups of unilateral strategies are, hopefully, self-explanatory. The third, that of the attempt to influence policies and behaviour of other states, is conditional upon the exact nature of policy and the structural 'importance' of the monetary authorities whose policies and behaviour one is attempting to alter. British short-term intervention policy, to smooth out 'irrational' movements of sterling, exchange rate, (see HC (82–83) 21-II, Evidence of the Treasury and Bank of England) and its longer-term goals of harmonization, would be easier to implement if the US monetary authorities were acting in harmony. Hence the apparent British attempt to persuade the US authorities of the efficacy of either short-term and limited intervention or harmonization of policies. The fourth strategy comes from the influence of implementing agencies within the international and world structure itself, and can sometimes provide the quickest and most efficient means of implementing policy. Here the informal meetings which involve the sharing of viewpoints and experience (such as the Group of Ten, the OECD's Working Party Three and discussion at the Bank of International Settlements), and the daily, working contact of the Bank of England with other European banks (particularly those in the European Monetary System) are important. Their effect is hard to measure in precise terms, but if these processes did not exist the implementation of British IMP would, no doubt, be much more difficult and its impact even more uncertain.

Multilateral implementation strategies are an explicit confirmation of the difficulty of achieving IMP goals through unilateral action. Co-ordination and rule establishment are a structural response to the policy inadequacy of the state, an attempt to set up international mediating structures between the state and the world economy. The Director-General for Economic and Financial Affairs of the Commission of the European Committees recently made the point that

> No country – and certainly no small or medium-sized country – enjoys total autonomy in the conduct of its economic affairs. Fundamentally, external constraints come from openness, not from formal arrange-

ments. Refusal to participate in arrangements which entail certain obligations on all sides will not remove these constraints, although it may to some extent alter their nature. (HC (82–83) 21-II, p. 251)

This and other perspectives (such as Panić, 1982) reinforce the necessity of adopting multilateral implementation strategies in order that desired outcomes be achieved and be mutually supportive.

International co-ordination is a necessary strategy given the nature of the world monetary structure and the position of the state within that structure: 'In the absence of agreed world-wide arrangements governing exchange rates and monetary control, *ad hoc* policy coordination is of particular importance' (HC (82–83) 385, p. xlii). Policy co-ordination is necessary on two levels – design and implementation: 'When national authorities pursue unilateral policies whose design fails to take account of policies [and conditions] abroad the outcome is likely to be unsatisfactory' (HC (82–83) 385, p. 1). The impact of purely national policies can be severely muted or altered if co-ordination over design and implementation does not take place. This has taken place at the highest political levels at the economist summit meetings, initiated in 1975 (Maddock, 1980), and in the OECD's Economic Policy Committee. It is reasonably clear, however, that strategies of IMP implementation through *ad hoc* co-ordination, although necessary, present many problems for the state, and the present arrangements are on the whole unsatisfactory. The Bank of England claims that: 'Existing well-tried arrangements provide for extensive discussion of the implications of interdependence, so that countries [*sic*] implement policy in full knowledge of the effects it is perceived as having on others, as well as of policies being pursued elsewhere' (HC (82–83) 21-II, p. 39, para. 5). This view is, however, optimistic and not really supported by the impact of policy. This kind of discussion does take place in the form of the IMF and the OECD's Working Party Three, but it is a retrospective review of extant policy and implementation with little chance of altering the process. The Bank was only able to point to two occasions (both within the European Community) on which policy was changed or modified implementation procedures adopted (HC (82–83) 21-II, pp. 79–81).

Conventional explanations for the problems of IMP co-ordination are here only part of an explanation. Mr Padoa-Schioppa of the European Communities sums up the conventional view very well:

It is not the lack of procedural rules that makes the exercise of policy coordination so difficult. Difficulties arise from the fact that national authorities have to respond to electorates who do not express the same priorities at the same time, nor always advocate objectives that are mutually consistent internationally. Moreover, the complexities of the policy process, and of its widely differing institutional frameworks, makes coordination quite difficult even when broad policy orientations are compatible. (HC (82–83) 21-II, p. 254)

But this view, while correctly stating part of the problem, ignores the further problem of the wider implications of capitalism and the structural problems of the state–world economy relationship. It also skates over the fact that we do not actually know the real and detailed policy implications of interdependence and, therefore, policy co-ordination is a broad strategy with many potential flaws.

The establishment of a set of international rules is defined by the House of Commons Treasury and Civil Service Committee as the attempt to 'influence the incentives each country perceives in such a way as to increase its national interest in taking acts that are in the general international interest' (HC (82–83) 385, p. li). Of course, this approach in common with the analysis of 'regimes' in general has certain important but limited uses, but it emphasizes the existing international status quo and notions of order, as opposed to the dynamic structural evolution that has occurred (see Strange, 1982). It might be that the 'general international interest' is only a temporary definition; moreover, who defines what this interest actually is? Stability and low inflation are expressions of political–economic choices and values: instability and inflation may benefit certain groups or be of political importance. International rule establishment is, then, an efficient and desirable means of implementing IMP because it legitimizes and enforces the expression of 'the general international interest'. It is, and has proved to be, an extremely difficult strategy – during the period of US hegemony in the international political economy the convergence of ideology and perceived national interests encouraged (on the basis of continuing growth) adherence to a series of monetary norms. The faltering of this hegemony and the emergence of recession means a necessary re-emphasis on the means of ensuring adherence to general norms. The authorititative institutionalization of rules clearly reinforces major international structural values and ensures complementary policies (that is, comple-mentary to a particular definition of the international monetary structure). In the latest moves to reaffirm support for the IMF, which had tended to languish in the heady days of 'surplus funds' and lax discipline (see Aronson, 1981), it is clear that the intention is 'that the I.M.F. will be used ... as an investigative and disciplinary agency' on a 'worldwide basis' (HC (82–83) 21-II, p. 421). This will need, at least, the formulation of general rules that support system goals (now taking place within the existing institutional framework) plus the active participation of the major entities – governments, central banks and commercial banks. If this can be achieved (and it seems as if it will be), this will be an important framework for the implementation of IMP.

It might be the case, however, that neither unilateral nor multilateral implementation strategies will have much success until these strategies encompass the structure of world economy. If we consider the possibility of governmental (British) influence on the exchange rate, or the possibility 'influencing the influences' on the exchange rate, any success beyond the short term seems elusive. Sir Jeremy Morse, representing the Committee of London Clearing Banks, puts the position thus:

> On the more broad question of whether I feel the Government can, if it wishes, have some influence on the exchange rate, certainly in the short run but it is evident from the history of the last period that it does not control that by any means, but of all the agencies in the market it has probably more influence than anybody else. (HC (82–83) 21-II, p. 44)

This statement highlights both the limited power of government to influence the world monetary structure and the limited nature of our understanding of that structure. Clearly, implementation strategies which work with, rather than against, structural processes are more likely to be successful, but government knowledge of the monetary structures and international monetary policy do not yet reflect this kind of analysis. In fact, most governments are still only in the process of developing linked national economic models to help understand the international economy, and most now rely on 'single small country' analyses (that is, using the 'simplifying assumption that domestic policy actions induce no policy responses in the rest of the world, and that domestic economic developments do not significantly affect global magnitudes': HC (82–83) 385, p. 1). But it is precisely the point that the assumption that 'foreign policies can be taken to be exogenous' is not warranted in the real world of political economy. Or for that matter, is it warranted to ignore the domestic policy of another state, particularly when that state wields structural power. Given the high governmental salience of IMP and the wide range of troublesome issues that do not have a 'solution' within the present power structures, how wise is it for the state policy process to assume the 'exogenous' nature of foreign policies?

The implementation of British IMP is marked by its secrecy and its elitist nature. This does not mean it is badly implemented, only that the criteria by which to judge implementation are formulated and applied within a relatively closed policy subsystem. Strategies of implementation are conditioned more by the influence of the Bank of England than by the Treasury, and the informal network of interbank communication is probably the most efficient means of co-ordination and of influencing the structure. As one might expect, a wide range of implementation strategies are carried out, although they are not all mutually reinforcing, within the context of the British medium-term financial strategy. Change in political emphasis at the highest level, for instance, the present Prime Minister's hard-line stance on Brazil, sometimes makes consistent and successful IMP implementation extremely difficult. But what is most striking is the apparent lack of an overall implementation strategy that relates efforts and probabilities of success in one area to those in the others. The whole process is also dominated by a changing ideological overlay which provides the world view, policy prescription and (implicit) implementation strategies, against the background of a fairly limited knowledge base. Consequently most of the IMP strategies, where these are explicitly considered, contain large elements of uncertainty, sometimes obscured by a veneer of pragmatism. The political and conditional context of implementation of British IMP is further reinforced by the fact that successful implementation takes place within a structure dominated by the USA and, therefore, no real change in the collective management of the system, engaging multilateral strategies, can take place without at least the tacit consent of the US authorities and support of the US banks (see, particularly, Strange, 1976).

The Implementation Perspective

Because of the nature of the process of implementation of international monetary policy, we have been unable to do full justice to the explanatory framework suggested in Chapter 1 of this book. What is very clear, however, is that the analysis of implementation is of fundamental importance. Given the extent of knowledge about the international monetary process, the degree of complexity of the structure and the levels of risk and uncertainty presently prevailing, implementation is the key to the success or failure of IMP. And the process of implementation itself – whether within the institutional confines of 'Banks' or 'Treasuries' or the arena of international political activity – is political. Implementation can no longer be assumed to be a matter of the technical application of objective criteria, as was the tendency in the Bretton Woods period.

This chapter has attempted a conceptual review of the implementation perspective applied to international economic policy, and the analysis points to several conclusions for that perspective, apart from reaffirming its importance. First, it is difficult to confine the analysis to 'foreign policy'. We argued initially that the category of 'foreign policy' was inappropriate, and a general consideration of international economic policy indicated the problem. The analysis of international monetary policy confirmed the nexus of domestic and foreign policy, particularly in domestic monetary and fiscal policy. It is, then, not appropriate and is in fact counterproductive to separate 'foreign' and 'domestic' policy in this area. To understand the implementation (and significance) of international economic policy we must neither isolate nor underestimate the importance of domestic policy processes. Secondly, much of the 'policy' involved in international economic policy is the result not so much of decisions, but of non-decisions. Characteristically non-decisions reflect the continuance of present policy or the acceptance of the existing processes and/or support for the existing structure. In many cases these non-decisions are more important than decisions. Non-decisions are not only more important, but more common in international economic policy. This means that the decisions that are taken and implemented need to be put in the context of the many non-decisions, and are only understandable within this context.

As a related point, it is not enough to look at the 'actors' in the policy process. The structural influences leading to non-decisions also influence implementation – the timescale, actual strategies and processes and, of course, impact. The inherent bias of an action-based political analysis has been discussed, but this bias is difficult to counteract in detailed decision analysis as it seems built on to the decision framework.

The success of implementation for much of international economic policy is largely outside the control of the implementing agencies, unless these agencies have a degree of structural power. And here the question posed initially, namely 'whether the implementation process led to very different outcomes from those intended by the decision-makers?', is critical. The only successful way to implement many international economic policies is now through multilateral strategies, and much of the time implementing agencies have to take the situation as they find it rather than 'make it' according to their desires. Again the exception is if the implementing agencies have structural power or the political authority which gives them indirect structural power (see, particularly, Calleo 1982).

Current levels of uncertainty in the world economy and in its institutions make the arena of international economic policy implementation a very difficult and problematic one. It is, as we have argued, a highly complex arena with unique difficulties of analysis and implementation, and until we have a greater understanding of its structure(s) and processes, implementation will retain a fair degree of uncertainty and risk. Clearly, the most favourable strategies of international economic policy implementation involve multilateral activity in the collective management of the international economy, and an attempt at some management of the world economy (for instance, the creation of a code of conduct for transnational corporations). Collective management is more effective and efficient with the creation of international rules. To the extent that the international economic policy of states can be implemented within an agreed framework of rules the burden on unilateral strategies is lessened, although unilateral strategies may be necessary to support that framework and to co-ordinate with international action.

We need detailed case studies to support or attack these preliminary comments. These will not be easy to do given the limited public nature of the processes, but nevertheless they are necessary. More than this the problems are understandable only in the context of history and only within the framework of some kind of structural analysis. David Calleo's admonition (1982, p. 194) to those who promulgate and follow 'fashionable theory' is appropriate for us who would study the policy process: 'Political–economic systems are not cast from the mould of theory; they grow out of the soil of history.'

7

Multilateral Decision-Making and Implementation: the Case of the European Community

David Allen and *Paul Byrne*

This chapter examines the question of implementation within a multilateral context. Rather than concentrating upon a single decision or policy within a single state, we shall consider a range of decisions and actions taken within the framework of the European Community (EC) – including both policies made within the provisions of the Treaty of Rome and more recent co-operative endeavours in the fields of foreign policy (European Political Co-operation – EPC) and monetary policy (the European Monetary System – EMS). Hopefully, this concentration on breadth rather than depth will not further obscure what is already a rather murky area of analysis – implementation, which is an area of study in which a common approach among analysts is noticeable by its absence.

The Context of Implementation

Studying implementation within the EC, however, does provide one important advantage. Much of the debate among students of implementation is concerned with the validity or otherwise of adopting a 'top–down', hierarchical perspective. While much of the early writing on implementation did assume that implementation was simply that which followed decision-making in a neat sequential manner, and sought to prescribe effective solutions to problems of securing control and compliance within a hierarchical framework, more recent studies have argued that this is an oversimplistic approach. Pressman and Wildavsky (1973), for example, have made the point that even where there is goal-consensus among implementors each will be operating within their own timescales and differing constraints, and that this poses severe problems of organizing effective implementation. Hood (1976) and Dunsire (1978b) have both offered persuasive arguments about the difficulties of securing control, even within unitary organizations. Many other authors have criticized the 'top–down' perspective for its authoritarian or managerial assumptions, arguing that effective implementation has to be secured by bargaining rather than directing. All these authors are fighting against the implicit assumption that, within a unitary organization or single nation-state, implementation is simply a problem of authority. When looking at the EC, we have no need to dispel such an assumption, as (in most cases) the EC has no such effective authority, and must proceed by bargaining and consensus-building.

Focusing upon the EC offers another advantage in that it highlights the difficulty of isolating foreign policy from domestic policy. The distinction between these two types of policy is conventionally held to cover both substance and procedure, but this distinction has come under attack, not least because of changes in the international environment. The traditional substance of international politics (towards which foreign policy is directed) had widened to include almost any issue that is the subject of governmental concern (Wallace, 1977). Thus, for example, the 1970s was a decade in which the traditional politico-military issues of East–West confrontation were overshadowed by the international significance of oil prices, currency fluctuations, inflation and employment problems, and so on. The 1980s have seen the resurgence of more traditional issues (notably in the cases of the Falklands, Afghanistan and the debate over Cruise), but these have supplemented rather than replaced the issues which arose in the 1970s. The traditional substance of domestic politics (sometimes inaccurately referred to as 'low' politics) has become the substance of international politics, and will remain so. Students of foreign policy have no alternative but to take notice of this, and to take into account this blurring of the distinction between foreign and domestic policy. Such a lack of clear distinctions between the two types of policy has, of course, always been evident in the EC where, under the largely economic provisions of the Treaty of Rome, individual nation states have engaged in multilateral negotiations about customs rates, levies, quotas, agricultural prices, transport, social security provisions, and so on. It is not surprising that not only academic observers, but also the participating governments remain confused as to the correct nomenclature for their pursuit of policy objectives within the EC. For example, the British Embassy to the EC (in Brussels) reflects this refusal of reality to conform to academic categorization – its staff consists of members of the Home Civil Service and members of the Foreign Service, in roughly equal proportions. Throughout member states of the EC opinions differ on whether policy within the community should be assigned to the functionally appropriate domestic departments or, as such policy inevitably involves relations with foreign countries, whether primary responsibility should be given to the various foreign offices. In short, substance is no real guide to making a clear distinction between foreign and domestic policy.

The same is true when one considers procedural distinctions. Characteristics of the domestic policy process – such as interest group activity, the need for legislation, the arousal of interest among the mass electorate – are rapidly becoming significant features of foreign policy-making in Western democracies. As the West becomes more interdependent, so actors who used to restrict themselves to the domestic sphere perceive a legitimate role for themselves in the foreign policy process. Again this blurring of procedural differences has been an endemic characteristic of the EC since its inception. National domestic ministers are able to enjoy some of the features of a foreign policy process when they engage in multilateral diplomacy in Brussels. Meeting in such a forum as the Council of Ministers, they are distanced from their domestic roots, freed perhaps from the close scrutiny of Prime Ministers and Chancellors and (with the exception of Danish ministers, whose negotiating mandate is rigorously controlled by the Danish Parliament) relieved of the immediate burden of being effectively accountable to national parliaments. In a similar fashion foreign ministers participating in the Council find themselves discussing (in a rather more public forum than they are accustomed to) such technicalities as the size of fishing-nets or the axle weights of lorries – subjects that they do not traditionally associate with foreign affairs.

The point of our argument, then, is that any discussion of the foreign policy process must incorporate an acknowledgement of the diminishing validity of a clear-cut distinction between domestic and foreign policy, and that this is especially the case in the context of the European Community. Having said that, there is one crucial distinction between the two types of policy that does remain valid, and which is equally applicable at the level of the nation state and at the Community level. This is that in seeking to implement foreign policy, both the individual nation state and Community institutions are operating in an environment over which no one identifiable body has sovereign authority in the way that a national government can at least lay claim to within its own nation state. Decisions which are taken collectively in Europe – whether they are backed up by the Treaty of Rome or not – have to be implemented in an environment which national sovereignty renders largely uncontrollable. Community institutions face the same kind of implementation problems whether they are trying to get member states to comply with internal measures, or non-member states to respond to an external initiative. In neither situation can the Community act as the controller of the sole legitimate means of coercion. This is similar to the situation faced by the framers of foreign policy within individual states; they too seek to implement their policies in an external environment over which they have limited control, legitimacy and authority. Just as international law and agreements may be flouted, so Community law is not backed up by effective sanctions.

The fact that individual states and the Community share these common problems should not lead us to ignore the very real differences which exist between them, or the features which make the Community different from other international organizations. The Community has a unique identity in the international spectrum, as the institutions and procedures that have evolved within the EC since the 1950s are clearly different from those found in either nation states or other international organizations. First, although few would dispute that the Community has a long way to go before it realizes the supranational aspirations of its founding fathers, it does have a less nebulous character than other international institutions. It has a substantial budget; which (unlike most other international organizations) it spends on common policies rather than mere administration. It has a set of recognized institutions that can claim at least a degree of authority and legitimacy *vis-à-vis* member-states and the rest of the international system. It has its own developing legal system, which (subject to national intransigence) is accepted as having precedence over the legal systems of its member states, and which covers a wide range of subjects. For all these reasons the Community represents a different context for implementation from other international organizations. On the other hand, the Community is clearly not a separate political system in its own right, in the way that a nation state is. The Community is a forum for its constituent member states, who retain their formal claims to sovereignty. Although one can identify a number of policies and programmes as being 'European', they remain to a large extent an uneasy compromise of national policies formulated within familiar national frameworks. It would be a mistake to conceptualize implementation at the Community level as just the end-product of decisions taken by individual member states, however, because these states are dealing with one another continuously over a broad range of issues, and clearly this interplay has a significant effect upon domestic position-taking. One must recognize that the interconnections between policy-making and implementation at the national level and at the European level present new phenomena to describe and analyse. Of particular note is the process evident in the Community whereby policy decisions are arrived at in a multilateral context, and implemented primarily within a national context.

It is tempting to draw a parallel with the division of responsibilities between central and local government in Britain whereby much of central government policy is implemented by local authorities. This would be misleading, however, as the Community process is characterized by a much greater input from those charged with the responsibility for implementation, and the whole relationship between decision-making agencies and implementation agencies is in any case in a constant state of flux. The Community is still evolving, and its continued existence is always under threat; this is by and large not a significant problem in the realm of national policy-making and implementation. Such structural uncertainty has an impact both on the sorts of decisions that are made, and on their implementation. For example, member states may agree to certain proposals at the European level not because they are impressed by their substance, but only because they wish to be seen to be supporting the principle of integration and to be behaving as 'good Europeans'. In these circumstances there will be a high level of support for the declatory principle, but a marked lack of enthusiasm for its implementation. Such 'posturing' decisions are, of course, not unknown in the sphere of national politics, but the structure of the Community makes them much more likely to appear at the European level. In general terms those involved in the Community (be they member states or Community institutions themselves) share a perception that the continued existence of the Community must be justified by performance – either by successfully implementing policies or, where important national interests are adversely affected, by adopting a low-key, gradualist approach. This performance orientation is much stronger at the Community level than it is within individual nation states (at least in the developed West), and is an important factor affecting implementation within the EC.

To summarize: implementation is concerned with getting things done – whether those things are what were originally intended by the formulators of policies and programmes is another matter. In the context of the Community getting something done is never easy; it is too complex an environment for that to be the case. Nevertheless, it is precisely this complexity, and the way in which this complexity is overt and institutionalized, that makes the Community a worthwhile area of study if one is concerned with the implementation of foreign policy. Whereas conflicts of interest, and bureaucratic 'interference', may be largely covert within an individual nation state, they are usually out in the open in the Community's policy process. It is this kind of empirical data, together with the Community's unique status in the international system, that allows for a discussion of not only decisions, but also behaviour – an essential prerequisite of any analysis of the problems posed by implementation.

Problems for Community Implementation.

The success of any attempt at implementation is dependent upon the provision of adequate resources. Finance must be available, there must be suitable staff with the time and expertise that is needed and – not least – the political will and political climate must be conducive to the proper implementation of any policy. Where such factors are lacking or inadequate, then we may talk of a resource problem existing, and expect this to have some impact upon implementation. The Community faces a number of such resource problems, stemming principally from the capabilities of its own institutions, and from the political interplay between Community interests and national interests.

The Community itself has relatively little money. Although the size of its budget is often criticized, it amounts to only about 1 per cent of community GNP, or about 2–3 per cent of the combined budget of the member states. Similarly the Commission of the European Community, which is the most important Community institution in the realm of implementation, is a relatively small body. It has about 10,000 staff, half of whom are engaged in translation, interpreting, or scientific research work. Although the Commission is charged with the task of acting as guardian of the treaties which for the basis of the Community, it is not the sole implementing agency. In most instances implementation will also involve the national bureaucracies of member states. The extent of commission involvement in implementation is largely dependent upon the type of policies involved. Thus, for example, Community policy towards private enterprise is governed by Articles 85 and 86 of the Treaty of Rome, concerned with restrictive trade agreements between member states and the control of monopolies – in broad terms, the realm of competition policy (Allen, 1983). Here the Council of Ministers has given the Commission the independent power to interpret and implement Articles 85 and 86. The Commission has fared well in its efforts to deal with restrictive practices, but has run into serious difficulties when in attempting to deal with potential abuse of monopoly power it has tried to create a policy on mergers. This is quite simply because whereas the Commission had the necessary resources to confront restrictive practices, both technically and politically (as the issue is unlikely to arouse significant political responses in member states), it has neither resource when dealing with mergers. On the technical front the Commission's problems were highlighted by its attempt to prosecute the Continental Can Co. in 1973 (Allen, 1983, p. 225); although the European Court agreed with the Commission's argument that Continental Can has pursued a number of mergers that laid the way open to abuse of monopoly power, it found in favour of the company because it adjudged the Commission to have failed adequately to define the market it was seeking to regulate. In other words, the Commission's attempt to apply general rules was held to be inadequate yet, unlike national bureaucracies, the Commission does not have the technical resources and expertise to make sophisticated economic judgements about the exact parameters of a complex market. On the political front any attempt by the Commission to develop and pursue an effective policy on mergers is inhibited partly by member states expressing opposition in principle to any significant expansion of

Commission powers, partly by domestic political pressures (as most member states have their own, differing policies on mergers) and partly by criticism of the Commission's technical competence.

It is rare for the Commission to be able to work independently of the bureaucracies of member states. For example, when managing the price support system of the Common Agricultural Policy it must work in conjunction with national experts within the framework of the Special Committee on Agriculture (Pearce, 1983) and the numerous management committees for each product. In general terms, it has to rely on national bureaucracies for much of its data – and has to contend with the problem that such national data is often not directly comparable. Working within these constraints, the Commission can find itself in a vicious circle – deprived by member states of adequate resources (especially on a political level) it must then suffer these same member states expressing a lack of confidence in its capability, and using such a lack of confidence to justify further denial of resources. There may be sound reasons for such criticism. As the Commission is not solely responsible for the minutiae of implementation, it is perhaps less likely than a national bureaucracy to be inhibited by considerations of practicality. On another front the Commission is criticized for a lack of internal co-ordination, with individual commissioners jealously guarding their own spheres of interest and knowing or caring little about those of their colleagues. On yet another front the Commission is attacked for its lack of political sensitivity; appointed rather than elected, only loosely accountable to the European Parliament, commissioners are argued to be somewhat careless as to the political repercussions of their own actions. For example, the decision to sell surplus butter supplies to the USSR may well have made sense from the Commission's essentially technocratic perspective, but the public outcry which this decision caused did create political problems for the governments of the member states. Similarly the Commission's initial reluctance warmly to embrace the application of Greece for membership of the Community, while understandable from the more limited economic and administrative perspective, attracted the ire of the more politically sensitive Council of Ministers. They argued that it was important to accept Greece, despite the obvious difficulties, because to do otherwise would have threatened the newly re-established democratic process in Greece, and would possibly drive Greece out of the Western camp – a repercussion they did not wish to contemplate given the strategic significance of the eastern Mediterranean.

Thus the Commission has to be considered an imperfect agency of implementation; although quite successful at removing barriers to trade within the Community, it has a less happy record when it has attempted to implement positive change. This is largely because member states, wary of their national interests, will not grant it the resources it would need to improve its capability in this latter area. Member states have developed a self-reinforcing doubt about the Commission's competence when it comes to dealing with any policy that represents radical change, and tend to bypass or ignore the Commission in such circumstances. An example is provided by the initiation of the European Monetary System (EMS). This system of linking the values of member states' currencies actually originated with the then President of the Commission, Roy Jenkins. This was a case of the exception proving the rule, however, as Jenkins's thinking and role conceptualization was very different from his predecessors' and colleagues in the Commission. They had been convinced by the lack of progress towards monetary union during the preceding decade that if it was to come at all, it would have to come gradually. Even after Jenkins had announced his radical initiative, his fellow Commissioners publicly cast doubt upon it and advanced their own piecemeal suggestions (Ludlow, 1982). Jenkins's response was simply to bypass his colleagues, and direct the whole force of his argument towards Europe's political leaders – with the result that thereafter the Commission had little role to play in the process.

Clearly, the Commission is in a different position and subject to different constraints than are the national bureaucracies in nation states. Although national bureaucracies also have to cope with overseeing implementation of their policies by subsidiary agencies (state governments, regional and local authorities, and so on), they at least have in the final analysis the legislative power to compel. The Commission, and the Community as a whole, lacks this threat of coercion. It may attempt to utilize the power of the European Court – and it should be noted that the Court has generally taken a pro-integration view, being willing (unlike some national judiciaries) to interpret the spirit rather than the letter of the law – but even the Court cannot cope with determined national intransigence. The Community often finds itself in a situation where it simply lacks the appropriate tools of implementation (as compared to those at the disposal of a nation state) or has to try to cope with the relative inflexibility of those that are available. An awareness of such problems can mean that certain issues are kept off the policy agenda of the Community – for example, the Commission has never really sought to challenge seriously the way in which member states disrupt the working of the market by granting selective aid to their own industries. On a more general level this problem of a lack of suitable implementative tools can be seen most clearly in the attempt to develop European Political Co-operation (EPC).

European Political Co-operation

European Political Co-operation represents an attempt by the member states of the Community to extend significantly the scope of integration/co-operation at the European level. It was devised in response to a decision of the Hague Summit in 1969, which instructed Community Foreign Ministers to 'study the best way of achieving progress in the matter of political unification within the context of enlargement'. It is intergovernmental (Allen *et al.*, 1982), essentially comprising co-operation between the Foreign Offices of member states, but has no fixed institutions and is not governed by any treaty. Particular problems of implementation have led to attempts to give EPC more concrete expression within the Community. While the more limited British proposals have been incorporated in the London Report of 1981 (these proposals made the calling of emergency meetings easier and also tried to get around the problem of the lack of a fixed secretariat by linking preceding and succeeding presidencies), the more ambitious attempt of the Germans and the Italians (the Genscher–Colombo proposals) to initiate a 'European Act' (similar in style to the Treaty of Rome) has to date failed. In terms of implementation the significant point is that EPC represents a commitment to consult within the Community on selected questions of foreign policy towards the outside world, but there is *no* commitment to joint action.

It has to be said that in many areas of EPC it is procedural decisions rather than substantive ones that stand most chance of being eventually implemented. Sometimes while Foreign Ministers and their officials are able to agree, they are not able to 'carry' their domestic constituencies (Wallace, 1983), sometimes they are unable to mobilize Community resources and often they are just unable to agree on the basis for common action. This latter problem has been highlighted recently as EPC has become a more public process attracting the attention of both the European Parliament and the media. Even when agreement is possible, implementation may well require inaction rather than action (it is perhaps worth noting that within the framework of the United Nations the members of the Community are best able to express solidarity with one another when abstaining on a vote rather than committing themselves either way). During the era when EPC was less public the lack of specific tools of implementation was if anything an advantage for the participants. They were able to make joint statements and declarations, secure in the knowledge that little in the way of specific action could, or would be expected. As the activites of EPC attract a wider audience, both within and outside the Community, the gap between posturing and programmatic decisions is becoming more embarrassingly obvious.

Even if they wanted to, there is little that the participants in the EPC process could do about this, as they lack the procedural devices to ensure implementation of their decisions. The Community has always tended (admittedly more rigorously in the past than present) to distinguish between the 'high politics' discussed in the EPC framework and the 'low politics' of the Community's external relations (Allen, 1978; Morgan,

1973). This latter sphere, unlike EPC, is covered by the treaties (especially in relation to trade, commercial and development policies), and the Commission has the responsibility of acting on the community's behalf as representative, negotiator and agent. The Community and its institutions are on more familiar ground when it comes to pursuing this kind of 'economic' foreign policy. It has been able to use its collective strength to exert a degree of influence over trade and monetary affairs in relation to the outside world which individual member states could not aspire to. Similarly the Community has proved to be a quite effective framework for those member states seeking protection for their industries (steel, textiles and shipbuilding) most threatened by a combination of recession and competition from non-member states (Tsoukalis and de Silva Ferreira, 1980; Farrands, 1979).

Generally speaking, the Community's various representatives (the presidency, the Commission, and so on) have had little difficulty in being accepted as a legitimate negotiating agent/partner by other states (over 100 states now maintain an official representation to the European Community in Brussels). The significant exception has always been the USSR (and here too the Russians were forced to negotiate with the Commission over fishing access), who caused the Commission some difficulty during the CSCE negotiations in Helsinki – the Europeans got around the problem by including the Commission representative in the delegation of the country holding the Community presidency.

In the area of development policy the Community's role has been greatly advanced by an early decision to allocate funds to a European Development Fund. Given a financial resource to distribute, as well as its power under the treaties to set the terms of less developed countries' trade with the Community, the EC in a sense could not fail to develop and implement a 'European' policy. Setbacks have occurred at the implementation stage, however; the Community's policies have aroused the suspicions of the USA (who have seen them as being neo-colonialist and discriminatory against US trading interests) and the frustration of those countries who find the Community's regulations too complex and bureaucratic to be taken full advantage of. By and large, however, the Lomé Convention (Lomé 3 is about to be concluded) can be cited as an example of a policy that works at the European level because there are (for the Europeans) no major resource problems.

If the Community's strengths are apparent in the realm of 'economic' foreign policy, its weaknesses are equally clear when it has to respond to a crisis situation. Neither the Commission nor the EPC framework are very good at implementing crisis management or a rapid response. The member states do have significant differences of interest and strategy on many of the issues which arise – unplanned and unexpectedly – in the international environment. Such differences lead to the Community seeking the lowest common denominator of agreement, and then attempting to implement the resulting weak common statements – arguably this is less effective than a more determined pursuit of contradictory national positions. On the other hand, freed from the pressure of having to respond quickly, the Community has developed the ability to formulate a common approach, and stick to it under pressure. For example, at the long and complex CSCE negotiations the Community's common line (developed through the EPC procedure) held up in the face of strong pressure on individual states – particularly from the USSR – to abandon the common European position (Allen *et al.*, 1982, pp. 60–9). Its relationship with the other superpower also demonstrates an enhanced capability for co-operation. It used to be the case that the Europeans could develop and implement common policy guidelines as long as they did not clash with the views of the USA, but that when there was a clash, Community solidarity was broken. In recent years, however, the Community has been able to maintain a relatively independent position over such issues as Poland, the gas pipeline, and the reaction to Afghanistan and Grenada. Collectively member states are able to resist the force of US arguments to a considerably greater extent than they would on their own.

To summarize: the Community has more concrete procedures and institutions at its disposal when seeking to implement foreign policy in the sphere of 'low politics' – it is, after all, in essence an economic community. It does not have the same devices available in the sphere of 'high politics' in terms of its foreign policy. This can lead to weaknesses in implementation, especially in a situation where the outside world thrusts a problem upon the Community. However, the point must be made that this lack of implementative capability can be a positive asset to member states. They can find themselves in situations in which the outside world expects some kind of European response, but in which the member states do not wish to pursue substantive policies. One example would be the Euro-Arab dialogue and the political situation in the Middle East (Allen *et al.*, 1982, pp. 69–83), where the prime concern of the Europeans was to respond to Arab demands that they distanced themselves from the US position, without actually having to give their response any real substance. The lack of procedural devices to implement such 'high politics' positions can be actually functional as far as the interests of member states are concerned. The same phenomenon could be observed during the Falklands crisis; the Community was able to proffer the necessary support for Britain in the shape of a common statement and the short-term declaration of economic sanctions but those states who were reluctant to be any further involved (especially Ireland and Italy) could rest secure in the knowledge that posturing would suffice given the lack of further common implementative tools. While this may aid the survival of the Community system, however, it should not obscure the fact that foreign policy formulation and implementation within the Community framework is subject to considerable systemic confusion. Because there is no single decision-making centre, the EPC framework and the Community institutions can find themselves working at cross-purposes. There is often poor co-ordination between the two processes both at the Community and the member state level. Those working within EPC often remain in ignorance of developments within the EC; the very essence of EPC was its exclusiveness and its relative secrecy (this is often cited as a 'resource' by practitioners wary of the very public bargaining that occurs within the Community proper). Furthermore, of course, the European level (EPC or EC) represents only one of a number of implementation alternatives for the member states in their pursuit of national objectives. They can still rely upon bilateral relations (Britain and France in particular value their considerable national capabilities), upon more restricted multi-lateral dealings (the global economic summits of the major Western states spring to mind here) and upon wider groupings than the Community, such as NATO, OECD and, in some cases, even the United Nations. There is, then, a confusion *between* levels and *within* levels of implementation.

Implementing Integration

System survival in a hostile environment is probably the greatest achievement of the Community in the sphere of foreign policy. In this sense it is not unlike most nation states but it, of course, has to cope with the additional problem of the perceived national interest of member states. This is important not only in the sphere of foreign policy, but in *all* aspects of Community decision-making and implementation. We noted above that one prerequisite of successful implementation was the provision of adequate political resources, and we must now turn our attention to the question of whether member states display sufficient commitment to the aim of European integration to allow us to dub their political commitment as adequate. All the participants in the Community process are aware of the importance of European unity as an issue that has a significant impact upon the composition of the policy agenda. For some member states, a perceived advance towards integration provides the justification for the implementation of unpopular and difficult decisions. Conversely other member states are motivated by the domestic unpopularity of European integration to keep issues off the Community agenda (often by ensuring that they are considered in a less controversial forum, such as the OECD). This is all despite the fact that the term 'integration' has remained undefined in the European context; there has never been more than a very generalized agreement among member states as to the ultimate purposes of full European co-operation.

To reiterate the point made above concerning the permanent state of flux in which the Community exists major questions about its future development have been on the agenda since its inception. These questions take both procedural and substantive form. They centre on such issues as enlargement (from 6 to 9, to 10, to 12), the extension of common policies (from a common market and an agricultural policy to an Economic and Monetary Union, perhaps a common foreign policy, maybe even security policy), the institutionalization of majority rather than unanimous voting, the powers and role of the European Parliament, the introduction of direct elections to that Parliament, and the role of summit meetings and the European Council. One could extend this list, but in this context the point to note is that all these issues have arisen and have been (partially) resolved as a result of intense intergovernmental negotiation, and that this has kept the relevance of the issue of further integration very firmly in the minds of member states. When the Community was established, many commentators assumed that the progress of integration would come incrementally and inevitably without the need for major renegotiations. The belief was that gradual implementation of the detailed provisions of the Treaty of Rome would lead to the need for further economic integration, and that European political institutions would have to develop in parallel. This has not happened: member states have tended to see their relationship with the Community as one based on zero-sum assumptions; an increase in the power of collective institutions being related to a decrease in the power of of the individual member states. Hence the attitude of member states towards the notion of integration has remained a powerful factor in their willingness to devote adequate political resources to Community programmes.

This can be seen in general terms if one considers the early history of the Community. One can argue that it was precisely the successful implementation of the initial objectives of the Treaty of Rome that inhibited further developments towards integration. The relatively successful economic performance of the Six in their early years may well have attracted the interest of the previously sceptical British, but it also led some of the Six (particularly France) to feel that they were now, once again, capable of pursuing an independent course. In other words, the successful implementation of one phase of integration can inhibit member states from further entanglement in collective action – a classic instance of anticipated outputs leading to unanticipated outcomes.

The fact that the symbolism of European integration is always present on the policy agenda has an appreciable impact on the other issues. Member states may agree on the goals to be pursued in a particular area, but may differ on the means to be adopted because of the relationship between those means and the advance of integration. For example, Britain is anxious to resolve the question of its contributions to the

Community budget – as are the other member states, who regret its constant appearance on the Community agenda – but successive British governments have not been prepared to contemplate solutions that entail a significant increase in the powers of the European Parliament or in the overall level of Community economic activity. Similarly, albeit from a different viewpoint, countries like Holland or Italy are reluctant to support any initiatives that do not involve all member states equally, for fear of the long-term impact on Community solidarity and further integration. Another example is provided by the attitude of those member states with relatively weak economies towards the creation of the European Monetary System; although worried by the possible economic consequences of linking their currencies with such strong currencies as the Deutschmark, the smaller member states allowed their concern not to be seen as 'bad Europeans' to override these fears.

Attitudes towards integration, then, are an important determinant of the degree to which member states are willing to commit political resources to policy implementation. It is possible to generalize about the impact of these attitudes; because of them, it has proved easier to implement policies concerned with the removal of restrictions within the Community (especially concerning trade) than it has to implement proposals for common policies. Theorists of integration have described the former as 'negative' integration and the latter as 'positive' integration (Pinder, 1968). Negative integration has proved susceptible to incremental implementation, and has posed relatively few political resource problems; attempts to implement positive integration policies have required more transfers of authority and encountered severe political resource problems. For example, measures designed to enhance the development of a common market among member states have proved less contentious to agree upon and implement than have measures which entail the transferral of significant economic policy authority from the national to the Community level. One illustration of this would be the Community's response to the problem of surplus capacity in the 'crisis industries' (textiles, steel, shipbuilding); while, as we have noted, the Community is able to manipulate the market conditions for these industries – by offering a degree of protection from external competition – it is not able to restructure effectively the economies of member states, or direct investment within these (Tsoukalis and de Silva Ferreira, 1980).

Where political resource problems are encountered, decisions tend to get pushed up the European hierarchy – a familiar phenomenon in nation states. This can have two possible consequences for implementation, both of which are again familiar to students of the policy process in nation states. One is that solutions and decisions are arrived at which are politically acceptable to all concerned, but are so ambiguous that they are either impossible to implement or are ineffective once implemented. A classic instance would appear to be the 'Dublin Formula', which Harold Wilson accepted as resolving the problem of budget payments when he was involved in renegotiating Britain's terms of entry to the Community. The other possible consequence is that one or more of the political leadership attach their personal prestige to a particular project; the evidence suggests that when this happens, the chances of slippage and distortion in implementation are much reduced. A good example of this can be found in the creation of the European Monetary System. The overt and persistent commitment of Chancellor Schmidt (and, to a lesser extent, President Giscard d'Estaing) would appear to have been the only factor powerful enough to overcome resistance to the concept of an EMS among bureaucrats and financial experts in both the Community and member states (Ludlow, 1982).

A consideration of political resource problems highlights national differences in the degree of commitment to European integration, but these are not the only significant national differences that have an impact on implementation within the Community. Member states have what might be termed differing administrative traditions, and these can pose severe internal environmental problems. Each member state's bureaucracy had developed its own way of working, its own way of approaching and resolving problems. Thus, for example, Britain had gained a reputation within the Community for taking its commitments to action very seriously; once Britain has agreed to a particular course of action, its bureaucracy is noted for the thorough manner in which it
pursues that course. Other member states have been criticized for being willing to reach common agreements without a serious intention of implementing them to the full. For example, the way in which the Italian government readily agreed to the proposal to introduce Value Added Tax in the late 1960s is often contrasted with its considerable reluctance to implement this policy once it became a Community commitment (Puchala, 1983). This behavioural phenomenon can have a significant impact upon decision-making. Some member states (particularly the British) are reluctant to reach common agreement on issues where they are not convinced that their partners will properly implement any decisions. The Community's attempt to develop a policy on fish is a case in point. As well as a number of substantive and well-documented disagreements (Volle and Wallace, 1977; Shackleton, 1983) between the member states as to the nature of a Common Fisheries Policy, problems also centred upon the question of implementation. Fishing is an industry that cannot be sophisticatedly policed at sea, and so boats, equipment and catches have to be inspected in port to ensure that they comply with any regulations that have been agreed. The alternative is simply to ban certain boats or types of fishing wholesale.

The Common Fisheries Policy ran into trouble partly because some states (in particular Britain) voiced doubts about the enthusiasm that other states (most notably France) would apply to ensuring that any agreed regulations were observed by their fishermen fishing in what used to be national – but which would become Community – waters. This was a problem that had arisen in other organizations (such as the North East Atlantic Fisheries Commission) in the past, so it was not exclusive to the Community. The situation was, of course, further complicated by the need of all the Community fishing countries to harness the collective bargaining power of the Community in dealings with non-member states over reciprocal fishing rights. The member states all needed a Community regime for external purposes but did not trust the implementation of that regime for internal purposes.

Differing national attitudes towards implementative responsibilities are not restricted to single issues like fish, but can be seen in many other relatively minor areas. The Community has made some attempts to police its own members in this area; under article 169 of the treaty it may institute proceedings against member states who fail to fulfil their obligations, but there is little it can do in the face of persistent national intransigence. It may be of interest to note that, in 1982, Italy attracted the most proceedings under this heading, fourteen cases; France attracted eight; while Britain – for all its resistance to the concept of integration – was the subject of only two cases (European Community, 1983). Be that as it may, it is not only national irresponsibility that has an impact on implementation. It is also the case that national bureaucracies can , if they are allowed to, use their influence as policy advisers to have a major impact on decision-making. The best example of this in recent years is provided by the creation of the EMS. We have already noted that the EMS came into being largely as a consequence of the personal commitment of the German and French leaders. Originally they had hoped to persuade the British leader (Callaghan) to lend his support to the proposal. However, while Schmidt and Giscard d'Estaing quite deliberately entrusted the early negotiations to their own nominees rather than members of their respective financial bureaucracies, Callaghan allowed his Treasury officials to become involved in the negotiations from the outset. This meant that while the French and German negotiators kept a fundamentally political perspective, the full weight of Treasury caution (and distaste for grandiose schemes that did not spell out all the details) was allowed to colour the British attitude throughout the negotiations, and was an important factor in Britain's eventual decision not to participate in the EMS (Ludlow, 1982). The EMS is a classic example of entrenched bureaucratic attitudes only being overcome by firm and consistent political leadership. As the Commission itself noted, the decision to create the EMS was very different from earlier initiatives in the field of monetary union: 'instead of plans being drawn up before the basic political decision was taken, the political decision was taken first and experts then commissioned to resolve the final technical problems' (European Community, 1979). Entrenched bureaucratic attitudes are clearly as much of a problem at the European level as they are within nation states.

The EMS also offers an example of the impact of domestic political constraints. The clear political leadership evident in the creation of the EMS was only made possible by the strong political position in domestic politics enjoyed by its main protagonists. Schmidt was only able to coerce his own bureaucracy in the way that he did because he was not under effective challenge within the Federal Republic; similarly Giscard d'Estaing's unexpectedly good showing in the French parliamentary elections of 1978 gave him the political freedom to endorse a policy that did not attract much enthusiasm in his domestic constituency. As the domestic political situation changed so too did the attitudes of political leaders. Thus, for example, at the penultimate stage of implementation of the EMS, the French leader suddenly became much less enthusiastic, and announced that France would only continue to support the scheme if it was linked to reform of the Common Agricultural Policy. Ludlow (1982) offers a persuasive argument that this change of heart was caused by domestic disquiet over the imminent European Parliament elections, and the dissatisfaction of the French farming community with the working of the CAP. It is a good example of the way in which apparently unrelated issues become inextricably linked in the Community implementation process.

The process of domestic constraints intruding upon European initiatives can of course, work in reverse. National governments are able to implement measures under the Community mantle that they would find difficult to bring off unilaterally. In this sense Community membership serves a 'cover' function. Thus, for example, the British government faced considerable domestic resistance to the introduction of tachographs in lorries; because of this, the government dragged its feet over the implementation of this European initiative and was successfully prosecuted in the European Court by the Commission, and was then able to use this as a counterargument to its domestic pressure groups – that is, the policy that one suspects the British government favoured all along got implemented because of the European commitment. The same phenomenon can be observed in the sphere of external relations; the German government was able in the 1970s to resist Israeli pressure (successful previously, for obvious reasons) and gradually extend support to the Arab and Palestinian cause as a response to the imperatives of oil politics, principally because it could plead the necessity of supporting its European partners and implementing the collective Community position.

There are limits to the political utility of the Community in domestic politics, not least because it can be argued that the cornerstone of the Community – the Treaty of Rome – has become increasingly inapplicable in the current world economic climate. The treaty embodies an essentially *laissez-faire* view of the role of governing authorities in economic management, but now has to be implemented in a world that is becoming increasingly protectionist. The Community is often divided between member states that can stand a measure of competition (for example, Germany) and those that cannot (for example, Britain and Italy). All the member states are faced with the problem of attempting to reconcile domestic pressure for intervention and protection with their commitment at the European level to the development of a free market. Enlargement of the Community has made this problem more acute. The Community no longer looks like a natural unit in either economic or political terms, as enlargement has incorporated disparate states. The diversity that now exists within the Community (and, indeed, its sheer size) means that even where there is general agreement on a principle, it can be very difficult to secure detailed implementation; indeed, it is becoming equally hard to *maintain* the implementation of policies that in the past had presented little or no problem. This is partly because of the new situation in which the Community finds itself, and partly because the implementation of policies in the past has produced a number of unanticipated and unwanted side-effects (of which the most obvious are the large and costly surpluses that the CAP generates).

Finally, we should refer to the implementation problems that arise inevitably from attempts to harmonize the activities of, at present, ten sovereign states. Although the theorists of integration made much of the similarities between the member states of the Community, citing their shared heritage, their similar systems of pluralist democracy, their similar economic systems and their similar predicament, they perhaps underestimated the impact of their differences on the detailed process of implementation. We have already mentioned the differing administrative styles that distinguish the individual member states of the Community; we should also extend this line of argument to include all those aspects of political culture that while encouraging the search for common decisions, sometimes inhibit the clear implementation of those decisions. Thus, for example, member states have experienced considerable problems in creating the system of direct elections to the European Parliament – having to cope with national differences over electoral systems, the timing of elections, the allocation of seats, and so on. This is an issue on which the political will exists, and where there is little in the way of bureaucratic resistance, but where simple size and diversity pose very real problems of implementation.

Conclusion

In summary, it can be seen that implementation at the European level faces many problems that we also find at the national level – ambiguous goals, imperfect procedures and instruments, bureaucratic resistance and inadequate control mechanisms. In addition to these, however, the context of multilateral decision-making introduces new complications – the interplay between national and European interests, the lack of a clear central authority, doubts about the competence and commitment of partners and working within a relatively inflexible ideological framework. Nevertheless, the fact that despite all its problems the Community has continued to exist suggests that the member states still consider it worth while to try and decide upon and implement policies within this particular framework. The European Community does seem to be quite good at 'muddling through' – a well-recognized process of policy activity at the national level. The member states express frequent dissatisfaction with the outcome of Community output but they show little inclination to rectify any discrepancies between aspiration and implementation. Perhaps when all other advantages cease, the Community remains a convenient framework for implementing that which is necessary but unpopular at the national level, and for transferring responsibility for policies that cannot be implemented successfully by any one member state acting alone.

It does still remain very hard to assess the effectiveness of implementation at the European level, mainly because it is often impossible to determine the exact nature of the goal or goals sought. Thus EPC is regularly cited as a success; commentators suggest that its extensive development far exceeded the expectations of those who established it – a positive example of outcome differing from output? On the other hand, there are those who point out that EPC has achieved little in the way of implementation of substantive policy, but then who could argue otherwise about the foreign policies of most member states? As far as the EC proper is concerned the goals sometimes seem clearer, although even here a common market with perfect competitive conditions remains an impossible ideal. The European Community has proved to be more competent at implementing the *detail* of closely negotiated intergovernmental bargains than it has at implementing its original objective of developing an economic and political union capable of exerting supranational power and authority over its constituent states. In the implementation of multilateral decisions incrementalism is the order of the day.

8

The Implementation of Britain's CSCE Policy, 1975–84

Michael Clarke

The vocabulary of implementation surrounds the Conference on Security and Co-operation in Europe (CSCE). Since the signature of the Final Act at Helsinki, the degree to which that document has been 'implemented' and the measures to monitor others' implementation of it have been the subject of numerous studies and government reports, particularly in the USA. Yet most foreign policy accounts of the CSCE have not looked at it as an implementation issue, but rather as a study in diplomatic negotiation and détente. This is understandable, since the whole affair has become an institutionalized diplomatic process, and continued participation in such processes may seem to become an end in itself. So British 'policy' towards the CSCE can be seen quite credibly as amounting to little more than its negotiating stance and tactics at the various working groups and meetings that made up the institutions of the CSCE. And since the whole process has been proceeding for a long time, and will continue for the forseeable future, it inevitably becomes part of Britain's day to day diplomatic business and is difficult to define as policy in a discrete area; it takes on the aspect of diplomatic routine.

The CSCE as Diplomatic History

As a case study in diplomatic relations, the CSCE does indeed have a long and interesting history. The idea of a European security conference goes back to an original Soviet proposal in February 1954, but it was not until the mid-1960s that the idea was taken seriously in the West. In July 1966 the Warsaw Pact made a direct call for a conference in the Bucharest Declaration. Working through the East European members of the Pact, the Soviets pressed for a conference that would serve, in lieu of a postwar peace treaty, to codify and legitimize the boundaries of Europe and gain recognition for the German Democratic Republic. For precisely these reasons the West had always resisted such a conference. But with progress in other aspects of détente, the West was prepared, by 1969, to give the idea more credit (Russell, 1976). In practice, Soviet aims in the negotiations were probably less coherent than this, and the commitment to the process of both the West and the neutral countries was, at best, lukewarm. It was never clear that the CSCE was imbued with a single set of aims or objectives (Holsti, 1982). A series of protracted and often difficult negotiations followed and, in July 1973, Foreign Ministers of the thirty-five participating states met at Helsinki to adopt a series of recommendations for Stage 1 of the CSCE process. From September 1973 until July 1975 detailed negotiations proceeded in what was, at least in extent, the biggest European diplomatic conference ever held. It resulted in the signing of the Final Act (Helsinki Declaration) in August 1975 (HMSO, 1975).

The substance of the CSCE was, therefore, embodied in the four 'Baskets' of the Final Act. Basket I dealt with security matters: it included a declaration of ten principles concerning security and peaceful change in Europe and a series of specific commitments to so-called 'confidence-building measures' (CBMs) designed to improve the information of East and West about the military manoeuvres of the other. Basket II was broadly economic, covering trade relations, industrial policy, science and technology, and environmental matters. Basket III concerned 'humanitarian' issues; in particular, matters related to improving human contact, access to information, cultural co-operation and educational exchanges. Basket III has been broadly characterized as the human rights part of the CSCE. Basket IV concerned 'Follow-up to the Conference', in which it was resolved to continue the dialogue in an institutionalized form and to instigate regular review conferences. The Final Act is not a treaty and does not possess the force of law. Indeed, when Western commentators seem to lament the fact that the provisions of Helsinki are not legally binding in any way, it should be recalled that it was the Western powers who were most determined to ensure that the Final Act was a political, and not a legal, document in order to avoid giving to the Soviets *de jure* recognition of the ten principles, which they would have liked to make into a legal cornerstone around which the rest of the document would be cast (European Community, 1976, pp. 7-9). The Final Act is, therefore, an agreement – quite literally, a political declaration of intent between thirty-five states whose interests are affected. It includes all European states except Albania, and it includes the USA and Canada – an extension of geography which was a prerequisite to the West's participation in the negotiations. Apart from the detailed negotiations surrounding the drafting and signature of the Final Act itself, the CSCE has moved through a first review conference at Belgrade from June 1977 until March 1978, a series of meetings of scientific experts in Bonn during 1978, a meeting to discuss the peaceful settlement of disputes in Montreux in October 1978, a meeting on Mediterranean security in Valetta in February 1979, a scientific forum in

Hamburg during February 1980, and then a marathon second review conference in Madrid from November 1980 until September 1983. The direct outcome of this last conference included an agreement to participate in a conference on disarmament and confidence-building measures in Europe which began in Stockholm on 17 January 1984. Throughout these various sessions Britain's diplomacy had been co-ordinated within the European Community (in the framework of European Political Co-operation) with its NATO partners, and bilaterally with other European states with whom Britain feels common interests in various aspects of the CSCE.

Viewed in this way, the CSCE seems to offer an obvious example of a negotiating process. The most usual way to interpret the issue is, firstly, to assess the different perspectives and motives of East and West. The East was concerned primarily with the outcome of basket I negotiations, and would have liked to restrict the conference to only those matters. The West would only discuss basket I as long as equal weight and attention were given to basket III. The neutrals and non-aligned countries (NNAs) had interests in all of the baskets and usually played a constuctive mediatory role between East and West. To begin with, Britain was sceptical about the purposes of such a conference and certainly not optimistic about its prospects and the USA was relatively disinterested in the early stages. The USSR seemed to have everything to gain from the signing of the Final Act, and although it had been bargained into some important concessions by the time it was concluded, the Western powers were persuaded to engage in the dialogue not because it seemed favourable in itself, but because the CSCE had been packaged with the other institutions of détente, in particular, the Mutual and Balanced Force Reduction (MBFR) talks, in which the West was far more interested (Howard, 1977, pp. 243-4).

Secondly, however, it became clear immediately following the signing of the Final Act that it was not a diplomatic victory for the USSR. The contents of basket III attracted far more attention than those of basket I, in both East and West (Loescher, 1981). Basket II was essentially uncontroversial, though nevertheless the subject of some friction between both sides. Neither the Soviets nor the West could have foreseen the degree to which 'Helsinki' would come to represent a commitment to human rights, despite the fact that such matters are only one part of a carefully balanced diplomatic formula. And by the time the Final Act was signed in 1975, many of the original diplomatic Soviet motives in pressing for a conference had been overtaken by events: East Germany had achieved diplomatic recognition, *Ostpolitik* had added greatly to territorial legitimacy in Europe and in reality détente had not threatened Soviet interests in Eastern Europe. The initiative in the process switched to the West. The USA became much more attentive to the CSCE, and along with other West European states, Britain found the

Final Act a very convenient document with which to nag the USSR over its behaviour in Eastern Europe. By the time of the Belgrade review conference in 1977 the Soviets were distinctly less enthusiastic about the whole process. The West, in contrast, was determined to keep the Soviets and East European delegations at the conference. They would not agree to any time limit on the conference which would allow ritualized filibustering by the East, and were equally determined at the second review conference in Madrid not to let their adversaries off the hook. Basket I had proved, in fact, to be of very little help to the USSR. Basket III has emerged as a source of propaganda and a diplomatic windfall for the West. It stimulated dissident 'monitoring groups' in Eastern Europe and the USSR, created some publicity in the West which could only present the Soviets in a poor light, and it established a permanence to the process which guaranteed that the USSR could not easily leave the dock.

Thirdly, it was apparent early on in the drafting of the Final Act document that co-ordination between Britain and its European Community partners was surprisingly good. Many of the diverse matters in the CSCE related directly to European Community concerns, and the Nine were able to co-ordinate their diplomatic negotiations to a very high degree. So effective was this that as the process became institutionalized into the routine work of the Foreign and Commonwealth Office (FCO), the objective of deepening co-operation with Britain's European partners began to assume even greater importance than that of agreeing to common commitments among the thirty-five participating states. Of course, the first might be regarded as a prerequisite to the second, but nevertheless it helps explain the shifting attitudes that Britain displayed between 1975 and 1984. Here was an arena in which Britain could take a principled stand against Soviet behaviour, and do so in an integrated fashion with its European community partners. Policy co-ordination among the broader group of NATO countries was not as close, not least because European co-ordination was so time-consuming. European political co-operation, it has been said, was effectively built on the need to negotiate the CSCE process.

This, then, would be the bones of the story of the CSCE as an act of diplomacy. It describes policy in the broadest sense. We say 'Britain's policy' was to use the CSCE in order to pressure the Soviets. This gives us a possible explanation of motives, and a fairly accurate characterization of the conventional wisdom on the matter among the policy-making establishment. For the policy analyst, however, it does not get us much nearer to the policy Britain actually had in relation to the CSCE, or to understanding what were the outputs of that policy. Hence we tend to see British policy in this matter as a series of essentially abstract manoeuvres concerning wording and agreed interpretations, among state actors who are represented by their various national delegations. This has been the focus of the well-worn debate on the usefulness of the CSCE process. Its critics charge that it has had no discernible impact upon any of the areas that the baskets were intended to cover. Improvements, where they have occurred, have been patchy and cannot be pinned down to initiatives taken through the Final Act. Thus an independent British study concluded that two years after the Final Act it was impossible to say that there had been any *general* improvement in East-West relations resulting from the meeting (Helsinki Review Group, 1977). The Belgrade Concluding Document was a thorough disappointment to many, since it merely recorded that a meeting had been held, consensus was not reached on a number of proposals and that future meetings would be held (HMSO, 1978a, pp. 52–3). Its proponents assert that it is in the nature of the exercise that a direct impact will be impossible to discern. The most common phrases used in the FCO, for instance, to characterize the process were that it was a 'balanced package', a 'seamless web' of undertakings or a 'yardstick' against which to measure future behaviour. Thus it must be judged on its own terms. It is a dialogue and is important for that reason alone. Since it has a diplomatic rationale, it may be judged a success in those terms, as it has provided a mechanism where governments can posture over certain issues, go on the record over particular questions and indicate to each other their various priorities and differences.

Within these two positions some important elaborations of what the Final Act constituted were implied in various public statements. In the House of Commons alone, from being described (accurately) by Harold Wilson in 1975 as 'a set of political undertakings', the Final Act by 1976 had been described by Roy Hattersley as 'absolute obligations'. In 1980 Peter Blaker spoke of possible Soviet intervention in Poland as a 'flagrant breach' of Helsinki. While, technically, all of these descriptions were sustainable, the implications of them invest the Final Act with a quasi-legal status. Neither critics nor proponents help us to decide more clearly what this particular type of foreign policy – as policy – is all about. Let us, therefore, examine it not as diplomacy, but more strictly as policy commitment and execution.

The CSCE as Policy Execution

To examine the CSCE as an exercise in Britain's policy execution it is, first, necessary to determine more precisely what commitments it implied for Britain. The Final Act is a very wide-ranging document. It covers not only a large number of diverse states, in different groupings, but also a multitude of political and politico-social matters. In itself this is nothing new, since many international agreements make sweeping calls for action to improve social conditions. The Final Act is, however, unique to the extent that it mentions highly specific measures that could be taken across a broad spectrum of subjects to improve conditions. It speaks of specific exchanges of information, of feasible economic and cultural projects, of particular measures of military confidence-building, of the costs of visas, or the working conditions of journalists and business people. Yet while it is unusual to find such an array of specifics in a multilateral diplomatic agreement, almost all of them are commitments only in a relative sense. The rubrick which covers these matters invariably commit the participating states 'to take measures further to improve', or to 'endeavour to ensure' that something is undertaken, to 'declare their readiness' or 'make it their aim' to do something. The section of the Final Act dealing with human contracts, which has been the focus of so much Western attention, is couched in extremely relative terms. It speaks of the 'freer' movement of people (HMSO, 1975, p. 33), and though it mentions many specific areas in which improvements might be made, there are only two sentences, under the heading 'Reunification of families', which provide categorical commitments (p. 34, lines 14–21). The whole document, therefore, presents an interesting set of contrasts. It covers many humanitarian and social areas, and mentions many very specific measures which would be desirable, while it leaves generally vague the criteria by which the performance of such measures could be judged.

If one breaks down the text of the Final Act itself, it emerges that 33 per cent of the document (671 lines) is composed of statements of principle. A further 15 per cent (302 lines) concerns procedural arrangements, either in specific commitments to further meetings or, more vaguely, in a commitment to future consultation through existing channels. That portion of the document which indicates that particular action is required, unilaterally, bilaterally, or through existing multilateral fora, covers some 27 per cent of the text (567 lines). Within this category where the more specific commitments to action can be inferred, the only part which spells out in detail what action is required, and under what circumstances, is that section dealing with confidence-building measures, and eight lines concerning some mechanics of application procedures for the reunification of families. Apart from this, the 'further action' that is required is not tied to any time limit or to any specific test of behaviour. The other 25 per cent of the text (521 lines) does not require action directly, but rather indicates desirable areas of action that might be explored in some other (unspecified) structures of co-operation at some time in the future. Here, for instance, desirable co-operation on environmental matters, where the subjects of concern are spelt out – information-gathering, industrial pollution, water pollution, and so on – is treated as a set of topics for future 'organisation of conferences, symposia and meetings of experts' or for 'relevant international conventions'. In this category governments are required only to encourage, or at most 'facilitate', the endeavours of some other organisations.

When it is broken down in this way, it is clear that the Final Act commits the signatories to a number of quite different things. Many principles are reaffirmed; this requires no action from anyone. It is a matter of record that they have been stated and can be referred to in the context of the other issues involved in the CSCE. Beyond that, the document largely commits the signatories to favouring certain attitudes rather than taking action, and action which is to be judged in relative rather than specific terms. In so far as the Final Act demands changes in behaviour – that things will definitely happen that would not otherwise have happened – they are encompassed in the CBM document and in the commitments to future meetings and 'follow-up' procedures.

What does this sort of analysis imply about the way we should study the CSCE as *policy*? Clearly, it indicates that if we view the Final Act as mere diplomatic verbiage and follow its negotiating history through the subsequent meetings up to 1984, then we will be analysing an argument that becomes almost theological in its abstraction. We will ignore a whole series of important questions concerning how the story might have been different or the impact of the whole process greater on East-West relations. We will only discover something of the general attitudes of the British foreign policy establishment towards the issues as intellectual problems raised by the negotiations. We will not discover much about how the British goverment, *as an organization*, handled the CSCE. On the other hand, if we concentrate only on the limited, but specific, behavioural changes demanded by the Final Act, then we will miss a great deal of the posturing and declaratory activity that is a vital part of foreign policy outputs. One of the dangers in applying the rigorous behavioural analysis that can be highly appropriate to some aspects of the execution of domestic policies is that it can render foreign policy as sterile as the opposite approach renders it abstract. Dunsire's analysis (1978a), for instance, of implementation in a bureaucracy, or Pressman and Wildavsky's study (1973) of the administration of an aid programme, are valuable as analyses of a particular type of policy, but foreign policy, characteristically, does not involve as much behavioural modification as evidence of success. Much more in foreign policy is intentionally vague and highly declaratory. It is not good enough, therefore, to analyse the CSCE merely as a set of behavioural demands. The demands of the Final Act, as we have seen, are intellectually and behaviourally various, and the scope of governmental concern that they cover is very wide. So we should be aware that when we refer to 'Britain's policy' towards the CSCE, we are in fact referring to a whole series of different policies and *types* of behaviour that are co-ordinated, mainly in the mind of the observer, under the general heading of 'CSCE policy'.

For our purposes, then, the usual way of examining implementation – through an analysis of each of the four baskets of the Final Act – is not appropriate, as this only defines diplomatic subject-areas. It is more useful for us to try to find the hazy demarcation lines between the different types of implementation that were required. Three quite distinct areas suggest themselves – not so much because they required completely different types of behaviour as such, but because the circumstances of each created different demands on the policy-making machine.

First, we can define the problem of Britain's own internal implementation of the Final Act. It is curious that so little attention is ever given to Britain's own compliance with the document. Secondly, there is a rather different implementation task in conforming to the further procedures that had been agreed; for CBMs, for follow-up meetings and conferences. It was necessary, in other words, to implement the diplomatic procedure of the CSCE process. Thirdly, there is the government's attempt to implement its 'CSCE policy' so as to affect the behaviour of the Eastern bloc countries in more favourable directions, by appealing to the statements of principle in the Final Act, pointing to the relative commitments and opening avenues of further action between the signatories.

Britain's Own Implementation of the Final Act

This is an interesting, and almost entirely neglected, area in the study of the CSCE. It is largely neglected because the focus of CSCE analysis has normally been on the improvements we discern in the East as a result of the Final Act. It is interesting because it reveals a good deal about Britain's own bureaucratic attitudes to the process, and tells us quite a lot about how the foreign policy-making machine has worked in relation to the other two areas.

Two years after the signing of the Final act, the FCO gave evidence to the Defence and External Affairs Subcommittee (DEASC) of the House of Commons Expenditure Committee that, 'there are no major British interests requiring special treatment within the framework of the Final Act' (House of Commons, Expenditure Committee, 1977, p. xii). More particularly, over basket I the Ministry of Defence reported in a memo to the DEASC that: 'there are no foreseeable implications for UK defence policy in the implementation of the provisions of the Final Act' (ibid., p. 81). The action required to honour Britain's commitments on CBMs, in any case, were carried out within NATO, and hence became a matter largely of agreeing procedures with allies and then allowing the multilateral organization to enact them (though in some cases Britain voluntarily notified the Warsaw Pact of national military manoeuvres as part of its commitment to CBMs). On basket II the Department of Trade noted that: 'As far as the UK is concerned we believe that (with one exception) we already fully implement the Basket II provisions' (ibid., p. 53). The exception concerned the existence of quotas on textile and electronic imports, which the Department of Trade had no intention of removing. The Foreign Secretary at the time, Anthony Crosland, told the Council of Europe that Britain approaches basket II from a 'very high threshold' of existing achievement, and that present restrictions were at an 'irreducible minimum'. In basket III the FCO dealt with a number of Eastern complaints over the first two years, but was only inclined to take seriously the problem of the time taken to issue visas for travel from Eastern Europe to Britain. This was attributed to technical difficulties in handling a large number of applications (ibid., pp. 67, 79). In an unpublished memorandum the FCO agreed to help reinforce staff numbers in its Visa Section. In response to this work of the DEASC the government produced its own observations on the subcommittee's report (HMSO, 1978b). Of the fourteen detailed proposals made by the DEASC, the government described its existing practice in eleven of them as being adequate to meet the requirement, and expressed qualified disagreement on two and outright disagreement with one of the proposals.

It seems, then, that none of the ministries involved, nor indeed the central Cabinet machinery, felt much obligated by the terms of the Final Act. Indeed, as Andrew Shonfield pointed out in a memo to the DEASC (House of Commons, Expenditure Committee, 1977, p. 34), there were distinct advantages to making future proposals which would put the Western powers under some real obligation to implement changes in certain areas; to give the East, in effect, a higher motive to honour the spirit of the agreement. The Western powers in general, for instance, were very wary of allowing the technological transfer sections of the basket II agreements to become real commitments that would benefit the East, and imposed criteria on the transfer of technology which deprived the Eastern countries of the most obvious advantage they could derive from that basket. The East was not noticeably keen thereafter to implement any of the major provisions of basket II.

In fact, apart from the ten principles, the drafting of the Final Act both in its structure and in its terminology inclines very much to Western views and norms of behaviour. The question of Britain's own implementation, therefore, was very much concerned with the need to be seen to act somehow in pursuit of the Helsinki objectives and to deflect criticisms on specific, though minor, points. Nowhere in Britain's own implementation of the Final Act is there evidence of any ministry or government body which wanted to elevate the importance of the document by a specific attempt to implement it vigorously or imaginatively. No one seems to have felt that Britain's own implementation of Helsinki was a salient part of the issue.

The Final Act commits all the signatories to publish and disseminate the text in all states 'and make it known as widely as possible' (HMSO, 1975, p. 52). The government published the text as a Command Paper, and reprinted it in a later collection of documents (HMSO, 1977). It could never claim, however, to have given it much publicity. The FCO spent a certain amount of time discussing the dissemination of the Final Act and decided that beyond its general availability in libraries and as an official document, it would be too expensive to provide any sort of mass circulation – though there was an idea that it should be circulated in schools and colleges throughout the country. And there was no sympathy for the idea that a balanced summary could be produced that would be more easily accessible – the document was a carefully agreed text and should not be reinterpreted for the sake of brevity. So the Final Act has remained a piece of diplomatic record and has had a minimal impact on the informed public. Indeed, references to it in the British press since 1975 have concentrated so much on the basket III provisions that the Helsinki Declaration is widely interpreted as a provision only for human rights.

More significantly, Britain's implementation required the provision and disbursement of certain funds. The FCO allocated £100,000 annually in what was described as 'follow-up expenditure'. In the first year, 1976-7, only £44,000 of the sum was spent, though in subsequent years the total amount available was increased annually. By 1983-4 this amount had been increased to a figure of just over £190,000. Of this allocation, £128,000 (67 per cent of the total) is channelled through the British Council. £56,000 (29 per cent) is assigned to the existing funds for FCO cultural relations and just under £6,000 (3 per cent) goes to women's organizations.

In interviews FCO officials have argued, quite reasonably, that the money was only intended to initiate worthwhile projects that would eventually support themselves. They would, therefore, have to assess possible projects very carefully. They have also pointed out that the scope for financial action, particularly under basket III, was limited by the lack of suitable organizations in Britain that could facilitate exchanges and contacts with Eastern Europe. In communist countries the party organization can easily activate cultural groups, youth organizations, academic exchange schemes, and the like, and direct them centrally. In the case of Britain, however, there is no natural network of organizations that can be galvanized by an easy injection of cash, so it was not immediately obvious that British and East European government actions could be easily meshed.

Nevertheless, the total amount available must be regarded as small by any standards. In 1977-8 (when CSCE expenditure was most significant in view of the first review conference in Belgrade) Britain was spending over £2 million on cultural, scientific and educational exchanges with Eastern Europe, and increased that amount by only £43,500 of follow-up money – an increase of less than 2.5 per cent (House of Commons, Expenditure Committee, 1977, p. 9). The largest proportion of the total follow-up money has always been allocated to the British Council. This is not surprising, since the British Council is engaged in a good deal of the sort of work that falls under basket III and some of that under basket II. But from 1978 with the controversy surrounding the Central Policy Review Staff report on the administration of foreign policy, and the economic thrust of the Conservative government from 1979, the British Council has been subjected to a range of economic cuts and a curtailment of its work. Other small amounts of the follow-up money were given to selected organizations: an extra £6,000 to the British Youth Council, for instance; some extra funding to the GB/USSR Association, or the GB/East European Centre; and some funding for visits to Eastern Europe by officials of the Royal Society and the British Academy. The fate of this CSCE financial commitment is interesting, since the scale of activity involved is in marked contrast to the scale of activity that both politicians and officials seemed to have expected from Eastern Europe. Western spokesmen maintained that the Final Act was a political document, whereas the Soviets always stressed that, aside from the ten principles, the improvements that were required were overwhelmingly administrative. The pattern of expenditure undertaken by the British government rather supported the Soviet interpretation. There were no real initiatives, no significant organizations brought into being; a small amount of money was channelled through the existing system with the purpose of doing a little more of the same.

Implementing the Procedures of the CSCE

The second broad type of implementation that involved Britain was what could be described as the procedure of the diplomatic process. As in all other signatory states British decision-makers were committed to continuing participation in all of the various CSCE meetings. Certainly, no one was prepared to walk out, or bring the process to an end, and although there was a certain amount of diplomatic brinkmanship, not just by the two superpowers but also by states such as France, Romania and even Malta, everyone was prepared for a long haul and had accepted that dialogue would continue indefinitely. In this respect, at least, implementation was more tangible and the aims of foreign policy-makers clearer. Their responsibility was to take advice, collect information, co-ordinate their positions internally and with allies, and follow through the various conferences. In this category the concentration of implementation was on form rather than substance. And in this area of implementation it is clear that the form came to determine a great deal of the substance. Whereas the 'aims' of that part of the general CSCE policy dealing with Britain's own implementation were largely determined centrally, from the level of the working groups of the secret Cabinet committee on defence and overseas policy (Sims, 1983, pp. 107, 115) down to the level of the FCO; the aims of this part of the policy were determined very much by the actions of the negotiators themselves and the momentum of the talks. To a much greater extent this type of policy implementation was made from the bottom up.

For all that has been written about the CSCE very few accounts consider the actual negotiations that have taken place between the first Belgrade review conference through the interim specialist meetings, to the second, marathon review conference in Madrid and then the Security and Disarmament conference in Stockholm in 1984. Those studies that do exist almost always view the CSCE as a case study in bargaining theory (Holsti, 1982). Yet major elements of Britain's general CSCE policy were formulated in this procedural part of the implementation process.

The diplomatic procedures which were enacted by Britain were unexceptional and ran efficiently. The FCO established a CSCE Unit to co-ordinate its work and held a small programme of seminars with non-governmental organizations (NGOs) to prepare for the first review conference at Belgrade. The approach was a restrained one; FCO officials pointed out at such seminars that the CSCE must be seen in long-term perspective, and it would be a mistake to expect too much from the first review conference. The emphasis would be on tightening up the existing Final Act by introducing new proposals that would be more precise. The balance of new proposals would reflect the existing balance between the baskets of the original document. Nothing would be done to upset the carefully packaged principles of Helsinki, since they were still somewhat fragile. Nevertheless, officials at these seminars hoped for some modest but specific progress, particularly over CBMs and on some basket II issues. They acknowledged that human rights issues in basket III had become highly sensitive since 1975, but at one seminar in September 1977 made the point quite clearly that they did not intend to let Belgrade break down over such issues (unpublished memoranda, 1977-8).

In the event the Belgrade conference was a disappointment even by these modest standards (Edwards, 1978). The Eastern bloc was clearly on the defensive and was not forthcoming on the West's new proposals; Eastern countries tabled a number of larger, but vague, proposals of their own, on disarmament and environmental matters, and suggested more declarations of principle. The conference quickly became deadlocked. The US delegation launched a series of strong attacks on the human rights record of the East; the Western allies appeared somewhat embarrassed by this, but supported the leader of the US delegation, Arthur Goldberg – 'the unguided missile' as some journalists christened him – in his approach (Sherer, 1980). The NNA states became progressively more exasperated with the blocs as the conference appeared on the verge of collapse, and played a crucial role late in the proceedings to achieve at least a compromise communiqué. It was a short document which recorded that they had met, had disagreed and specified how the follow-up process would continue (HMSO, 1978b, pp. 52–3). In the interim between the Belgrade meeting in March 1978 and the opening of the second review conference in Madrid, in November 1980, there were three meetings of specialist working groups. In all cases these were held because of the specific insistence of particular delegations at Belgrade. The Scientific Forum in Hamburg was regarded as marginally useful but no one viewed any of them with much enthusiasm, and their communiqués (unpublished) reflected a series of generalized recommendations for Madrid.

By the time of the Madrid conference the British diplomatic machine was well prepared. Co-operation with allies was improved, there was agreement on how to handle human rights issues, and though the leaders of most major delegations were new (and generally more senior than their Belgrade counterparts), there was a good deal of Belgrade, and Helsinki, expertise in the FCO on which to draw. From the point of view of the FCO Madrid was a very well-prepared meeting, but it took place in a deteriorating climate of East–West relations. The agenda itself presented major problems. When they were solved, the conference proper opened to the accompaniment of Afghanistan and the Polish crisis, was bedevilled by accusations surrounding the discovery of Soviet submarines in Swedish waters, reached its crisis in 1982 as martial law was declared in Poland and, finally, concluded in public acrimony at Foreign Minister level over the Soviet destruction of Korean Airlines flight 007. In these circumstances political deadlock again arrived quickly (Skilling, 1981, pp. 11–13). The nub of the political problem was the old issue of reaching a deal between what the Soviets wanted for basket I and what the West regarded as acceptable in basket III. As such, Madrid proceeded much more as an East–West confrontation than had been the case at Belgrade. It was very obviously a barometer of the Cold War and yet, beneath the level of the political deadlock, more detailed work than might have been expected did eventually take place. In late 1982 when political discord seemed to jeopardize the whole affair, most of the detailed textual work was being done. Basket II issues in fact had been settled before the end of 1982 and merely waited to be slotted into an overall package. And in September 1983 when Madrid concluded, the results were not as meagre as might have been supposed; CBMs were extended to cover the whole of Europe, rather than only the borders. The West had inserted references, inevitably 'balanced' ones, to the rights of free trade unions and the Soviets had at last secured their CSCE European disarmament conference that had been little more than a negotiating ploy until the opening of Madrid. And here it was agreed that the conference would first discuss CBMs – close to the heart of the West – before going on to a second stage to discuss disarmament. Ironically, with the collapse of the Intermediate Nuclear Force Talks in Geneva in December 1983, and the doubts hovering over the other arms control talks as a result of the deployment of Cruise and Pershing missiles in Europe, the CSCE's Stockholm conference emerged as the only major forum for East–West security discussions. By default the CSCE process took centre-stage at the beginning of 1984, despite the fact that little of substance was expected from it.

On the face of it this outlines the story of a set of negotiations which became progressively divorced from political reality and in which British policy is not of great interest. In fact, however, the procedural implementation from Belgrade to Madrid produced a significant change of emphasis in the whole CSCE policy and became, to a large degree, the substance itself. This occured in two particular ways.

First, the development of European political co-operation among the members of the European community became increasingly important as the procedural implementation progressed. As Burrows and Edwards note (1982, p. 135) prior to 1975 Western co-operation was generally framed within the NATO grouping. Co-ordination at this stage, however, remained fairly general. European Community co-ordination became steadily closer, though, as the specifics of the Final Act were addressed. By the time of Belgrade the CSCE had become a perfect vehicle for the development of political co-operation. Ministers stressed the importance of maintaining it in their preparations for the conferences; and FCO officials called it, 'the fundamental work and the most systematic' of its co-ordination among the European Community, NATO, the Council of Europe and necessary bilateral contacts with other NNA states (House of Commons, Expenditure Committee, 1977, p. 14).

Co-ordination took place both through working groups operating under the Political Committee of the Nine, and through the work of DGI in the European Commission. At the conferences themselves co-ordination became part of the weekly routine. The Nine met regularly as first business of the day at least three times a week during conference sessions. At Belgrade this caused some friction between the Nine and those other non-Community members of NATO who became known as the 'outer Six', since NATO found it impossible to co-ordinate its approaches until the Community members had emerged from their early morning discussions. And within basket II and parts of basket III where direct Community policies were involved, DGI officials co-ordinated Community delegations and parcelled out the introduction of new proposals on a roughly equitable basis. This very cohesion among the Nine, however, was part of the reason why the overall Western approach at Belgrade became ragged. When Ambassador Goldberg began to attack the East over human rights, the embarrassment of the Western states was not so much because they disagreed with the tactic, but more that they had not taken a clear view within the Nine on this question and had allowed themselves to be cut off from a combative US delegation.

By the Madrid conference, Community–NATO co-ordination had improved considerably, though the structure of meetings remained generally the same. But Madrid revolved more around basket I, and hence issues more related to NATO's concerns: the US delegation, led by Max Kampelman, was in any case more in sympathy with Community attitudes, and political co-operation was by then a well-understood and efficient machine. This close co-operation did not prevent some intense annoyance in the community during February 1978 at the end of the Belgrade conference: the French delegation broke ranks and unilaterally submitted compromise proposals to try to break the deadlock over the concluding document, and began to support the principle behind the long-standing Soviet proposals for a European disarmament conference (Yost, 1982). At root, however, these were symbolic acts, undertaken for public consumption to accommodate some statesmanlike speeches by President Giscard. Such grand gestures made little difference to the development of co-operation. Similarly the high-level meetings of the European Council of Foreign Ministers (and the other regular Foreign Minister meetings) had little direct impact on co-operation. The Foreign Ministers discussed the CSCE in February 1977 but thereafter appear not to have considered it in any detail. French action in Zaire in April 1977 dominated their next meeting and the CSCE was subsequently pushed off the agenda.

In practice, political co-operation was a success because of the sheer intensity of the contacts at the detailed level. The draft proposals produced by the community group were solid enough to command respect and the wording would frequently carry not only other allies, but the NNA states as well. The existence of common 'community' interests, the intensity of contact, and the existence of a working secretariat in DGI, all made the Community the most powerful group in the negotiations (Lemaitre, 1977). None of this was inevitable; European political co-operation was a fledgling process in the mid-1970s (Arbuthnott and Edwards, 1979, pp. 167–72) and, as ministerial meetings repeatedly showed, was not guaranteed success over any issue. Whereas political co-operation in general was more procedural than substantive during the period, at the CSCE it was a reality and it had a significant impact on the course of the negotiations.

For Britain, this was unexpected. British diplomats did not anticipate being part of such a strong group. Co-operation was expected from the beginning, but largely within the framework of NATO and the more general interests of Atlantic relations. By the end of the Belgrade conference, however, with a US delegation that had a different set of priorities and East European contributions that were often unskilled, European political co-operation had clearly emerged as a major bonus for British policy, taking precedence over everything else – agreements with the East, the favour of the NNAs, the favour even of the other

NATO partners. One FCO official who was intimately involved in Helsinki and Belgrade commented in 1978 that the 'context of the Nine was absolutely basic to the positions we took'.

Secondly, and very much as a function of this situation, the negotiations from Belgrade to Madrid went increasingly in the West's direction. It was not just that the Soviet and East European governments became defensive after the Final Act was signed, nor that the general East–West conflict worsened, to provide an anti-Soviet backdrop to the negotiations. It was also the case that the Eastern states were consistently and significantly thwarted in negotiations. The very diplomatic success of the West contributed to a significant change of emphasis in British policy between 1975 and 1983.

The Final Act, as we have seen, was a laboriously constructed and carefully balanced document. Nevertheless, both in the scope of its coverage and in a great deal of the wording it employs, it favours the West, more particularly the West Europeans. Moreover, because of the very nature of the wording the Final Act is constantly subject to further reinterpretation. Unlike a treaty, its clauses do not always have a commonly understood meaning. And unlike a treaty, it did not spring from a positive sense of mutual advantage. It was part of a mutually advantageous package, but most of the rest of that package has now disappeared. The CSCE, therefore, is a dynamic rather than a stable arrangement and very much at the mercy of its immediate political environment. In this situation the West has relentlessly won the battle of reinterpretation. It turned the drafting of the Final Act to its own advantage – in the event, the Soviets paid a high price for their ten principles (Davy, 1980). The West ensured at Belgrade that assessments of implementation could not logically be curtailed and that the review process must continue. This does not mean that the East was bludgeoned into agreement – far from it. But the East was reduced to stalling, then trying to flood the conference with new proposals, then stalling again, then threatening a walk-out. The Soviet delegation in particular was outmanoeuvred by the way in which the Community states circulated draft agreements on which all but the Soviets, East Germans and Czechs could virtually agree. The West won the argument, though not the battle, as the Soviets were forced into simple obstruction, so that no substantive document was possible. At Madrid the East again had to agree to an open-ended conference and to argue its various interests in terms defined by the West. In the detail of the discussions the Eastern delegations did not display sufficient skill to gain anything, even intellectual satisfaction, from the process.

A major factor in the explanation of this was the greater degree of discretion and flexibility that Western delegations enjoyed. The review conferences took on lives of their own, appearing to be largely abstract battles of words and meaning. Western delegates were put on a long leash by their home governments, and in a forum where there was a generally high turnover of diplomatic personnel, certain figures who were permanent began to emerge with great authority and influence. As expectations that anything substantive would emerge from the whole process declined, so Western delegates exercised more freedom of manoeuvre. This too made it easier for the West Europeans to co-ordinate their proposals.

Both these developments – European Community solidarity and Western intellectual victories – contributed to a shift of emphasis in British policy. For success in the negotiations was unlikely to produce success in the real-world outcome of the process; the East would simply continue to be defensive and obstructive. After the disappointment of having nothing to show for all the effort at Belgrade, British policy became tougher in the approach to Madrid. There was a new, and more co-ordinated, emphasis on the need to stress human rights issues. Little was now expected from the process and there seems to have been a greater inclination in the Conservative government to use Madrid as a public forum. The role of the NNAs as mediators visibly declined at Madrid and the conference became far more a bipolar negotiation between the alliances. Having discovered that the process of negotiation had brought greater solidarity and skill, but not greater prospects of diplomatic success, there was a natural tendency for British policy to move in a more uncompromising direction. This also reflects a clarification of British policy aims in the CSCE. By the opening of Madrid the momentum of the diplomatic process had filtered out a number of possibilities. There would be no new initiatives (as the Soviets kept trying to introduce), but a constant attack on the definitional problems of the Final Act. European Community solidarity was a first priority; NATO solidarity was a close second. There would be no particular attempt to build political bridges by trying to involve the NNAs in the structure of European relations. If the Soviets would not co-operate within the rubrick of the Final Act and continued to defend themselves by recourse to inept propaganda, then the West would make political capital from it. On human rights issues at Madrid the British government (though not with the wholehearted support of the FCO) was prepared to name individuals and cases. This was something the delegation at Belgrade specifically had not done. Certainly, by 1981, in contrast to the attitude before the Belgrade conference, the government *would* have been prepared to see the process break down over human rights issues if the USSR was prepared to accept the onus of walking out. What, in effect, had happened in the policy–making process was that having been left to their own devices, the negotiators had fallen into a pattern which was favourable, though not in itself significant, to British diplomacy.

Implementing the Aims of the CSCE

Finally, let us turn to the business of implementing the formal purposes of Britain's CSCE policy: that of working to induce a change in attitudes and a growth of confidence between East and West in Europe. Clearly, this is different in kind to the other types of implementation we have examined. The first placed the emphasis on domestic, administrative action; the second on co-ordination and influence among allied delegations. This, however, emphasized the need to find ways of influencing unsympathetic states on a broad range of matters. It was obviously the least tangible area of implementation. Its lack of tangibility, however, is not a satisfactory explanation for its fate. How was it that the formal purposes of the CSCE policy became the least relevant objective?

First, let us consider how this objective might have been pursued. It would be naïve to suppose that merely quoting the Final Act at the Soviet and East European governments would have any marked effect on them. No British policy-makers ever felt that the posturing side of the policy would have any direct impact, though some NGOs who were consulted by the FCO seemed to hope that it might. Curiously the USSR appears to have pursued *its* CSCE implementation rather in this way. Unwilling to implement the CSCE domestically, being manipulated by the West in the diplomatic process, the Soviets appear to have resorted to a series of declarations about the CSCE which did not noticeably change until well into the Madrid conference when a disarmament session became a real possibility (Wood, 1979). The whole process in fact was too much at the mercy of the general East-West climate to be a political weapon in its own right. Brandishing the Final Act would achieve nothing outside one's own political community. How, therefore, is it possible to influence broad changes in behaviour through a vaguely worded agreement?

In so far as a British strategy of implementation did emerge for this side of policy it was articulated before the Belgrade review conference. It was a two-handed strategy, to hold to a restrained, realistic posture in the further negotiations, putting the onus always on the East to respond to specifics, while at the same time opening avenues of further communication – facilitating, as the Final Act indicates, the work of other organizations. This approach was clearly outlined, as we have seen, in the round of confidential meetings that the FCO had with NGOs before Belgrade. The intention of such meetings was to gather information and formulate specific proposals, while drawing the organizations into the process in the hope that they would also take their own initiatives identifying areas of mutual self-interest. In theory, this was a sensible way forward. In practice, the first half of the strategy changed and the second half faltered.

The aim of holding to a restrained position in the negotiations changed, as we have seen, through the exasperations of Belgrade. The fact that the West was clearly winning the arguments at Belgrade and that the USA was leading the chase, led to the breakdown of any hopes that East–West relations would move forward as a result of the conference. As an FCO official commented in 1979, Belgrade *did* fail as a negotiation because basket III issues were allowed to loom too large. This is not to say that the British approach became unrestrained after that. Clearly, it became tougher but was still concerned to be seen as realistic. As we have seen, however, the increasing success of the negotiators created a momentum which put the West on the offensive and which meant that they could keep the diplomatic process alive without taking any real risks. As Andrew Shonfield warned before the Belgrade conference; 'A no-risk, or even an obsessively low-risk, strategy, would just as effectively stultify the process that has been set in motion as a formal abrogation of the Helsinki Accord' (House of Commons, Expenditure Committee, 1977, p. 35). At the end of Belgrade this warning was echoed by an influential independent observer group, in its conclusion that the West 'should also look closely at the needs of the Soviet Union which could be accommodated' (Helsinki Review Group, 1978, p. 22).

As the Madrid conference became more East–West-oriented, so this trend continued. The irony of Madrid is that it *did* produce a result but, as in 1975, the Soviets may have paid a high diplomatic price for their disarmament conference. It remains to be seen whether the Soviets and East Europeans can define a specific self-interest in complying more closely with an increasingly 'Westernized' Final Act.

The second part of the strategy was always weaker in conception and appears simply to have run out of steam quite early. The scope for opening 'new avenues' was initially limited by the fact that the government took the view, from the top downwards, that the CSCE should not duplicate, and certainly not interfere with, the work of other organizations and negotiating structures. Thus before 1982, the CSCE Goronwy-Roberts, who opened the Belgrade conference for Britain repeated the FCO's insistence that disarmament and arms control questions were better dealt with elsewhere (HMSO, 1978b, p. 10; House of Commons, Expenditure Committe, 1977, p. 2). In 1980 Lord Carrington, as Foreign Secretary, was quite clear that nothing in Madrid could be allowed to interfere with the prospects of the MBFR talks (House of Commons, Foreign Affairs Committee, 1981, p. 4). Similarly the United Nations Economic Commission for Europe was seen as the most appropriate organization to handle most of the basket II issues (House of Commons, Expenditure Committee, 1977, p. 3), and the majority of new proposals made by Britain were channelled through that. Basket III was unique to the CSCE and, by nature, the hardest to monitor. Again, however, both the government and the FCO favoured reliance as far as possible on existing machinery. Routine monitoring took place through the FCO's standard communications network. There was no counterpart of the USA's special commission to monitor the CSCE process (US Congress 1978), though the FCO kept abreast with the vast amount of material which that commission produced and helped initiate, informally, the establishment of the independent Helsinki Review Group (1977), though this only operated on an *ad hoc* basis. Elsewhere on basket III the government was able in 1976 to conclude some reciprocal arrangements with the USSR concerning travel restrictions on journalists, and made some proposals to East European governments on travel and information issues, which in the event were not successful.

More significantly, there was no sustained attempt to galvanize NGOs into self-interested action on the CSCE. The small number of organizations directly concerned in basket III issues (that is, those which receive some money) are required to submit proposals for funding which the FCO will scrutinize. It has become uncommon for the FCO to initiate any new projects. On basket II issues, where a great many firms and organizations might have become involved, action was again limited. Some action was taken to brief regional chambers of commerce on the possible benefits of basket II. Most liaison, however, took place directly with the Confederation of British Industry. The Department of Trade should have been most directly concerned, but in practice DoT officials never saw Helsinki as a specific trade arrangement and preferred to view CSCE as a Foreign Office responsibility. The FCO had good liaison with the East European and Soviet Directorate in the CBI but, in truth, the CBI's contacts in Eastern Europe were (and are) better than most, and there was little the FCO could do for them. No financial sponsorship was made available to the CBI. The CBI acted as co-ordinator of British companies' reactions to East European conditions. In fact there was minimal interest among British companies. While the DoT and the FCO may have been lacklustre in their approach to this problem, they were clearly operating in difficult circumstances. Those British companies operating in the Eastern bloc produced specific complaints when directly asked to respond, but they did not complain individually before they were prompted. CBI officials understand as well as anyone else that Eastern Europe, in the words of one head of department, 'is a place for professionals only'. There are many problems for Western businesses in trading with Eastern Europe: having to deal through the official foreign trade organization, the lack of access to end-users, the lack of accurate information, and so on (Business International SA, 1979). It is not an environment for the fainthearted, the impatient, or the poorly financed business concern. The Final Act, it was argued, would be of little practical help either to those who already do, or those who will never, trade with Eastern Europe. Contacts between the FCO and the CBI, therefore, seem to have been only marginally useful to either of them.

This, then, provides us with a clearer idea of why implementing the CSCE in relation to changing conditions in the East has been so unsuccessful. It was, from the outset, the hardest part of the 'CSCE policy' for Britain, and results in this direction have been negligible. The Final Act has not proved to be a framework for political evolution, since it is at the mercy of other political forces. Nor has it been a codification of existing practice, since practice differs from state to state in Europe and over time. There is no consistent trend of behaviour in relation to any of the baskets. Our analysis suggests, however, that the failure, to date, is not solely because the task was difficult, but also because that part of the policy was carried out on too narrow a basis. The objective of modifying Eastern behaviour took second place to the objective of out-negotiating the East, and the need to open up new avenues of co-operation conflicted with a natural bias to maintain existing structures of contact. Above all, there was never a perception that Britain, or the West, should modify its own behaviour in any significant way. As negotiations have proceeded this has come to seem even less necessary.

Conclusion

Whether or not the CSCE is judged to be a diplomatic success, it is a fascinating example of the politics of policy implementation, since it raises the issue in a number of different contexts: domestic implementation; procedural processes; in relation to allies; and in relation to non-allied governments. The very ambiguity of the original commitment, the Final Act, has meant that CSCE policy is largely being made in the process of implementation. However meagre its results appear, it provides a very good example of a case of 'policy process' as opposed to 'decision-making' in the more traditional sense. The analysis suggests both methodological and substantive conclusions.

In terms of methodology the CSCE raises some important questions. On an issue that has seemed to revolve more around diplomatic form than political substance it is easy to confuse description with explanation. Once we have described Britain's attitude to the negotiations, we have, we may feel, explained the outcome of them, since the results of the CSCE are generally intangible. But this does not explain why the 'British attitude' took the form it did. British CSCE policy since 1975 spans four administrations, three Prime Ministers and five Foreign Secretaries. Who, then, was determining the attitude over time? Who determined the degree of priority to be accorded the CSCE at any given juncture? More particularly, could it have been different? When we consider the different implementation demands made by the Final Act, it is clear that its applicability is potentially very wide. yet it was implemented very narrowly. Why? The usual answer is that it was so vaguely worded and such a lowest common denominator between different interests that nothing else was possible (Geusau, 1978). But vagueness and compromise does not, in itself, prevent action, say, within NATO or the European Community. In those arenas a great deal of action flows from vaguely worded declarations. Why should not the Final Act have been viewed as a great opportunity for self-interested initiatives? Why was the British foreign policy–making machine, as a mechanism, prepared to settle for minimal results? To answer these sorts of question we have to analyse the implementation of the policy.

Turning to substantive issues, several answers suggest themselves. First, the general aims of Britain's CSCE policy were always relatively ambiguous. There was no single aim because it was, of necessity, not a single policy, but a mixture that was drawn not just from different areas of activity (culture, trade, defence) but which required a range of implementing activities (co-ordination, financial disbursement, conference diplomacy, publicity). The CSCE was, intellectually, always the poor relation of successive governments' arms control or détente policies. This meant that particular choices between one political priority and another were being made at a fairly low level in an incremental process that was concerned more with co-ordination than initiation.

Secondly, the formal stucture of the policy-making machine for the CSCE was narrow. The vast majority of CSCE work was done by the FCO in consultation with the Cabinet Office. The MoD and DoT were also involved, though not as extensively. The range of NGOs that became involved was also very small. The FCO made efforts to include a cross section of relevant NGOs, but the number was never great. The organizational structure of the policy was thus highly centralized around the FCO. This made for efficient liaison, both domestically and internationally, but the FCO never saw its role as being more than that of liaison. In theory, initiatives were supposed to arise elsewhere.

Thirdly, however, initiatives seldom did arise from elsewhere. There was no organization either in or out of government that galvanized others into action. There was no organization – and for that matter no individual politician – whose fate was bound up with the outcome of the CSCE. The determination of the FCO from very early in the game to work through existing channels and organizations merely added a residual responsibility to a number of bureaucrats whose main function was to do something else. The CSCE, therefore, had no institutional backers.

Fourthly, within the structure of CSCE policy, patterns of behaviour favoured the formally diplomatic over the practical. This was partly because the FCO, rather than any other department, was at the centre of the process, and partly because the whole CSCE had grown up as a diplomatic initiative which branched out into other areas – rather than growing from activity in other areas which required diplomatic co-ordination. Also because the areas of potential interest were so wide and Britain – whether in the context of the European Community or NATO –.

had to work in a large multilateral forum, the task of co-ordination became an end in itself. It was both time-consuming and difficult to harmonize the interests of even close allies. Since allied unity always assumed first priority in the minds of policy-makers, a co-ordinated negotiating draft was, in itself, a mark of success. As we have seen, this became the key to achieving diplomatic success which in fact may have inhibited progress in other fields. And where practical action was required and undertaken, it was generally administrative rather than overtly political.

Fifthly, the view of both politicians and officials was that the CSCE was a barometer of the Cold War. It grew out of a particular optimistic era of détente, it became acrimonious when the optimism wore off and became deadlocked when détente was at a standstill. This, of course, is understandable, but again is not inevitable. Other negotiations find themselves shielded from the public hurly-burly of East–West relations, sometimes on the ground that they are too important to suffer, as was the case in the SALT process during the mid-1970s, or on the ground that they are involved in specific, detailed work among experts, as until 1983 was the case in the MBFR talks. The CSCE, however, met neither of these requirements. Moreover, because the CSCE was based essentially on a negotiation between blocs, the prevailing view of policy-makers seemed to be that it always *would* be a barometer of relations. Where that expectation exists, it becomes the reality.

None of this is an attempt to judge whether Britain's CSCE policy has been good or bad, successful or not. Some would argue that it has been 'good' policy but not 'successful', because it was never intended to be a success. Others argue that it has been as 'successful' as the circumstances could have allowed. Others argue that it has been 'bad' policy and hence unsuccessful, because it has not been able to escape from its Cold War context. We have not tried to evaluate policy in this way here, but rather to explain it from the implementation perspective. We are concerned with how the aims, the priorities and the expectations of the policy were evolved in the process of implementing it. In a case such as this there was never a point at which Britain decided to 'have' a policy of a certain type. We have used the Final Act as our reference point. This was a foreign policy commitment into which Britain entered and its subsequent policy was largely determined by the gradual and incremental way in which it honoured that commitment. None of this changes the result but it helps to explain it.

Note: Chapter 8

I am grateful to all the people both inside and outside government who granted me interviews during the research for this chapter, and to Jane Brooks and Michael Lydon for their research assistance.

9
Conclusion

Michael Clarke and *Steve Smith*

The Implementation Perspective

Nothing that happens in foreign policy is inevitable. Studies in foreign policy behaviour, however, are retrospective and in retrospect it seems easier to attribute a great deal of foreign policy behaviour to the problem of 'limited options', or even 'no options'; to stress, in other words, the constraining nature of the international environment in which foreign policy is played out. Indeed, many traditional explanations of foreign policy define the international environment as that which makes foreign policy distinctive – operating, as it does, in a state of essential anarchy. Thus, it is argued, the foreign policy of a state can be compared to a hand of cards that have to be played out to best advantage in an international arena where mistakes are heavily punished. There is a tendency, in other words, not to consider the messy problems of foreign policy implementation too carefully. The special nature of the 'international environment' is sufficient explanation for the obvious difficulties of carrying a policy through.

The analysis of implementation does not dispute the reality that foreign policy takes place in a constraining environment. But it does emphasize the need to explain more precisely how those constraints operate in a given case. As we pointed out in Chapter 1, there is a gap in the literature on foreign policy analysis between policy *outputs* and real-world *outcomes*. Where outputs and outcomes are not consistent, we tend to look back at the decision-*taking* stage and conclude that the policy-makers must have misperceived the real nature of the issue, or the real nature of the world, and hence made poor decisions. In our implementation analysis, however, we have tried to look specifically at the relationship between outputs and outcomes in various circumstances not just to fill the gap, but to throw a different light on the whole business of foreign policy and the assumptions we make about analysing it. Implicit in this focus too is an attempt to evaluate policy more carefully. As Jenkins points out, a consideration of the politics of implementation raises all the issues concerning policy objectives, expectations, means, measurements of success, and so on; all the matters (usually left implicit) on which an evaluation of policy is based (Jenkins, 1978, p. 203). We are not trying here to outline specific criteria of evaluation, but we recognize that all of our questions are implicitly evaluative.

We deliberately chose a wide range of cases, all within the Western world – where policy-making is both more complex and more consequential – and allowed contributors a wide brief within a very general framework. Five of our cases concern state-centred foreign policy in three different states, and two cases concern multilateral policy-making that is less state-centric. Our cases range from the exclusively unilateral (the hostage rescue attempt) to the deliberately multilateral (the European Community). They range from intensely centralized decision-making structures (the White House at the end of Vietnam) to highly decentralized ones (in the case of making international economic policy). And they cover the range of policy instruments: from using brute military force, to take hostages that could not be negotiated to safety; to symbolic and coercive military force, to impress adversaries in North Vietnam or in Africa; to economic measures, both as direct sanction and subtle pressure; to pure diplomatic persuasion and domestic administration, in the form of conference diplomacy. In every case the importance of the international environment of those policies is reaffirmed. But it is reaffirmed in ways which give us a greater insight into the discrepancies between policy outputs and outcomes. The implementation perspective, even over this range of cases, offers some interesting *explanations* about foreign policy as *behaviour*.

This question, of course, has been tackled before in another attempt to account for the difficulties in carrying out policy. The work of Allison (1971), and the related approaches in foreign policy analysis which stemmed from it, laid great stress on the problems of bureaucracy and organization. Whereas the traditionalists had laid stress upon the nature of the international environment as sufficient explanation for policy limitations, a new wave of analysts now concentrated on the performance of the foreign policy machine, as management, as a key explanation of why there was such an apparent gap between outputs and outcomes. Allison's 'bureaucratic politics' hypothesis was a persuasive, though limited, explanatory device and he may have backtracked a little by 1976 in placing greater emphasis on the more obvious proposition that 'organization matters' (Allison and Szanton, 1976, pp. 3–23). A major debate has occurred in fact around the perspectives advanced by Allison (Smith, 1981). As Goldstein points out (p. 55), a fierce argument rages over the US failure in Vietnam: was the policy intellectually wrong, or did it fail because the bureaucratic system did not implement it properly? These are interesting questions but they are not exhaustive ones. A concentration on Allison is a concentation on bureaucracy as the key variable in foreign policy implementation, and this rather misses the point (Jenkins and Gray, 1983, pp. 185–90). For as our studies here demonstrate, there is a more subtle relationship between outputs and outcomes of a foreign policy machine. To attribute foreign policy failures only – or even chiefly – to bureaucratic and organizational malfunctions makes too many assumptions about the rest of the process: that there *was* a decision of some sort that required organizational action; that the decision was inherently capable of being carried out; that someone powerful wanted it to happen; and so on. Our cases demonstrate that these are hardly universal truths. In one of our cases, the American attempt to rescue the hostages, there was a clear decision – indeed, a desperate throw that would either succeed or fail, and which failed because of the way in which it was carried out. The British attempt to impose economic sanctions on Rhosesia was also clear enough in itself, though the aims were rather more broad. In all other cases under discussion a direct causal relationship between decision and action is not present. We are not examining *a* decision, or even a single, discrete policy, which was implemented either well or badly. Rather we are examining the way in which the implementation process *is* the decision process to a greater or lesser extent. Even in the one clear case of decision as the direct cause of action, Smith finds that the implementers (the military) did not in fact directly do anything wrong. They kept to the plan in so far as it existed. The events which brought disaster resulted from factors which were simply not foreseen in the original policy. So the 'decision' to attempt the rescue is not the same thing as the plan to employ eight helicopters, train in a certain way, decentralize command, and so on. Decisions on such key aspects of the plan that was to be 'carried out' were themselves decided in the process of implementation.

In this perspective, therefore, we are concerned with something more than organizational failures. We are trying to occupy an ill-defined intellectual area between the more traditional assumptions of rational actor behaviour, with its concentration on decision-making, and the analysis of foreign policy chiefly as an organizational system, with its concentration on (usually American) bureaucracy. In the introductory chapter we tried to clear the ground by defining three areas which implementation studies emphasize: the nature of decision, the characterization of the international environment as an arena of policy implementation and the question of types of control which foreign policy-makers can exercise within that environment. On the evidence of the studies in this volume we return to these questions, though not as separate issues. They are all clearly interdependent, so let us reconsider them as such by attacking some of the important issues which these studies have suggested.

The Implementation Environment

First, let us consider what it is about the international environment that makes policy implementation so difficult. The answer is not as obvious as it seems. The traditional view is that the international environment is lacking in order and authority. The lack of *authoritative* international institutions is regarded as important; governments are seen as acting as essentially single entities in the international sphere, enhancing a distinction between the stable institutions of government and the transitory and subordinate institutions of the international system. Governments must ultimately rely on self-help and cannot engage in the form of role specialization which makes domestic society integrative. The international system, because it does not perform in this integrative way, is traditionally seen as being uniquely competitive and challenging to the authority of governments. Foreign policy is thus more difficult to formulate and implement with any consistency, so it is in the very nature of the international environment that the problems arise. This, however, is not a satisfactory assumption from which to begin, for there is a tendency to overdraw the distinction between international and domestic society.

This assumption has behind it the shadow of 'last resort', that is, 'in the final analysis governments must stand alone/acknowledge no higher authority, etc.'. But students of foreign policy are no more preoccupied with last resorts than anyone else. After all, in the last resort governments can, and have, made war on substantial proportions of their own populations. It is interesting to note that in Hood's conclusion (1976, p. 192) on the limits of administration in a domestic context he comments that; 'The degree of hostility in the environment is the key factor.' He certainly does not interpret the domestic environment as necessarily consensual. More specifically, foreign policy is conducted at a number of institutional levels in the international world – the governmental, the private and public transnational, and the international organizational. It is clear also that governments have a fair amount of discretion in choosing which institutional level to employ, or intervene in, or refrain from intervention in, as they perform their functions. The *Yearbook of International Organization* records that in 1981 there were just under 7,000 inter- or non-governmental organizations operating in the international arena. While few would argue that the state is rendered obsolete by this fact, it nevertheless indicates that behind the rhetoric of statehood and sovereignty governments have powerful interests in *not* asserting final authority over their environment and in encouraging high degrees of predictability in international behaviour. Just as in the domestic sphere, governments are both more and less powerful given the range and complexity of modern political organization, and must establish predictable relations with other governments and with the network (or morass) of institutionalized, organizational behaviour. Assertions of sovereign authority are much more a characteristic of weak governments than strong ones in international relations.

Then too there is a much greater degree of role specification in the international world than most traditional views of foreign policy imply. There is obvious role specification among various international organizations, and hierarchical orders between them. But governments do not have to perform a complete range of functions which keeps them 'in the final analysis' politically self-sufficient and therefore an autonomous entity, even though in some cases they may try to. It is normally sufficient that they regard the functions performed by other organizations as, at least, not incompatible with their purposes and hence are able to coexist with most of them without having to battle for authority.

On this general point, therefore, we may question the degree to which the international environment is really different from the domestic one as an arena of implementation.' And as four of our seven cases (on sanctions, the CSCE, European Community policy and economic policy-making) make clear, the implementation process must involve a mixture of domestic and international, public and private institutions. In these areas of policy implementation the distinction between domestic and international environments really is not very important. It assumes an importance in our two cases involving the USA, but both policies were enacted in a situation of overt and recognized conflict. Clearly, if we are searching for the magic ingredient which makes the international environment a uniquely difficult arena of implementation, it is not to be found in traditional assumptions of 'anarchy' or 'disorder'. Even if we assume a significantly greater *degree* of disorder in the international environment, our cases indicate that we need to explain 'disorder', and so on, in more specific terms.

If disorder is an obstacle to implementation, then it is not because it stems from necessarily antagonistic views among participating actors. It is more that the nature of their policy environment is made up of a complex mixture of different types of actor and agency. Compared to the scale of the problem that Tooze outlines, for instance, the number of people who make decisions directly about the global economy is extremely small. The same is true of the European Community, even more so of NATO. Yet in all three cases that small number of people represents a highly complex mixture of types of agency, all with their own structures, legal requirements and special interests. It may be that there is a unanimous consensus among the policy-makers in the global economic regime that world growth is a necessity and should be made the chief aim. There may well be a near-unanimous consensus on how to achieve it: that certain countries should reflate faster than others and, if necessary, incur a deficit. But as Tooze makes clear, a high degree of consensus still leaves the problem of working through national financial agencies, private financial organizations (both national and multinational) and different types of international institutions who all have differing responsibilities. In other words, it is not 'disorder', in the sense of overt disagreement or the possibility of conflict as a last resort that is the problem, so much as sheer complexity and marginally differing priorities among a morass of different organizations (Dawson, 1979).

In saying this we are not trying to wish away genuine conflicts of interest or differences in ideology between states. Certainly, the international environment is rent with conflicts of interest and many policies cannot be pursued simply because of the opposition of other actors. By and large, however, states do not aim their particular policies at unyielding opposition. They may harbour aspirations, say, to break down the cohesion of the Eastern bloc, or to destroy the force of apartheid in Southern Africa, but these are not normally particular policies. A particular policy may be to support sanctions, to offer economic rewards, or to score diplomatic and propaganda victories – all with mixed aims and multiple purposes. The point is that while the policy may be *generally* directed at the source of overt opposition, it will only be a policy of *action*, in so far as it tries to do something much nearer to home. It will proceed through certain agencies wherein some general consensus exists that the action is desirable and technically possible.

It is here that we see the real nature of the international system as the constraining arena of policy implementation. In Chapter 1 we referred to the metaphor of decision 'coalitions' being more useful than that of 'chains of command'. This is true of all policy-making, even in the case of the military. In other words, to pursue a policy the initiator must build and maintain over time a coalition of implementing agencies who will accord an appropriate priority to that policy in some meaningful way (Dunsire, 1978a, pp. 124–31). It may be necessary to get one agency to agree to add another function to its workload, another to make itself primarily responsible for the necessary action, another to change the way in which it has been doing something, another to stop performing one of its usual functions, and so on; and to continue to do these things, probably for an unspecified period. Central policy-making, of course, may be more like a chain of command at the level at which it operates. All the cases we have studied contain an element of central decision-making, where key policy-makers such as the French President, senior White House staff, the British Cabinet or the Treasury have made broad political decisions – sometimes analytically, other times incrementally. In such cases it is clear that formal authority does matter and due deference is paid to it. As Farrands pointed out, for example (p. 77), President Giscard took a personal interest in France's African policies and consciously tried to redirect them in the mid-1970s with a series of measures that he was able, with his authority, to initiate. But like all policies that are initiated or redirected 'from above', they very quickly require specification and redefinition by other agencies. Giscard's redirected policy required changes in a number of economic and cultural agencies to give it effect. Once we think of policy at this first remove from overall authority, the chain of command metaphor increasingly gives way to that of the 'coalition'.

So the focus of our interest as students of policy implementation is on the way in which agencies can be aggregated to perform a policy in the international arena. Clearly, the international environment increases the diversity between agencies whose co-operation is required. Even in our simplest case involving the US attempt to rescue their hostages, Smith reveals that it was necessary to compromise and balance agencies *within* the US military in order to construct the operation (p. 28). Simply issuing orders, even to your own military, is no guarantee of action. As the studies by Tooze and by Allen and Byrne also make clear, the international agencies involved in more common concerns of foreign policy are not only diverse in representing public and private interests, different cultural values, and so on, but they also exist, as it were, in a vertical plane; a multinational agency may try to co-ordinate the work of a group of national agencies, who in turn are partly dependent on other multinational agencies, working at a deeper level of detail. Added to this, as both chapters demonstrate, is the fact that some of the implementing agencies are working explicitly on behalf of an international structure or regime, others are national agencies having an involvement in the structure, while still others will be national organizations whose actions simply happen to affect the structure. Complexity, therefore, more than hostility, characterizes the problems of aggregating agencies in the international arena.

This is hardly surprising, but it has important implications for our study of policy implementation, and the way in which we explain the discrepancies between what policy-makers say they are doing and what is actually achieved. For one thing, it emphasizes the transitory nature of most international implementation coalitions. It is not that agreement deliberately dissolves over time but more that priorities change, and shifts in policy are generated frequently by low-level agencies. In effect, decisions are constantly having to be remade, bureaucratic and ideological resources have to be rededicated, and with each renewal the policy evolves in a modified direction. As we see in the case of Britain's CSCE policy (p. 154), and in relation to the European Community (p. 136), the 'remaking' of decisions at successive stages alters the emphasis on what is possible and achievable at a given moment. This is often referred to as the 'feedback loop' in decision-making analysis; the process by which policy-makers observe the effects of their policy in the real world and modify it as they learn. But the process should be characterized more subtly than this. For 'learning' in policy-making can be either an expansive or a narrowing and reinforcing process (Steinbruner, 1974, pp. 136-8). And our analysis indicates that if dissolving implementation coalitions *are* a key determinant in policy evolution, then the learning process is more likely to be narrowing rather than expansive. For the apparent failure of a policy may not be because it is intrinsically impossible, or unacceptable to the outside world, but because the coalition of domestic and foreign organizations necessary for its implementation did not hold together long enough. In short, we should try to distinguish between a failure of the structure and a failure of the policy. They are not the same, and it is useful to recognize that governments often accept the failure of the former as an indication of the failure of the latter. Our examination of the CSCE, for instance, suggests that a good deal more could have been done to give a higher priority to the official aims of Britain's policy. The British government seems to have started with a reasonably open mind on the possibility that the CSCE could make some difference to East–West relations, but the coalition of domestic and foreign implementing agencies necessary to carry this overall policy out was never constructed deliberately or maintained systematically. Within a year the coalition that mattered was that between the Foreign Ministries of the European Community states and the Commission; the British government 'learned' that little was to be expected in future, only the detail of the CSCE could be successfully pursued, and Community solidarity was crucial to the achievement of anything. Or again, over Rhodesia, the coalition of implementing agencies that was necessary to carry through an effective oil sanction included the British services, foreign government agencies, British and multinational oil companies, and many British government diplomatic agencies. As White shows (p. 48), the policy was redefined to achieve little more than symbolic purposes. The government 'learned' from it that there was little it could do to prevent oil reaching Rhodesia. This too is questionable. There were many possible ways in which Rhodesia could be denied oil – there was an overwhelming international consensus that it should be. The coalition of agencies simply did not operate as an effective force; as time went on without a result the government's ideological commitment to the policy became tepid as it weighed the costs and it increasingly allowed the implementation agencies to define the chief purpose of the policy, which was not action but posture.

There is, therefore, a necessary interaction between governmental priorities and the transitory nature of many implementing agency coalitions. Just as longstanding coalitions that handle routine policy are difficult to break when a government wants to do something different, so they are equally difficult to assemble and maintain in a new configuration unless a government is able to sustain an active high priority – *and pay the necessary price for it.* Where foreign and multinational agencies must be involved in any coalition, it is unlikely that appeals to common values will be sufficient to sustain action.

Our awareness of this also helps to explain why so much of the international arena is characterized by declaratory policies. One of the noticeable differences between foreign and domestic policy is the greater intangibility of foreign policy. This is not because things do not happen in the international arena – clearly, they do. But foreign policy is not directly concerned with the production of goods and services, or transfer payments for redistributive purposes, or with the business of maintaining and controlling large populations. It may be designed to facilitate other policies which do perform such tasks, and as most of our cases show, there is a shifting boundary between foreign and domestic concerns, but Foreign Ministries do not rank among the big spenders, or the big employers, in any government. It is hard to characterize the precise nature of foreign policy work in the way that other categories of governmental activity can be defined. So students of foreign policy tend to fall back again on implicit assumptions about the international environment, and say that because action is often not possible, declarations must be made and a game of posturing is played. We could also understand such posturing, however, not just as a substitute for action – though it often is – but also as an attempt to establish procedures on which coalitions of various implementing agencies could be built. The complexity to which we have referred means that most international structures, or arrangements to make up a regime, are likely to be in the process of change. So declarations and posture statements are often an attempt to indicate commitment or to renew the cement which is holding a particular coalition together. In other words, the international arena demands a great deal of purely procedural foreign policy work; not directed at adversaries, or those who simply disagree with a policy, but at client and sympathetic agencies, both domestic and foreign, in order to create an environment favourable to their co-operation. Tooze, Allen and Byrne, and Clarke (pp. 113, 128, 160) are acutely aware of this phenomenon. In the situations they examine governments are clearly not themselves competent to carry out the actions that are implied in most of their policies. Much of their activity, therefore, is devoted to try to create the conditions in which those agencies which are competent to affect practical outcomes can operate, and operate in some way *together* against the grain of their more established routines.

Characterizing Decisions in Foreign Policy

These ideas also offer ways of explaining a second major issue in policy implementation – the degree of clarity there is in anything we define as a decision, or choice. Given that we are examining the relationship between policy outputs and actual outcomes, it is important that we do not assume that there is always a discrepancy because implementation, in some sense, fails to work. As we pointed out, we are trying to define the ways in which implementation may affect the whole policy process: not just explaining how policy is or is not carried out, but also the more routine process by which the outcome – the implementation – *is* the policy.

We have characterized the international arena as one of great complexity because of the range of different agencies which bear on any issue. In this situation there is a natural tendency for decision-makers to favour policies that seem consistent with established routines and stable structures of co-operation; to be cautious, above all to take short-term views. Another expression of this complexity is in the concept of interdependence. The range of organizations which have an involvement in international arrangements is such that there is a high cost involved to any actor in trying to withdraw from, or rupture, the arrangement. It is one of the ironies of interdependence that while this well-recognized phenomenon poses problems of an acutely international nature, it nevertheless encourages governments to dash for short-term, national, even xenophobic, solutions.

It is possible to define a relationship between decision and outcome, then, which is not quite 'incremental policy evolution' nor simply 'feedback and learning', but something more interesting and less deliberate. Many foreign policy decisions are performing a range of functions other than initiating action. That is, what the analyst characterizes as a 'decision' for the purpose of defining a governmental choice – such as Nixon's decision to 'pressure' Hanoi (p. 63), Giscard's decision to initiate a new approach to French African diplomacy (p. 76), or the case of many European political co-operation decisions (p. 131) – is actually a mixture of policy directives, some of which cannot be implemented, others of which can only be implemented through a small number of agencies to a limited extent and still others of which implement themselves. To the extent that a government may want to announce its preferences in making public its decision to do something this part of the decision is self-implementing. This was an integral part of the decision that White analyses, for instance (p. 34). A good many decisions fall into this category (Anderson, 1979). To the extent that the decision implies long-term action taken within the international community, such as the decision to lead a universal boycott against Rhodesia, it was incapable of implementation. As it turned out, the 'international community' – governments, organizations, public and private companies – was simply too complex to be effectively organized to this end, even though there was a strong consensus in favour of the British government's position on this issue. To the extent that some of a decision *is* implementable it will normally be through national agencies operating on a short-term basis. Thus, over Rhodesia, Britain was able to initiate a boycott using its military, its trade ministry and its diplomatic network. But as White also makes clear (p. 38), it was unsure how this boycott would really work, what would be its effects, or how long it would last.

In effect, then, we can see a range of purposes involved in any recognizable decision. We can also see that the components of a decision demand implementation at different specific levels. The self-implementing declaration, paradoxically, is the most specific. When it is declared, it is enacted. And it may be that the least specific part of the decision is that which seems to initiate action, for it will be action demanded of national, and controllable, agencies. It will set them, by an exercise of central authority, to do something, and have to rely on them to build the coalitions of other agencies that are necessary to have an impact or an outcome. Central decision-makers cannot know much about how the agencies near them will perform in relation to other agencies further away. They have to wait and see. So a decision may be clear and centralized in terms of its declaratory purposes, but quite decentralized in terms of its requirement for action. At this level it may in fact be a decision to let the implementation agencies make the policy, to define its purposes and its priorities. The less specific the action component of a decision, the more the implementing agencies – pushed by their superiors to act in *some* way – will define the scope and strength of the action itself. As Allen and Byrne conclude (p. 141), the European Community has proved more effective at implementing the detail of specific intergovernmental policies than the broader objectives it was designed to pursue. And the 'Community policy' of its member states is made more by what the Community actually does than by what national decision-makers, somewhat vaguely, hope or intend it will do.

Defining Control in Foreign Policy

This introduces a further issue into our perspective, which is to define more clearly the strengths and weaknesses of governmental control over its foreign policy. Building on our previous conclusions, it appears that there is a large gap between the organizational structures that governments require to control the implementation of policy and those which they generally have. This too helps account for the prevalence of declarations and short-term actions with limited prospects.

We have stressed the decentralized, and shifting, nature of the international environment as an arena of policy implementation, and the need to build and maintain coalitions of agencies within it. Yet the foreign policy-making structures of all the states under discussion here are highly centralized. Outside the Western world this is even more the case. Given that we assume that authority and 'chains of command' only go so far in promoting implementation, the fact that centralized foreign policy structures are trying to operate in a decentralized environment poses some interesting issues of control. It is not difficult to explain why foreign policy organizations tend towards centralization. For one thing, foreign policy is normally an executive prerogative and surrounded by the symbolism and secrecy of national security. More significantly, it is important to have a fairly tightly structured liaison system, where interdependent foreign policies involve so many public and private, domestic and foreign, organizations. When Britain's foreign policy machine was last under the microscope in the mid-1970s, the logic of the problems it faced was that either the Foreign Office should be very big to cover all areas of government, or very small to liaise effectively between them. There is a logic to centralization at the decision-making level, but this may tend to conflict with the requirements of implementation in a complex environment. As the studies of the economic system and the European Community show, things which *are* done, either as routine or agreed policy, are done in a decentralized way. Similarly Farrands shows how a highly centralized foreign policy machine, working through unitary, national agencies (the military and other ministries) in an environment where opposition was no match for French resources, nevertheless was blown off course by the sheer complexity of its more particular aims and the volatility of local African politics. Clarke is concerned to point out how the very centralization of the implementation structure for Britain's CSCE policy led to a highly conservative attitude, and low expectations for the policy, on an issue which required above all else a large measure of decentralized action if it was to fulfil any of its declared aims.

What does this discrepancy imply about the process of policy control? For one thing, it is clear that control works differently even within unitary organizations close to the policy-making centre. The military is a classic case. Most military establishments have a single basic structure, understood rules and the coercive ability to make them stick. Yet as Smith indicates, directing 'the military' to perform a particular task is not just a matter of giving an order. Bargaining, co-ordination and liaison all have to take place at every level at which 'the military' operates. The military can be provided with advice, but may have to be persuaded to take it; it can be ordered to work through certain channels, but may have to be bullied into them; and so one. Mere involvement of key decision-makers in the military machine counts for nothing, for specialist expertise soon begins to operate and decision-makers find themselves involved in the bargaining games that are endemic in all big organizations. Indeed, it is surprising that decision-makers continue to display so consistent a belief in the superior powers of military establishments to implement policy. This is understandable, since military structures are essentially unitary, close to government and susceptible to authoritative direction. But if this makes them a good bet for taking orders, it does not mean they are automatically competent to carry them out. American policy-makers in the attempted rescue of the hostages were partly manipulated by the lower-level activities of the military establishment they directed; French policy vainly placed a great deal of faith on the ability of its military to perform a complex politico-strategic role in Africa; and Nixon and Kissinger continued to believe that efficient military action could be sustained merely by issuing secret and personalized orders to particular sections of the armed forces. In all of these cases the policy-makers had insufficient control over the outcomes of their preferred policies. However decisive their individual choices appeared to be – even rational or analytical in terms of being consciously made – key areas of their policy was being made for them because of the sheer inability of individuals to control the way in which large organizations go about their business.

Structures of authority, then, are less relevant to control than organizational characteristics (Hood, *et al.*, 1979). The business of characterizing organizations is still in its infancy (Hood and Dunsire, 1981). Nevertheless, it alerts us to the fact that there are many different techniques of control which may be required even within a single organization. Some of these too have been pursued in the literature of policy analysis (Dunsire, 1978b; Hood, 1976, pp. 118–33). If we translate these ideas to the international level, the problems of control become extremely acute, for one is searching for ways of offering a mixture of rewards, incentives, threats, appeals to values, or whatever, in order to hold coalitions together in some sort of structure.

Moreover, because of the centralization of foreign policy machinery, this is normally being done at second hand or through an intermediary, perhaps another ministry or a private company. Whereas in, say, fiscal policy the government's agent, in the form of the revenue service, can directly affect the targets of the policy, in foreign affairs this is seldom the case even where the target may be a domestic organization. The political seniority of a Foreign Ministry, or of a Cabinet or presidential system, is therefore not a true measure of its implementing power, unless it can translate such seniority into an ability to sustain diverse coalitions. As we have argued, giving orders is not enough even in the case of the military. And if we consider other traditional policy instruments – economic, interventionist, diplomatic, propagandist – it is even more the case that policy works through intermediaries. The general literature of international politics still acknowledges the relevance of 'power' as a central concept in the relations between states, and these policy instruments are the means of exercising power. Yet all of these instruments have to be exercised, to a greater or lesser extent, at second hand. There are few economic levers a government itself can pull directly against another state; intervention and propaganda usually require the co-operation of many private organizations or low-level government agencies; and diplomatic instruments are not normally effective when exercised unilaterally. It is curious that so many writings on power assume in most cases an ability to engage in unilateral implementation, under tight government control.

From an implementation perspective the problem of foreign policy control is quite paradoxical. As the concerns of international politics become ever wider, both domestically and internationally, so the authoritative part of the foreign policy machine remains essentially non-specialist to perform a co-ordinating, directing role. Perhaps this is necessary. But if it is, effective control over government policy becomes harder to exercise. Horizons are narrowed, policies tend to become more piecemeal and it becomes easier to get agreement to veto international action rather than to initiate it.

Let us not give the impression, however, that foreign policy is a sham. The strength of centralization in the matter of policy control lies in the procedural direction. The foreign policy machine can deal at first hand with such matters as monitoring international behaviour, making statements and taking necessary policy stances, and trying to establish, or more likely reinforce, structures of domestic and international co-operation. Over these matters a high degree of direct control can be exercised. This is particularly important in the matter of regime construction at the international level. As we have pointed out, the key role for foreign policy in a complex, mixed-actor environment lies in the business of facilitating arrangements between the producers of goods and services, and encouraging a high degree of predictability in international behaviour. Foreign policy has a crucial role to perform in fitting a set of administrative arrangements around a particular structure of states. And as we have said, it is not necessary for states to control the activities of all organizations that affect them – indeed, foreign policy would be impossible to carry out if it were – but it is necessary for states to organize general structures which make international activities at least compatible with their core interests. This is the context in which foreign policy can be most effectively pursued. For this is where the centralization, the political authority, the co-ordinating function and the diplomatic skill of a foreign policy machine can be at its most effective.

There are, of course, no hard-and-fast rules about this. In the cases that have been examined there are different degrees of control exhibited in various ways. It is in the nature of things that foreign policy-makers try to exert influence and have controllable policies in all spheres of political activity. Nevertheless, on the basis of our view of the international system as an arena of implementation, of the mixed nature of decision-making complexities of policy control, we have tried to generalize to explain how the problems of control favour certain policy outputs over others.

In conclusion, we should stress that none of this is an attempt to rewrite what we intuitively knew about foreign policy. It is a generally conservative, constrained affair which takes place in complex circumstances. But for too long students of the subject have been content to ascribe its characteristics to an almost mythical belief in the unique circumstances of international politics, or the special but unspecified, nature of foreign policy. We have tried to explain these special characteristics in policy terms. Far from being inaccessible to the policy analyst, as both they and we have tended to assume, the sphere of foreign policy presents some of the sharpest examples of implementation processes becoming decision processes, of the need to aggregate various diverse agencies to achieve policy outcomes, and of the problems of complexity and control in an environment where there are few direct levers. The point of viewing foreign policy from this perspective is to obtain a better appreciation of the relationship between events in a highly complex international environment and the perceptions of those who are charged with making foreign policy decisions.

Bibliography

Allen, D. (1978), 'Foreign policy at the European level: beyond the nation-state?', in William Wallace and W. E. Paterson (eds), *Foreign Policy Making in Western Europe* (Farnborough: Saxon House), pp. 135–54.

Allen, D. (1983), 'Managing the Common Market: the Community's competition policy', in Helen Wallace, William Wallace and Carole Webb (eds), *Policy Making in the European Community* (London: Wiley), pp. 209–36.

Allen, D., Rummel, R., and Wessels, W. (1982), *European Political Cooperation* (London: Butterworth).

Allison, G. (1971), *Essence of Decision* (Boston, Mass.: Little, Brown).

Allison, G. T., and Szanton, P. (1976), *Remaking Foreign Policy: The Organizational Connection* (New York: Basic Books).

Anderson, J. E. (1979), *Public Policy-Making*, 2nd edn (New York: Holt, Rinehart & Winston).

Anell, L. (1981), *Recession, the Western Economies and the Changing World Order* (London: Pinter).

Arbuthnott, H., and Edwards, G. (1979), *A Common Man's Guide to the Common Market* (London: Macmillan).

Aronson, J. D. (1981), 'Banking and insurance', in S. Strange and R. Tooze (eds), *The International Politics of Surplus Capacity* (London: Allen & Unwin), pp. 111–24.

Barber, J. (1979). 'Economic sanctions as a policy instrument' *International Affairs*, vol. 55, no. 3 (July), pp. 367–84.

Bardach, E. (1977). *The Implementation Game* (Cambridge, Mass.: MIT).

Barnet, R. (1972), *The Roots of War* (New York: Atheneum).

Barratt, S., and Fudge, C. (eds) (1981), *Policy and Action: Essays in the Implementation of Public Policy* (London: Methuen).

Bergesen, A. J. (ed.) (1980), *Studies of the Modern World System* (New York: Academic Press).

Berman, L. (1982), *Planning a Tragedy: The Americanization of the War in Vietnam* (New York: Norton).

Berman, P. (1978), 'The study of macro- and micro-implementation', *Public Policy*, vol. 26 (Spring), pp. 157–84.

Bertrand, R. (1981), 'The liberalisation of capital movements – an insight', *Three Banks Review*, no. 132 (December), pp. 3–22.

Bingham, T. H., and Gray, S. M. (1978), *Report on the Supply of Petroleum and Petroleum Products to Rhodesia* (London: HMSO).

Bloomfield, L. (1982), *The Foreign Policy Process* (Englewood Cliffs, NJ: Prentice-Hall).

Bressand, A. (1982), *Ramses: The State of the World Economy* (London: Macmillan).

Brown-John, C. L. (1975), *Multilateral Sanctions in International Law: A Comparative Analysis* (New York: Praeger).

Bryant, R. C. (1981), *Money and Monetary Policy in Interdependent Nations* (Oxford: Blackwell).

Brzezinski, Z. (1970), *Between Two Ages: America's Role in the Technetronic Era* (New York: Viking).

Brzezinski, Z. (1983), *Power and Principle* (London: Weidenfeld & Nicolson).
Buijtenhuijs, R. (1978), *Le Frolinat et les révoltes populaires du Tchad 1965–1976* (The Hague: Mouton).
Burrows, B., and Edwards, G. (1982), *The Defence of Western Europe* (London: Butterworth).
Business International SA (1979), *Doing Business with Eastern Europe: Operating Techniques* (Geneva: Business International SA).
Calleo, D. (1982), *The Imperious Economy* (London: Harvard University Press).
Cardoso, F. H., and Faletto, E. (1978), *Dependency and Development in Latin America* (Berkeley, Calif.: University of California Press).
Carter, J. (1982), *Keeping Faith* (London: Collins).
Cerny, P. (1980), *The Politics of Grandeur* (Cambridge: Cambridge University Press).
Cerny, P., and Schain, M. (eds) (1980), *French Politics and Public Policy* (London: Pinter).
Charlot, J. (1971), *The Gaullist Phenomenon* (London: Allen & Unwin).
Chase-Dunn, C. K. (1982), 'International economic policy in a declining core state', in W. P. Avery and D. P. Rapkin (eds), *America in a Changing World Political Economy* (New York: Longman), pp. 77–96.
Chomsky, N. (1970), *At War with Asia* (New York: Pantheon).
Clarke, M. (1979), 'Foreign policy implementation: problems and approaches', *British Journal of International Studies*, vol. 5, no. 2 (July), pp. 112–28.
Cohen, S. (1977), *The Making of US International Economic Policy* (New York: Praeger).
Cox, R. W. (1981), 'Social forces, states and world orders: beyond international relations theory', *Millennium*, vol. 10, no. 2 (Summer), pp. 126–55.
Crandall Hollick, J. (1981), 'France under Giscard d'Estaing: a retrospect', *World Today*, vol. 37, no. 6 (June), pp. 204–10.
Crandall Hollick, J. (1982), 'Civil war in Chad', *World Today*, Vol. 38, nos 7–8 (July–August), pp. 297–304.
Cripps, F. (1983), 'A model revolution for the old school', *Guardian*, 27 September.
Cross, E. G. (1981), 'Economic sanctions as a tool of policy against Rhodesia', *World Economy*, vol. 4, no. 1 (March), pp. 70–6.
Davy, R. (1980), 'The historical importance of the Helsinki Final Act', *The Times*, 7 November.
Dawson, S. (1979), 'Organisational analysis and the study of policy formulation and implementation'. *Public Administration Bulletin*, no 31 (December), pp. 52–68.
Destler, I. M. (1972), *Presidents, Bureaucrats and Foreign Policy* (Princeton, NJ: Princeton University Press).
Destler, I. M. (1980), *Making Foreign Economic Policy* (Washington, DC: Brookings Institution).
Doxey, M. (1971), *Economic Sanctions and International Enforcement* (London: Oxford University Press).
Draper, T. (1967), *Abuse of Power* (New York: Viking).
Dunsire, A. (1978a), *Implementation in a Bureaucracy* (Oxford: Martin Robertson).
Dunsire, A. (1978b), *Control in a Bureaucracy* (Oxford: Martin Robertson).

Edwards, G. (1978), 'Belgrade and human rights', *Government and Opposition*, vol. 13, no. 3 (Summer), pp. 307–22.

Ellsberg, D. (1972), *Papers on the War* (New York: Simon & Schuster).

Emminger, O. (1979), 'The exchange rate as an instrument of policy', *Lloyds Bank Review*, no. 133 (July), pp. 1–22.

European Community (1976), *Coopération politique européenne*, GT (76) 4 rev. (Luxembourg: European Community).

European Community (1979), *European File*, 7/1979 (Brussels: European Commission).

European Community (1983), *Sixteenth General Report on the Activities of the European Communities, 1982* (Brussels and Luxembourg: European Commission).

Farrands, C. (1979), 'Textile diplomacy: the making and implementation of European textile policy 1973–1978', *Journal of Common Market Studies*, vol. XVIII, no 1 (September), pp. 1–18.

Fitzgerald, F. (1972), *Fire in the Lake: The Vietnamese and the Americans in Vietnam* (Boston, Mass.: Atlantic-Little, Brown).

Frankel, J. (1963), *The Making of Foreign Policy* (London: Oxford University Press).

Frears, J. (1981), *France in the Giscard Presidency* (London: Allen & Unwin).

Fulbright, W. (1966), *The Arrogance of Power* (New York: Random House).

Furtado, C. (1971), *Development and Underdevelopment* (Berkeley, Calif.: University of California Press).

Gabriel, R. A. (1980–1), 'A commando operation that was wrong from the start', *Canadian Defence Quarterly*, vol. 10, no. 3, pp. 6–10.

Gallucci, R. L. (1975), *Neither Peace nor Honor: The Politics of American Military Policy in Vietnam* (Baltimore, Md: Johns Hopkins University Press).

Galtung, J. (1967), 'On the effects of international economic sanctions, with special reference to Rhodesia', *World Politics*, vol. 19, no. 3 (April), pp. 378–416.

Gazit, S. (1981), 'Risk, glory and the rescue operation', *International Security*, vol. 6, no. 1, pp. 111–35.

Gelb, L. H., with Betts, R. K. (1979), *The Irony of Vietnam: The System Worked* (Washington, DC: Brookings Institution).

George, A. (1980), *Presidential Decisionmaking in Foreign Policy* (Boulder, Col., Westview Press).

Geusau, F. A. M, Alting von (1978), 'Détente after Helsinki: attitudes and perspectives', in *Yearbook of World Affairs*, pp 8–22.

Giscard d'Estaing, V. (1976), *La Démocratie Française* (Paris: Fayard).

Goldstein, W. (1970), 'Skepticism on Capitol Hill', *Virginia Quarterly Review*, vol. 46, no. 3, pp. 390–410.

Goldstein, W. (1971), 'The American political system and the next Vietnam', *Journal of International Affairs*, vol. 25, no. 1, pp. 91–119.

Grieve, M. J. (1968), 'Economic sanctions: theory and practice', *International Relations*, vol. 3, no. 6 (October), pp. 431–43.

Halberstam, D. (1972), *The Best and the Brightest* (New York: Random House).

Halperin, M. (1974), *Bureaucratic Politics and Foreign Policy* (Washington, DC: Brookings Institution).

Halperin, M., with Hoffman, D. N. (1977), *Top Secret: National Security and the*

Right to Know (Washington, DC: New Republic Books).

Hayward, J. (1973), *The One and Indivisible Republic* (London: Weidenfeld & Nicolson).

Helsinki Review Group (1977), *From Helsinki to Belgrade* (London: David Davies Memorial Institute).

Helsinki Review Group (1978), *Belgrade and After* (London: David Davies Memorial Institute).

Heritage Foundation (1980), *Iran, the United States and the Hostages after 300 Days*, Heritage Backgrounder, No. 126, (29 August).

Hersh, S. (1983), *The Price of Power: Kissinger in the Nixon White House* (New York: Summit Books).

Heskai, M. (1982), *Iran: The Untold Story* (New York: Pantheon Books).

Hilsman, R. (1967), *To Move a Nation* (New York: Doubleday).

HMSO (1975), *Conference on Security and Cooperation in Europe. Final Act*, cmnd, 6198 (London: HMSO).

HMSO (1977), *Miscellaneous No. 17 (1977). Selected Documents Relating to Problems of Security and Cooperation in Europe 1954–77*, cmnd 6932 (London: HMSO).

HMSO (1978a), *The Meeting Held at Belgrade from 4 October 1977 to 9 March 1978 to Follow up the Conference on Security and Cooperation in Europe*, cmnd 7126 (London: HMSO).

HMSO (1978b), *Fifth Report from the Expenditure Committee – Session 1976–77, Progress towards Implementation of the Final Act of the Conference on Security and Cooperation in Europe. Observations by Government*, cmnd 7112 (London: HMSO).

Hoffmann, F. (1967), 'The function of economic sanctions', *Journal of Peace Research*, vol. 4, no. 2, pp. 140–6.

Holsti, K. J. (1982), 'Bargaining theory and diplomatic reality: the CSCE negotiations', *Review of International Studies*, vol. 8, no. 3 (July), pp. 159–70.

Hood, C. (1976), *The Limits of Administration* (London: Wiley).

Hood, C., and Dunsire, A. (1981), *Bureaumetrics* (Farnborough: Gower).

Hood, C., Dunsire, A., and Thompson, S. (1979), 'Describing the status quo in Whitehall: a prerequisite for the analysis of change', *Public Administration Bulletin*, no. 31 (December), pp. 20–36.

House of Commons, Expenditure Committee (1977), *Fifth Report from the Expenditure Committee Session 1976–77, Progress towards Implementation of the Final Act of the Conference on Security and Cooperation in Europe*, HC 392 (London: HMSO).

House of Commons, Foreign Affairs Committee (1981), *Minutes of Evidence*, HC 41 (London: HMSO).

House of Commons, Foreign Affairs Committee (1982), *Minutes of Evidence*, HC 48ii (London: HMSO).

House of Commons (81–82) 449, Treasury and Civil Service Committee (1982), *Memoranda on International Monetary Arrangements* (London: HMSO).

House of Commons (82–83) 385 (1983a); *Second Special Report from the Treasury and Civil Service Committee Session 1982–83, International Monetary Arrangements* (London: HMSO).

House of Commons (82–83) 21-II (1983b), *Fourth Report from the Treasury and Civil Service Committee Session 1982–83, International Monetary Arrange-*

ments. Vol. II, Minutes of Evidence (London: HMSO).

Howard, M. (1977), 'Helsinki reconsidered: east–west relations two years after the Final Act', *Round Table*, vol. 67, no. 267 (July), pp. 241-5.

Hudson, M. (1977), *Global Fracture: The New International Economic Order* (London: Harper & Row).

Ingram, H., and Mann, D. (1980), *Why Policies Succeed or Fail* (London: Sage).

Janis, I. L. (1982), *Groupthink*, 2nd edn (Boston, Mass.: Houghton Mifflin).

Jenkins, B., and Gray, A. (1983), 'Bureaucratic politics and power: developments in the study of bureaucracy', *Political Studies*, vol. 31, no. 2 (June), pp. 177-93.

Jenkins, W. I. (1978), *Policy Analysis* (Oxford: Martin Robertson).

Jensen, L. (1982), *Explaining Foreign Policy* (Englewood Cliffs, NJ: Prentice-Hall).

Johnson, R. T. (1974), *Managing the White House* (New York: Harper & Row).

Jordan, H. (1982), *Crisis: The Last year of the Carter Presidency* (New York: Putnams).

Keohane, R. O., and Nye, J. S. (eds) (1972), *Transnational Relations and World Politics* (Cambridge, Mass.: Harvard University Press).

Keohane, R. O., and Nye, J. S. (1977), *Power and Interdependence* (Boston, Mass.: Little, Brown).

Kissinger, H. (1955), *Nuclear Weapons and Foreign Policy* (New York: Harcourt Brace Jovanovitch).

Kissinger, H. (1969), 'Domestic structure and foreign policy', in H. Kissinger (ed.), *American Foreign Policy* (New York: Norton), pp. 9-50.

Krasner, S. D. (1972), 'Are bureaucracies important? or Allison Wonderland', *Foreign Policy*, no. 7, pp. 159-79.

Krasner, S. D. (ed.) (1982), *International Organization*, special issue, 'International regimes', 36, no. 2 (Spring).

Kress, G., Koehler, G., and Springer, J. Fred (1981), 'Policy drift', in D. Palumbo and M. Harder (eds), *Implementing Public Policy* (Lexington, Mass.: Lexington Books), pp. 19-28.

Kurzweil, E. (1980), *The Age of Structuralism* (New York: Columbia University Press).

Ledeen, M., and Lewis, W. (1982), *Debacle: The American Failure in Iran* (New York: Vintage Books).

Legum, C. (1975), *Africa Contemporary Record 1974-1975* (London: Rex Collings).

Legum, C. (1976), *Africa Contemporary Record 1975-1976* (London: Rex Collings).

Legum, C. (1977), *Africa Contemporary Record 1976-1977* (London: Rex Collings).

Legum, C. (1978), *Africa Contemporary Record 1977-1978* (London: Rex Collings).

Lellouche, P., and Moisi, D. (1979), 'French policy in Africa: a lonely battle against destabilisation', *International Security*, vol. 3, no. 4 (Spring), pp. 108-29.

Lemaitre, P. (1977), 'Solidarity begins at home', *The Times*, 1 November.

Loescher, G. D. (1981), 'Human rights and the Helsinki–Belgrade process', in *Yearbook of World Affairs*, pp. 62-78.

Losman, D. L. (1979), *International Economic Sanctions: The Cases of Cuba, Israel and Rhodesia* (Albuquerque, NM: University of New Mexico Press).

Ludlow, P. (1982), *The Making of the European Monetary System* (London: Butterworth).

McFadden, R., Treaster, J., and Carroll, M. (1981), *No Hiding Place* (New York: New York Times Books).

Maclean, J. (1981), 'Political theory, international theory and problems of ideology', *Millennium*, vol. 10, no. 2 (Summer), pp. 102–25.

McManus, D. (1981), *Free at Last* (New York: Signet Books).

Maddock, R. (1980), 'A perspective on economic summits', *International Relations*, vol. VI, no. 6 (November), pp. 949–66.

Martin, D. (1982), 'Inside the rescue mission', *Newsweek*, 12 July.

Michalet, C. A. (1976), *Le Capitalisme mondial* (Paris: PUF).

Michalet, C. A. (1982), 'From international trade to world economy: a new paradigm', in H. Makler, A. Martinelli and N. Smelser (eds), *The New International Economy* (London: Sage), pp. 37–58.

Moody, S. (1981), *444 Days* (New York: The Rutledge Press).

Morgan, R. (1973), *High Politics, Low Politics: Towards a Foreign Policy for Western Europe* (London: Sage).

Morgenthau, H. (1978), *Politics among Nations*, 5th edn (New York: Knopf).

Morse, E. L. (1976), *Modernisation and the Transformation of International Relations* (New York: The Free Press).

Mountjoy, R. A., and O'Toole, L. J. (1979), 'Towards a theory of policy implementation: an organisation perspective', *Public Administration Review*, vol. 39, no. 3, pp. 465–76.

Moynihan, D. (1970), *Maximum Feasible Misunderstanding* (New York: The Free Press).

New York Times Magazine (1981), 'America in captivity', special issue, 17 May.

Odell, J. (1982), *US International Monetary Policy* (Princeton, NJ: Princeton University Press).

OECD (1978), *From Marshall Plan to Global Interdependence: New Challenges for the Industrialised Countries* (Paris: OECD).

Olson, R. S. (1979), 'Economic coercion in world politics', *World Politics*, vol. 31, no. 4 (July), pp. 471–94.

Palumbo, D. J., and Harder, M. A. (1981), *Implementing Public Policy* (Lexington, Mass.: Lexington Books).

Panić, M. (1982), 'Monetarism in an open economy', *Lloyds Bank Review*, no. 145 (July), pp. 36–47.

Pearce, J. (1983), 'The common agricultural policy', in Helen Wallace, William Wallace and Carole Webb (eds), *Policy Making in the European Community* (London: Wiley), pp. 143–76.

Pinder, J. (1968), 'Positive integration and negative integration', *World Today*, vol. 24, no. 3 (March), pp. 90–1.

Pressman, J. L., and Wildavsky, A. B. (1973), *Implementation* (Berkeley, Calif.: University of California Press).

Puchala, D. J. (1975), 'Domestic politics and regional harmonization in the European communities', *World Politics*, vol 27, no. 4, pp. 496–520.

Puchala, D. J. (1983), 'Worm cans and worth taxes: fiscal harmonization and the European policy process', in Helen Wallace, William Wallace and Carole Webb (eds), *Policy Making in the European Community* (London: Wiley), pp. 237–64.

Ravenal, E. (1978), *Never Again: Learning from America's Foreign Policy Failures* (Philadelphia, Pa: Temple University Press).

Richardson, J. (ed.) (1982), *Policy Styles in Western Europe* (London: Allen & Unwin).

Rose, R. (1976), *The Dynamics of Public Policy* (London: Sage).

Rosenau, J. (1980), 'Calculated control as a unifying concept in the study of international politics', in J. Rosenau, *The Scientific Study of Foreign Policy*, 2nd edn (London: Pinter), pp. 197–238.

Rosenberg, M. J., Verba, S., and Converse, P. E. (1970), *Vietnam and the Silent Majority* (New York: Harper & Row).

Rubin, B. (1980), *Paved with Good Intentions* (New York: Penguin Books).

Ruggie, J. G. (1983), 'Continuity and transformation in the world polity: towards a neorealist synthesis', *World Politics*, vol. 35, no. 2 (January), pp. 261–85.

Russell, H. S. (1976), 'The Helsinki declaration: Brobdingnag or Lilliput?, *American Journal of International Law*, vol. 70, no. 3, pp. 242–72.

Said. E. (1981), *Covering Islam* (New York: Pantheon Books).

Sales, A. (1982), 'World systems and national movements in the industrialised countries', in H. Makler, A. Martinelli and N. Smelser, *The New International Economy* (Beverley Hills, Calif.: Sage), pp. 287–321.

Salinger, P. (1981), *America Held Hostage* (New York: Doubleday).

Schlesinger, A. (1967), *The Bitter Heritage: Vietnam and America's Democracy 1941–1966* (Boston, Mass.: Houghton Mifflin).

Schmitt, H. O. (1972), 'The national boundary in politics and economics', in R. L. Merritt (ed.), *Communication in International Politics* (London: University of Illinois Press), pp. 251–73.

Schreiber, A. P. (1973), 'Economic coercion as an instrument of foreign policy', *World Politics*, vol. 25, no. 3 (April), pp. 387–413.

Serfati, S. (1976), 'The Fifth Republic under Giscard d'Estaing: steadfast or changing?', *World Today* vol. 34, no. 3 (March), pp. 81–9.

Shackleton, M. (1983), 'Fishing for a policy: the common fisheries policy of the Community', in Helen Wallace, William Wallace and Carole Webb (eds), *Policy Making in the European Community* (London: Wiley), pp. 349–72.

Sherer, A. W. (1980), 'Goldberg's variation', *Foreign Policy*, vol. 39, (Summer), pp. 154–9.

Sims, N. A. (1983), 'The arms control and disarmament process in Britain', in H. G. Brauch and D. L. Clarke (eds), *Decisionmaking for Arms Limitation: Assessments and Prospects* (Cambridge, Mass.: Ballinger) pp. 97–129.

Skilling, H. G. (1981), 'CSCE in Madrid', *Problems of Communism*, vol. 30, no. 4 (July–August) pp. 1–16.

Smith, S. M. (1981), The utility of foreign policy approaches', in M. Clarke and B. White (eds), *An Introduction to Foreign Policy Analysis* (Ormskirk: Hesketh), pp. 75–94.

Special Operations Review Group of the Joint Chiefs of Staff (SORG) (1980), *Rescue Mission Report* (Washington, DC: Government Printing Office).

Stavins, R., Barnet, R., and Raskin, M. G. (1971), *Washington Plans an Aggressive War* (New York: Vintage).

Steinbruner, J. (1974), *The Cybernetic Theory of Decision* (Princeton, NJ: Princeton University Press).

Steiner, M. (1983), 'Worlds of foreign policy', *International Organization*, vol. 37, no. 3 (Summer), pp. 373–93.

Stevens, R. W. (1976), *Vain Hopes, Grim Realities: The Economic Consequences of the Vietnam War* (New York: Franklin Watts).

Strack, H. R. (1978), *Sanctions: The Case of Rhodesia* (Syracuse, NY: Syracuse University Press).

Strange, S. (1976), 'International monetary relations', in A. Shonfield (ed.), *International Economic Relations of the Western World, 1959–1971*, Vol. 2 (Oxford: Oxford University Press, for RIIA), pp. 18–359.

Strange, S. (1982), 'Cave hic dragones', *International Organization*, ed. S. Krasner, special issue, 'International regimes', vol. 36, no. 2 (Spring).

Strange, S. (ed.) (1983), *Pathways to Political Economy* (London: Allen & Unwin).

Strange, S., and Tooze, R. (eds) (1981), *The International Politics of Surplus Capacity* (London: Allen & Unwin).

Sylvan, D. J. (1981), 'The newest mercantilism', *International Organization*, vol. 35, no 2 (Spring), pp. 375–93.

Thompson, G. J. (1974), 'French policies in West Africa: neocolonialism in action', School of Oriental and African Studies, London, mimeo.

Thompson, V., and Adloff, R. (1981), *Conflict in Chad* (London: Hurst).

Thompson, J. C. (1968), 'How could Vietnam happen? An autopsy', *Atlantic Monthly*, vol. 111 (April), pp. 47–52.

Tint, H. (1972), *French Foreign Policy since the Second World War* (London: Weidenfeld & Nicolson).

Tooze, R. (1983), '"Sectoral analysis", and the international political economy', in R. J. Barry Jones (ed.), *Perspectives on Political Economy* (London: Pinter), pp. 231–41.

Tooze, R. (1984), 'Perspectives and theory of international political economy: a consumer guide', in Susan Strange (ed.). *Pathways to Political Economy* (London: Allen & Unwin), .

Tsoukalis, L., and de Silva Ferreira, A. (1980), 'Management of industrial surplus capacity in the European Community', *International Organization*, vol. 34, no. 3 (Summer), pp. 355–75.

Tumlir, J. (1983), 'The world economy today: crisis or a new beginning?' *National Westminster Bank Quarterly Review* (August), pp. 26–44.

Ullmann, M. (1973), 'Security aspects in French foreign policy', *Survival*, vol. XV, no. 6 (November–December), pp. 251–64.

US Congress, House of Representatives Commission on Security and Cooperation in Europe (1978), *The Belgrade Follow up Meeting to the Conference on Security and Cooperation in Europe: A Report and Appraisal* (Washington, DC: Government Printing Office).

US Congress, House of Representatives Committee on Banking, Finance and Urban Affairs (1981), *Iran: The Financial Aspects of the Hostage Settlement Agreement* (Washington, DC: Government Printing Office).

US Congress, House of Representatives Committee on Foreign Affairs (1981), *The Iran Hostage Crisis* (Washington, DC: Government Printing Office).

US Congress, House of Representatives Subcommittee of the Committee on Appropriations (1980), *Hearings on Hostage Rescue Mission* (Washington, DC: Government Printing Office).

US Congress, Senate Committee on Banking, Housing and Urban Affairs (1981), *Iranian Asset Settlement* (Washington, DC: Government Printing Office).

US Congress, Senate Committee on Foreign Relations (1980), *The Situation in Iran* (Washington, DC: Government Printing Office).

US Congressional Research Service (1979), *An Economic Embargo of Iran* (Washington, DC: Government Printing Office).

US Congressional Research Service (1980), *Iran, Consequences of the Abortive Attempt to Rescue the American Hostages* (Washington, DC: Government Printing Office).

US Congressional Research Service (1981a), *Iran: Executive and Congressional Reactions and Roles* (Washington, DC: Government Printing Office).

US Congressional Research Service (1981b), *Iranian Hostage Crisis and Release* (Washington, DC: Government Printing Office).

Vital, D. (1968), *The Making of British Foreign Policy* (London: Allen & Unwin).

Volle, A., and Wallace, W. (1977), 'How common a fisheries policy?', *World Today*, vol. 33, no. 2, pp. 62–72.

Waites, N. H. (1983), 'French foreign policy: external influences on the quest for independence', *Review of International Studies*, vol. 9, no. 4 (October), pp. 251–64.

Wallace, W. (1975), *The Foreign Policy Process in Britain* (London: Royal Institute of International Affairs).

Wallace, W. (1977), 'How foreign is foreign policy?', paper presented to Political Studies Association Annual Conference, 4–6 April, University of Liverpool.

Wallace, W. (1978a), 'After Berrill: Whitehall and the management of British diplomacy', *International Affairs*, vol. 54, no. 2 (April), pp. 220–39.

Wallace, W. (1978b), 'Old states and new circumstances: the international predicament of Britain, France and Germany', in W. Wallace and W. Paterson (eds), *Foreign Policy Making in Western Europe* (Farnborough: Saxon House), pp. 31–55.

Wallace, W. (1983), 'Political cooperation: integration through intergovernmentalism', in William Wallace, Helen Wallace and Carole Webb (eds), *Policy Making in the European Community* (London: Wiley), pp. 373–402.

Wallensteen, P. (1968), 'Characteristics of economic sanctions', *Journal of Peace Research*, vol. 5, no. 3, pp. 248–67.

Wallerstein, I. (1979), *The Capitalist World-Economy* (London: Cambridge University Press).

Waltz, K. (1967), *Foreign Policy and Democratic Politics* (Boston, Mass.: Little, Brown).

Waltz, K. (1979), *Theory of International Politics* (Reading, Mass.: Addison-Wesley).

White, R. (1970), *Nobody Wanted War: Misperception in Vietnam and Other Wars* (New York: Doubleday).

Wigg, R. (1975), 'France and the raw materials question', *World Today*, vol. 31, no. 2 (December), pp. 498–505.

Williams, R. (1980), *The Nuclear Power Decisions: British Policies, 1953–1978* (London: Croom Helm).

Wilson, H. (1971), *The Labour Government 1964–70* (London: Weidenfeld & Nicolson).

Windrich, E. (1978), *Britain and the Politics of Rhodesian Independence* (London: Croom Helm).

Wodie, F. (1970), *Les Institutions internationales régionales en Afrique occidentale et centrale* (Paris: Pichon et Jurand-Auzias).

Wood, A. (1979), '*Pravda*, Europe and the Helsinki Act: a survey', *International Relations*, vol. 6, no. 4 (November), pp. 645–61.

Yost, D. S. (1982), 'Arms control prospects at Madrid', *World Today*, vol. 38, no. 10 (October), pp. 387–94.

Zagoria, D. (1968), *Vietnam Triangle: Moscow, Peking, Hanoi* (New York: Pegasus).

Index